The Past, Present, and Future of Accountancy Education and Professions

Nina T. Dorata
St. John's University, USA

Richard C. Jones
Hofstra University, USA

Jennifer Mensche
St. Joseph's University, USA

Mark M. Ulrich
CUNY Queensborough Community College, USA

A volume in the Advances
in Finance, Accounting, and
Economics (AFAE) Book Series

IGI Global
PUBLISHER of TIMELY KNOWLEDGE

Published in the United States of America by
IGI Global
Business Science Reference (an imprint of IGI Global)
701 E. Chocolate Avenue
Hershey PA, USA 17033
Tel: 717-533-8845
Fax: 717-533-8661
E-mail: cust@igi-global.com
Web site: http://www.igi-global.com

Copyright © 2023 by IGI Global. All rights reserved. No part of this publication may be reproduced, stored or distributed in any form or by any means, electronic or mechanical, including photocopying, without written permission from the publisher.
Product or company names used in this set are for identification purposes only. Inclusion of the names of the products or companies does not indicate a claim of ownership by IGI Global of the trademark or registered trademark.

Library of Congress Cataloging-in-Publication Data

Names: Dorata, Nina Terranova, 1957- editor.
Title: The past, present, and future of accountancy education and professions / edited by Nina Dorata, Richard Jones, Jennifer Mensche, Mark Ulrich.
Description: Hershey, PA : Information Science Reference, [2022] | Includes bibliographical references and index. | Summary: "The book will have a broad scope covering the ways accountancy will require new roles and knowledge for its constituents in the emerging future. The book will explore how technological, educational, professional, and societal changes will transform accountancy. Regulatory changes either from governmental or private sectors could also create changes as roles, knowledge and expectations change. This book will provide relevant frameworks and the latest empirical and non-empirical research findings in the area. It will be written for academics and professionals who want to improve their understanding of the strategic role in managing changes in accountancy education and the profession and understanding how past changes may impact the future of accounting education and the professions"-- Provided by publisher.
Identifiers: LCCN 2022041674 (print) | LCCN 2022041675 (ebook) | ISBN 9781668454831 (hardcover) | ISBN 9781668454879 (paperback) | ISBN 9781668454848 (ebook)
Subjects: LCSH: Accounting--Study and teaching. | Accounting--Social aspects.
Classification: LCC HF5630 .P37 2022 (print) | LCC HF5630 (ebook) | DDC 657.071--dc23/eng/20221107
LC record available at https://lccn.loc.gov/2022041674
LC ebook record available at https://lccn.loc.gov/2022041675

This book is published in the IGI Global book series Advances in Finance, Accounting, and Economics (AFAE) (ISSN: 2327-5677; eISSN: 2327-5685)

British Cataloguing in Publication Data
A Cataloguing in Publication record for this book is available from the British Library.

All work contributed to this book is new, previously-unpublished material.
The views expressed in this book are those of the authors, but not necessarily of the publisher.

For electronic access to this publication, please contact: eresources@igi-global.com.

Advances in Finance, Accounting, and Economics (AFAE) Book Series

ISSN:2327-5677
EISSN:2327-5685

Editor-in-Chief: Ahmed Driouchi Al Akhawayn University, Morocco

MISSION

In our changing economic and business environment, it is important to consider the financial changes occurring internationally as well as within individual organizations and business environments. Understanding these changes as well as the factors that influence them is crucial in preparing for our financial future and ensuring economic sustainability and growth.

The **Advances in Finance, Accounting, and Economics (AFAE)** book series aims to publish comprehensive and informative titles in all areas of economics and economic theory, finance, and accounting to assist in advancing the available knowledge and providing for further research development in these dynamic fields.

COVERAGE

- Economics of Innovation and Knowledge
- Risk Analysis and Management
- Taxes
- Economic Theory
- International Economics
- Health Economics
- Field Research
- Behavioral Economics
- Microeconomics
- Finance and Accounting in SMEs

IGI Global is currently accepting manuscripts for publication within this series. To submit a proposal for a volume in this series, please contact our Acquisition Editors at Acquisitions@igi-global.com or visit: http://www.igi-global.com/publish/.

The Advances in Finance, Accounting, and Economics (AFAE) Book Series (ISSN 2327-5677) is published by IGI Global, 701 E. Chocolate Avenue, Hershey, PA 17033-1240, USA, www.igi-global.com. This series is composed of titles available for purchase individually; each title is edited to be contextually exclusive from any other title within the series. For pricing and ordering information please visit http://www.igi-global.com/book-series/advances-finance-accounting-economics/73685. Postmaster: Send all address changes to above address. Copyright © 2023 IGI Global. All rights, including translation in other languages reserved by the publisher. No part of this series may be reproduced or used in any form or by any means – graphics, electronic, or mechanical, including photocopying, recording, taping, or information and retrieval systems – without written permission from the publisher, except for non commercial, educational use, including classroom teaching purposes. The views expressed in this series are those of the authors, but not necessarily of IGI Global.

Titles in this Series

For a list of additional titles in this series, please visit:
www.igi-global.com/book-series/advances-finance-accounting-economics/73685

Changing World Economic Order in the Post-Pandemic Period
Sushanta Kumar Mahapatra (The ICFAI Foundation for Higher Education (IFHE) (Deemed), Hyderabad, India) and Vishal Sarin (Lovely Professional University, India)
Business Science Reference • © 2023 • 305pp • H/C (ISBN: 9781799868965) • US $260.00

Principles of Financial Control in the Public Sector
Plamena Georgieva Nedyalkova (University of Economics, Bulgaria)
Information Science Reference • © 2023 • 190pp • H/C (ISBN: 9781668488836) • US $185.00

Accounting and Financial Reporting Challenges for Government, Non-Profits, and the Private Sector
Fábio Albuquerque (Instituto Politécnico de Lisboa, Portugal) and Paula Gomes dos Santos (Instituto Politécnico de Lisboa, Portugal)
Business Science Reference • © 2023 • 322pp • H/C (ISBN: 9781668472934) • US $240.00

Perspectives on Blockchain Technology and Responsible Investing
Sonal Trivedi (Chitkara Business School, Chitkara University, India) Rashmi Aggarwal (Chitkara Business School, Chitkara University, India) and Gurmeet Singh (The University of the South Pacific, Fiji)
Business Science Reference • © 2023 • 317pp • H/C (ISBN: 9781668483619) • US $250.00

Mainstreaming Cryptocurrency and the Future of Digital Finance
Hamed Taherdoost (University Canada West, Canada)
Business Science Reference • © 2023 • 330pp • H/C (ISBN: 9781668483688) • US $250.00

Handbook of Research on Designing Sustainable Supply Chains to Achieve a Circular Economy
Yanamandra Ramakrishna (Skyline University College, UAE) and Siti Norida Wahab (Universiti Teknologi MARA, Malaysia)
Business Science Reference • © 2023 • 697pp • H/C (ISBN: 9781668476642) • US $295.00

IGI Global
PUBLISHER of TIMELY KNOWLEDGE

701 East Chocolate Avenue, Hershey, PA 17033, USA
Tel: 717-533-8845 x100 • Fax: 717-533-8661
E-Mail: cust@igi-global.com • www.igi-global.com

Table of Contents

Detailed Table of Contents

knowledge in our graduates. The intent is to support the belief that more higher education institutions (HEI) will indeed increase their incorporation of sustainability topics into their accounting curriculum.

In the study, gamification method is suggested as an alternative or supportive learning method to traditional theoretical and applied courses in training the accounting staff needed by businesses in higher education institutions in the digitalized world. In this context, it is aimed to teach the measurement principles within the scope of IAS/IFRS to a total of 108 students studying at Uşak University, a state university in Turkey, and taking accounting courses, by gamification method. For this purpose, first of all, a theoretical lesson on the measurement principles within the scope of "IAS/IFRS" was taught with the students, and then a written test on each valuation basis was administered to the students. Afterwards, students were allowed to play the digital game "Let's Measure Its Value," which the authors created in line with a scenario in the digital environment and where each measurement basis was exemplified with visuals. The answers given by the students regarding the measurement principles with both methods were compared.

Interviews conducted by both forensic accountants and auditors are an important task associated with either role in gathering information that progresses inquiries. Auditors interview clients about the collectability of accounts receivable, or the appropriateness of significant accounting estimates such as goodwill impairment. Forensic accountants interview clients when financial fraud is suspected in cases of asset misappropriation, bribery, larceny, and financial statement fraud. However, training in the task and the literature concerning how the task should be undertaken is disjointed, outdated both by the science and developments in practice undertaken elsewhere. Anecdotally, although new auditors spend nearly twenty five percent of their engagement time performing interviews and partners spend nearly forty percent performing interviews, there is virtually no formal training on how to conduct an interview at the undergraduate and graduate level.

requirement that currently exists since the CPA exam was offered. That change, in addition to the knowledge requirement for technology application, has broad implications for the academy and the profession. These issues are explored in this chapter.

Covid-19 has affected the business methods and procedures of almost all professions as well as the economies of the countries. Many professions in Turkey have felt the adverse effects of the pandemic. One of these professions is Certified Public Accountant (CPA). The pandemic has significantly affected accounting practices and the roles of professionals. Therefore, the need to learn in detail from the experts has emerged. So, this study aimed to investigate the effect of the pandemic on the professional activities of CPAs. In this direction, using the interview technique, eight questions were asked to eight professionals, mainly problems, expectations, income status, workload, and work stress. The results of the research revealed that the members of the profession had problems with both government institutions and taxpayers. As a result of the research, the CPAs stated that they had difficulty finding an interlocutor during the pandemic and had severe communication problems. Emphasizing their income has decreased significantly, the CPAs also said that their workload has increased.

Accountancy departments across higher education have been experiencing enrollment declines and these declines will likely continue going forward. Program directors need to be innovative and diversify their offerings in order to attract students. Traditionally most accountancy programs in higher education have limited their program offerings to two tracks: 1) audit and 2) tax. This chapter provides program directors with strategic direction and guidance on alternative offerings that an accountancy department can implement to expand their offerings and to attract new students. These alternative offerings include higher education programs developed and endorsed by professional associations such as the Institute of Internal Auditors, Association of Certified Fraud Examiners, and ISACA. Program Directors can implement all these programs or in piecemeal. The authors have implemented these programs into their accountancy program at their university or college with success and share with readers how they can get these programs up and running quickly and with ease.

The pace of technological change is staggering. Together with the effects of the covid-19 pandemic and the entrance of Gen Z into the workplace, the content and nature of accounting is changing significantly. While much attention has focused on technology, several other competencies contribute to a successful accounting career. The more exposure that accounting students have to these competencies, and the more opportunities that they have to develop these competencies as part of their academic preparation, the more likely they are to successfully navigate the transition from university to the workplace. In this chapter, the author examines four competencies for professional success, how academic preparation currently meets those needs, how it might include more, and the influence of Gen Z on the profession.

This chapter is an overview of the many gaps accounting students demonstrate as they enter the business world. The gaps to be explored can be separated into two overall categories: technology (these gaps will be referred to in this chapter in a summary fashion as they will be addressed in detail in another chapter) and soft skills, which comprise several gaps that are centered in many ways around communication and management skills. Business demands for accounting graduates go beyond technical skills as they are viewed as future business leaders.

The accounting profession has undergone a major transformation, and while the academic community does its best to educate students and provide them with the core competencies required to ultimately achieve success in the profession, the traditional "tool kit" is in need of updating. The speed of change and the ever-increasing demands of business have further widened the expectations gap on newly graduated students' skills and on the universities that are preparing them for their careers. Larger universities have successfully addressed this issue by partnering with public accounting firms. While these collaborations have proven to be very effective for the students at larger and more established universities, smaller programs without such access are at a disadvantage. The road ahead for smaller accounting programs is going to be a challenging one, but creativity and outreach are the keys.

Preface

OVERVIEW OF THE SUBJECT MATTER

This book covers the implications for accounting educators, and those responsible for preparing individuals to enter the professional accounting environment, of changes in the professional business environment, including new technologies, demands for a broader range of business information, and changes to the Uniform Certified Public Accounting Exam. This book explores how changes in the professional environment and relevant issues influencing the practice of accounting, including societal changes will transform accountancy and the related skills and knowledge expected of those entering the accounting profession.

Additionally, the book provides insights of the role of certain academic institutions in enhancing the CPA pipeline and how their role is further challenged and threaten given the expectation of enhanced skills and technical knowledge expectations that CPA Evolution demands.

In presenting its implications for those entering the profession and discussing emerging issues influencing the practice of accounting, this book relies on relevant frameworks and the latest empirical and non-empirical research findings in the diverse areas referenced herein.

Perspectives on Preparing Those Entering the Profession and on Institutions That Supply and Educate Candidates for the Profession

As a service provider to businesses, governmental entities, and nonprofits, the accounting professional must be prepared to adapt to emerging changes in the diverse professional environments they serve. To do so requires that candidates entering the profession receive an education covering the technical requirements, the professional roles and responsibilities of an accounting professional, and the skills required to meet the demands placed on them.

This book introduces many of the emerging changes to the environment in which professional accountant provide their services and examines how those changes implicate the roles and responsibilities and professional skills necessary for and expected of new entrants into the accounting profession. The various chapters, explain how the accounting educational system, both academic and professional, must adapt so that, upon entering the accounting profession, accounting professionals are prepared to meet the demands that will be placed on them.

Lastly, the book provides significant awareness by analyzing accounting degrees completed provided by The Integrated Postsecondary Education Data System (IPEDS), which is a post-secondary education data collection program for the National Center for Education Statistics. The educational institutions that are heavily invested in accounting education and thus have the most to lose as declining enrollments persist are among the smallest institutions in the United States. The lesson and warning here are that these institutions must collectively establish cohesive and effective strategies to mitigate declining enrollments in accountancy education because their role is paramount in maintaining the accountancy pipeline.

Target Audience

This book is written for accounting educators, including academics and accounting education and training professionals, and accounting professionals interested in understanding changes in the accounting profession and understanding the implications of those changes for managing those entering the profession and how past changes may impact the future of accounting education and the profession.

Moreover, the book will provide insights and support to accounting and nonaccounting executives concerned with the management of expertise, knowledge, skills, information, and organizational development in accountancy in different types of settings, including for-profit and not-for-profit organizations.

DESCRIPTION OF EACH CHAPTER

The Essential Skills for Candidates Entering the Accountancy Profession

This chapter describes the alignment of essential skill frameworks prescribed by numerous professional organizations and accrediting bodies. It suggests that accounting curriculum should focus on these essential skills using a new approach that is arranged by essential skills, rather than technical content.

Accounting education is not only focused on technical content, but on helping students develop career-ready essential skills. It could even be said that there should be a greater focus on skills rather than technical content. Numerous professional associations and accrediting bodies prescribe such essential skills, including the American Institute of Certified Public Accountants, the Institute of Internal Auditors, the Association to Advance Collegiate Schools of Business, Middle States, and the National Association of Colleges and Employers. Each of these organizations have prescribed essential skills that students should have in order to be successful in the workplace. The skill frameworks of these organizations often overlap, with a focus on critical thinking, deduction/reasoning, problem solving, teamwork/collaboration, communication, and ethical reasoning. Yet, despite this clear demand for essential skills from professional organizations and accrediting bodies, the accounting curriculum is still largely focused on technical content. This paper proposes a new approach to the accounting curriculum, with essential skills being the primary focus of courses, with the technical topics being linked to the essential skills.

The Opportunity for Growth of Sustainability Accounting and Reporting in the College Accounting Curriculum

This chapter focuses on the reasons and advantages to including sustainability topics in a college accountancy program at higher education institutions. More and more investors, lenders and other users of corporate reports call for more sustainability-related disclosures, especially associated with the financial risk from climate change on business property, regulation, and litigation. Calls for more transparent and additional disclosures from market regulators, investors, and other professional organizations have grown significantly since mandated disclosures in 2010. Although evidence suggests that calls for knowledge and disclosures have been largely neglected, still candidates for the accountancy profession provide more value armed with sustainability intellect and risk exposures.

Public accounting firms, large and small expand their advisory business lines to include assurance for ESG disclosures. More and more professionals secure the Fundamentals of Sustainability Accounting (FSA) credential whose knowledge provides the link between financial sustainability information and a company's ability to enhance enterprise value. The SASB's, (Sustainability Accounting Standards Board), is now part of the International Financial Reporting Standards (IFRS) Board, purpose is also to link industry-based disclosures for sustainability risk and operations and its enterprise value (sasb.org). This chapter provides the evidence that supports the call for inclusion in the traditional accountancy curriculum to meet the goals of the SASB.

Gamification as a New Approach in Accounting Education in the Digitalizing World: Gamification Application in Teaching the Measurement Principles in the Scope of IAS/IFRS

Creative learning approaches for all disciplines at all levels of education enhances the learning process by actively engaging students. That approach improves motivation, interest, and attitude towards learning. Using gamification techniques, that include a multitude of sensory applications, such as visual, audio, in the context of prior knowledge provides a pathway for knowledge retention. This chapter provides an analysis of the successes of gamification in learning both theoretical and applied aspects of accounting knowledge. The conclusion reached is that students' active involvement in learning, rather than the traditional passive receipt of knowledge, is not only fun, but also makes learning more application relevant.

Investigative Interviews Conducted by Forensic Accounting and Auditing Professionals

This chapter examines the importance of interviewing skills as a major task of auditors and forensic accountants, including extensive coverage of one well-known interviewing framework. The chapter espouses the view that interviewing skills are not sufficiently covered in the accounting curriculum. A significant portion of forensic accountants' and auditors' jobs is conducting interviews. The AICPA's Pre-certification Core Competency Framework confirms that communication and critical thinking skills--important components of interviewing--are essential for those wishing to enter the accounting profession. Interviewing has progressed into an approach called investigative interviewing, which has a goal of obtaining information from the subject of the interview. Training in this area includes a respected framework called PEACE (Preparation and Planning, Engaging, Explaining, Account, Close, and Evaluate), which has been adopted worldwide. Studies have shown that although PEACE is an effective framework, without additional training, it may produce inconsistent results. The paper concludes that accounting curriculum has insufficient coverage of interviewing techniques, despite the AICPA's call for competency in the communication and critical thinking areas.

Changes, Challenges, and Choices: An Approach to The Future of Accounting Education in a Turbulent World

The future is influenced by the past. The future holds new horizons as the past has taught the profession. Pandemics and technology advances alter skill sets necessary for professionals to succeed in accountancy. This chapter focuses on the lessons of economic crisis and technological turbulence and their impact on skills and competencies for the future. The only constant is change in competencies and how institutions of higher education are responsible for changing education strategies to meet professional demands. The chapter concludes with a call for further research to explore strategies that education can keep pace with that demand.

The Uniform Accountancy Act and CPA Evolution: What the New Regime Means for Accountancy

This chapter considers wide-ranging changes in educational policy in the updated Uniform Accountancy Act and CPA Evolution. The chapter also discusses how these changes will impact the pipeline and CPA candidate decisions once Evolution takes hold.

Accounting education is substantially influenced by the content of the Certified Public Accountant (CPA) exam. The CPA exam content then influences US jurisdiction educational requirements, as well as accounting program curriculum. The upcoming changes to the CPA exam, called CPA Evolution (Evolution), include content and logistical changes to the exam. To assist jurisdictions in setting educational requirements, the American Institute of Certified Public Accountants (AICPA) and the National Association of State Boards of Accountancy (NASBA) issued the Uniform Accountancy Act, which has been recently updated to reflect Evolution. These new UAA model rules suggest degree requirements, specific accounting curriculum content, and evaluation of accounting programs based on the school's accreditation status. It also prescribes professional skills to be included in the educational process, and includes a suggestion that internships be permitted to allow candidates to develop these skills. The UAA does not speak to the "Sit 120" rule that many states have in place which allow students to sit for the CPA exam with 120 credits, rather the UAA suggests that 150 credits are necessary to sit for the CPA exam. This new educational policy is considered in the environment of a declining accounting pipeline and current pass rate trends. There is also a discussion on how candidates might select their discipline-specific part on the new Evolution exam.

The Effect of COVID-19 on Professional Accountants: The Evidence of Turkey

With recent years of pandemic experience, professional accountants have learned to pivot to providing professional services in a restrained environment. The effects of the pivot include augmenting how and when business was conducted. Communication structures changed too, from traditional face-to-face to a multitude of electronic means. This chapter provides evidence of how the delivery of professional services were modified during the pandemic and how the modifications affected profitability. The chapter also describes how clients' behavior and expectations changed during the pandemic and the impact of those changed behaviors and expectations on profitability. Overall, the chapter sets the course and outcomes should a pandemic-like event reoccur.

Department of Accountancy: Alternative Offerings

The future of accountancy education lies in keeping pace with the demands of the profession, not only with respect to professional skill, but also the requisite knowledge. As technology improves access to technical knowledge, the constant in accountancy is still the change in technical knowledge and the professional services that align with it. This chapter emphasizes the growth of related services that typical public accounting firms now provide, otherwise known as "advisory services." These services include internal audit, fraud examination, and information technology audit. In spite of the proliferation of these alternative lines of business, higher education curriculum in these disciplines has not kept pace with the demand for candidates with the requisite knowledge. The chapter provides a road map to grow such programs and thus meet the demands of the profession.

Professional Competencies for Student Success in an Increasingly Global, Digital, and Virtual World

The chapter is a testimony of the layer of skills demanded of students entering the accountancy profession. It focuses on skills rooted in tradition, but also advocates strongly for the soft skills, which the authors consider more challenging to acquire in a typical collegiate education. The soft skills require practice and mature with professional experience, yet are vital for success. The chapter provides solutions and suggestions for pathways where learning and practice is attained for skill development.

Business Demands of Accounting Students

This chapter uses survey data with responses from business executives to assess certain skill gaps between the knowledge provided by institutional education and those needed by industry for recent graduates entering the profession. Most of the skills are focused on expectations in technology application and the soft skills. The survey provides insights on what is not only needed but also exposes opportunities to enhance employment chances for candidates by program inclusion of desired competences for graduates upon entering the workforce.

Can Accounting Programs at Smaller Universities Survive?

Accountancy programs have experienced enrollment declines for several years. The changes brought by the CPA Evolution Exam create challenging program adjustments for all academic programs; however, smaller institutions, which are predominantly private schools, are particularly vulnerable to potentially expanding program to meet Evolution's core and discipline-based knowledge requirements. This chapter focuses on how smaller institutions can creatively meet Evolution's mantra and perhaps may find themselves at an advantage relative to larger programs. Creative solutions are provided for the significant number of small universities that provide accountancy education.

CONCLUDING COMMENT

The chapters of this book introduce, describe, and examine a diverse range of emerging professional accounting environmental, regulatory, and structural business factors influencing the way entrants into the profession are educated and trained.

After introducing and describing their focus area, the individual chapters examine the implications of the emerging environmental factors and offers specific recommendations for enhancing or modifying the accounting educational curriculum to address the environmental factor introduced.

The chapter contents address a broad range of emerging professional accounting topics and necessary skills and responsibilities required for entrants into the accounting profession, such as:

- The essential skills required of professional accountants that should receive enhanced coverage in existing accounting curricula. Emphasis is placed on the acceleration and progression of essential skills in an age of technological advances.
- The importance of introducing the emerging reporting area of sustainability into the accounting curriculum to align with the emerging "integrated", meaning financial and risk-based, company reporting framework. The importance is underscored as more stakeholders' demand sustainability-related disclosures to make informed investment decisions that may or may not enhance enterprise value.
- Structuring accounting courses in a manner that engages students and allows them to participate actively, rather than passively in their learning environment. Active learning through creative and engaging instruction leads

to student retention in the discipline, which is necessary for pipeline growth for the profession.

- A model for enhancing accounting students' interviewing skills, particularly for future assurance providers and forensic accountants, for whom such skills are essential. The profession significantly relies on the representations made by others. Being skillful on how the information is primarily obtained through interviewing is a skill often neglected in instruction during a typical formal education course of study.
- Preparing new professional entrants for the dynamic environment in which the professional accountant provides their service, including a chapter introducing the many "soft skills" necessary for success as a professional accountant and advocating strongly for an accounting educational model emphasizing these relevant soft skills.
- The new Evolution model established for the revised CPA Examination including a discussion of the revised Uniform Accountancy Act provided guidance for a state licensing authority to promote alignment of registered academic accounting programs with the Evolution model. Specifics for program content, including the appreciation of significant internship experiences, are described. A separate chapter discusses the challenges the new Evolution model introduces for smaller academic accounting programs and offers suggestions for complying with the Evolution examination and licensing model.
- Lessons learned by professional accounting organizations when conducting their business activities during the challenging COVID-19 period. The chapter discusses experiences of professional accounting practitioners in Turkey, but the observations and conclusions are generalizable to professional accounting practitioners globally. The chapter is a reminder of the pivot firms must take to successfully operate their business in conditions outside firm control.
- A discussion and roadmap for preparing the professional accounting firm to grow their advisory services practice to meet the demands of a changing client service environment.
- The challenges that "smaller" institutions have faced in educating candidates for the profession during the recent past. Paths to better outcomes for the future are provided, as these institutions are further challenged to meet new education paths for CPA Evolution. The discussion provides insights on the importance of smaller institutions role in supplying candidates to accountancy pipeline and the significant challenges they face in maintaining that status.

Overall, the book offers practical recommendations for preparing entrants into a professional accounting environment in which change might be the only constant. Further the book offers insights for the future as various stakeholders grapple with declining entrants to the profession and determine mitigation strategies for future growth.

Nina T. Dorata
St. John's University, USA

Richard C. Jones
Hofstra University, USA

Jennifer Mensche
St. Joseph's University, USA

Mark M. Ulrich
CUNY Queensborough Community College, USA

Chapter 1
The Essential Skills for Candidates Entering the Accountancy Profession

David Y. Chan
St. John's University, USA

Nina T. Dorata
St. John's University, USA

Mark M. Ulrich
CUNY Queensborough Community College, USA

ABSTRACT

The skills required to become a successful accounting professional are evolving. In the past, accountancy students that excelled in memorizing and retaining technical content have generally performed well in their professional careers. The advancement of technology such as robotic process automation and artificial intelligence has changed that status quo in the profession. Essential skills (ES) such as critical thinking, deduction, problem solving, teamwork and collaboration, inclusive mindset, effective communication and presentation, articulate writing, professionalism, ethical reasoning, and the ability to provide/receive constructive criticism are becoming paramount in this new environment. Professional and academic frameworks have promulgated the importance of these higher order skills. However, accounting programs have generally not adapted as well in preparing students with these skills. The authors provide directors of accounting programs with two different approaches in implementing these ES into their curriculums.

DOI: 10.4018/978-1-6684-5483-1.ch001

Copyright © 2023, IGI Global. Copying or distributing in print or electronic forms without written permission of IGI Global is prohibited.

INTRODUCTION

There are many professional associations that represent the Accountancy profession. Both the American Institute of Certified Public Accountants (AICPA) and the Institute of Internal Auditors (IIA) provide formal higher education with frameworks that prepare the next generation of professionals for success. The AICPA is a professional association that represents Certified Public Accountants (CPAs). Similarly, the IIA is a professional association that represents the Internal Audit profession. Through their frameworks, both associations express the importance of ES and emphasize their desirability for accounting professionals. Higher education and business school specific accrediting bodies such as the Association to Advance Collegiate Schools of Business (AACSB), Middle States[11], and National Association of Colleges and Employers (NACE) also recognize and emphasize the importance ES as part of their frameworks. The profession and higher education accrediting bodies have aligned views that ES are important for a student to succeed in the business world. Therefore, the authors propose that accounting programs must consider adjustments to their current curriculum to facilitate or parallel the delivery of the ES.

What is the ES necessary for candidates entering the profession? How do prospective candidates acquire skills that are valued and necessary for successful accounting careers? These are questions that Directors of Accountancy programs should be contemplating because the skillset for graduates has evolved and many traditional methods of delivering an accounting education are becoming less relevant. As many tasks once responsible for entry-level professionals shift to non-licensure candidates (i.e., community college graduates entering the profession) or to robotic process automation (RPA), the more likely ES will shift to a higher order of skills. Bloom's taxonomy of higher order skills is analyzing, evaluating and creating; whereas lower-level skills such as remembering, and understanding are those that do not manifest into higher order skills because technology allows immediate access to relevant information. That access lessens the requirement to remember technical knowledge. Therefore, what was deemed as higher order skills now represent ES for entering the profession tomorrow.

ES are defined as critical thinking, deduction, problem solving, teamwork and collaboration, inclusive mindset, effective communication and presentations, articulate writing, professionalism, ethical reasoning, and the ability to provide/ receive constructive criticism. Higher order stills require a critical perspective of interpretation and evaluation along with effective communication skills that require presentation skills to inform and persuade. The ES for candidates is not avoided of being questioned and challenged and thus possessing the emotional intelligence and fortitude of being challenged amidst of being praised.

The ES were prominently called for on November 7, 2022, when the AICPA released their Foundational Competencies Framework for Aspiring CPAs[22] ("Framework"). The Framework focuses on critical skills necessary for the long-term success of candidates entering the profession. The Framework does not prescribe traditional technical knowledge, which is reserved for the CPA exam. Rather the Framework posits that the ES are necessary for the variety of career opportunities that a prospective CPA may choose from. Because the Framework was created with direct assistance from accounting professionals, it does reflect the ES to enter the practice.

In this Chapter, we discuss select professional and academic frameworks in relation to the ES. We provide Program Directors two alternative approaches to implement ES into an accounting curriculum. The first strategy involves changing an entire accounting curriculum that transforms the curriculum from a traditional discipline approach to an ES development approach. And the second strategy provides a transitional approach that involves the offering of a required ES focused course in a curriculum. The proposed strategies will enable an accountancy program to comply with the applicable frameworks that call for ES.

The remaining Chapter is structured as follows; Section II discusses the profession and academic frameworks. Section III discusses two strategies to implement ES into an accountancy program curriculum. Lastly, Section IV concludes the paper.

INFLUENTIAL FRAMEWORKS

The ES--largely at the higher level of Bloom's Taxonomy--have been identified by numerous organizations that are stakeholders in the higher education and accounting professional environments. Professional organizations, accrediting bodies, and others promulgate suggested skills and competencies that students should develop while they are in college. There is significant crossover between the types of skills and competencies called for by these organizations.

Accounting Professional Organizations

The accounting profession values the importance of these ES and that is evident by content promulgated by professional associations such as the AICPA and the IIA curriculum recommendations.

The American Institute of Certified Public Accountants (AICPA)

A recent update of the AICPA's Framework includes their suggested ES for Aspiring CPAs. The Framework identifies three competencies: 1) Technical Competencies, 2) Organizational Competencies, and 3) Leadership Competencies. The Technical competencies are categorized as follows: risk assessment, analysis, and management; analysis and decision-making; measurement and reporting; research; and technology, systems, and process management. The Organizational competencies are categorized as follows, strategic management, performance management, resource management, and environmental, social and governance management. Finally, the Leadership competencies are grouped as follows: ethical behavior; critical thinking; collaboration; self-management; and communication.

Many of the competencies listed have action verbs that are considered higher levels of learning of Bloom's Taxonomy (analyze, evaluate, and create). Still, there are competencies, such as "Identify relevant information to measure" that are considered the lowest level (Knowledge) of Bloom's. The competencies are written at a very high level and from an academic point of view, virtually all the competencies could fit into any business or accounting course.

The Uniform Accountancy Act Model Rules (National Association of State Boards of Accountancy (NASBA))

While the AICPA determines CPA exam content, the individual states and jurisdictions control the educational requirements for sit and licensure eligibility. Many states utilize the assistance of the National Association of the State Boards of Accountancy (NASBA) to evaluate educational experience for candidates requesting to sit for the CPA exam. Although NASBA publishes education guidance for jurisdictions through the Uniform Accountancy Act (UAA), licensing jurisdictions are not obligated, to follow the UAA. The most recent update of the UAA, the Model Rules Update in 2020, speaks to skills as it suggests education policy.

Rule 5-2(a) mentions "(a) These requirements are intended to provide a foundation in accounting and business course subjects. The program should: (1) Develop the skills required to apply the knowledge attained (including skills in communications, critical thinking, research and analysis). (2) Include and emphasize ethical behavior, professional skepticism and judgment, and professional responsibility. (3) Provide the highest quality instruction in subjects that clearly contribute to the knowledge, skills, and abilities necessary to meet the public's expectations of a CPA" (NASBA 2020).

The Institute of Internal Auditors (IIA)

The IIA has issued a University/College model curriculum framework (IIA 2022) for their Internal Audit Education Partnership (IAEP) programs (IIA 2022). The IAEP program's curriculum is promulgated by global leaders in internal audit. The curriculum specifically recommends a course called "Business Communication Skills for Internal Auditors" be included in their IAEP program. Furthermore, the IIA provides guidance for evaluating interpersonal skills of students in their IAEP program. Many instructors associated with an IAEP program emphasize the importance of ES by focusing the internal audit course primarily on interpersonal skills. A case study approach course delivers the IAEP concepts.

Academia

It is not only the profession that promotes the ES, but also do accrediting organizations through accreditation standards. In particular, the AACSB emphasizes ES in their standards. The AACSB accredits business and accounting programs and is widely seen as the top-tier business-specific accreditation that a business school can attain. Regional accreditors, such as the Middle States also promotes ES in its standards. The National Association of Colleges and Employers (NACE) is another stakeholder organization that bridges academia with the professional world. NACE directs their curriculum based on skills and competencies that are needed in the workforce.

The Association to Advance Collegiate Schools of Business (AACSB): Business Standards

The AACSB is an important accrediting body that is looked favorably upon by prospective students and employers. The AACSB's mission is to "foster engagement, accelerate innovation, and amplify impact in business education." [reference 2020 standards] The AACSB 2020 Standards, lasted updated in 2022, provide a standard for "Curriculum". In part these standard states "Normally, business degree programs at the bachelor's level include learning experiences that address competencies characteristic of a successful business graduate of an AACSB-accredited school, as well as content from business disciplines, such as accounting, economics, finance, management, management information systems, marketing, and quantitative methods." The standard clearly emphasizes that skills beyond rote knowledge are necessary for business students.

Schools must then identify competencies and assess whether their students are attaining them, according to assurance of learning (AoL) standards. The process requires that "The school identifies learning competencies for each business degree program as well as appropriate direct and indirect measures that are systematically assessed to demonstrate that learning competencies are achieved across degree programs." Though vague in terms of identifying what competencies must be taught, guidance is given here: "Competencies and curriculum management processes reflect currency of knowledge and expectations of stakeholders, including but not limited to organizations employing graduates, alumni, learners, the university community, and policymakers." To adhere to AoL standards, accountancy programs should access the AICPA competencies for more specificity.

The AACSB: Accounting Standards

The AACSB also issues standards for accounting programs, which guides accounting programs who seek separate accounting accreditation. As of June 2022 only 192 accounting programs world-wide have the separate accounting accreditation. (AACSB 2022) Current accounting standards were developed in 2018, though updated in 2022. Standard A4 includes a list of suggested accounting content for different degree levels. For bachelor's degrees, standards include a mixture of what could be considered skills/competencies (critical thinking, professional skepticism) and what could also be considered more technical content (internal controls and security).

Technology has its own standard for accounting accreditation. The standard shows how technology--with a focus on data analytics--is being seen as crucial, and now, almost more crucial than the basic career competencies that are not technology related.

Middle States Commission on Higher Education

Middle States Commission on Higher Education is a regional accrediting body of certain states in the Northeast. The accreditation is important for financial aid purposes and for transferability of credits between institutions. The latest standards for Middle States, issued in 2015, include a standard that addresses "Design and Delivery of the Student Learning Experience". In this standard, Middle States prescribes that an institution should include in its curriculum content that includes cultural and global awareness, communication skills, critical thinking, and technological competency. The Middle States standards are consistent with the standards from the AICPA, NASBA, IIA and the AACSB.

National Association of Colleges and Employers (NACE)

NACE has issued a set of competencies called Career Readiness. The NACE competencies include skills that mirrors much of what has been previously represented, which further validates the importance of the skills.

The NACE eight competencies are: career and self-development, communication, critical thinking, equity and inclusion, leadership, professionalism, teamwork, and technology. The competencies also include "Sample Behaviors", such as "Communication": that is, "Communicate in a clear and organized manner so that others can effectively understand." (NACE 2021)

Competencies' Frameworks

Table 1 provides an overview analysis of the different professional associations and the academic accrediting bodies. The AICPA framework is the most comprehensive in covering all the different ES amongst the two professional associations and NACE has the most coverage for the academic accrediting bodies. Nevertheless, the frameworks from the profession and accrediting bodies all show evidence of the importance of academic programs teaching ES.

However, university accounting programs may not be adequately preparing their students in relation to the ES (Table 2). We analyzed the accounting programs that have separate AACSB accreditation in the top five states that produce the most CPAs (NASBA 2020)[33]. Of the forty-nine schools only seven offer a separate course covering the ES as part of their accounting curriculum. About eighteen percent of both public and private schools offer a course focused on the ES. The analysis sheds light that there is a significant difference between what the profession and accreditors deem as necessary skills and what accounting programs offer. It can be argued that the programs may not have a specific course for ES but, the instructors may integrate the skills into existing courses. Given the significant volume of technical content that is typically learned in an accounting curriculum, adding content that applies ES to that content may be a tall order. Alternate learning strategies that "does it all" may need to be considered.

New York State Board of Public Accountancy revised education regulations for CPA Evolution removed separate courses in 1) Professional Ethics and Responsibility, Accounting Research, and Business and Accounting Communication (NYSED 2022). The removal of these implies that ES (ES) taught in these courses are embedded throughout the licensure curriculum. There is no evidence that is presented that is the fact. Given what we have found above, it can be construed that it is unlikely that the ES are integrated throughout the curriculum[44]. It could be surmised that unless jurisdictions require ES, then it is unlikely to be implemented. The strong evidence is the lack of evidence.

CURRICULUM MODERNIZATION

Should the dissemination of technical accounting/auditing content be the priority or only a priority? Does technical knowledge prepare students for their future careers?

Table 1. Alignment of competencies framework

Professional and Academic Associations					
ES	AICPA	IIA[55]	AACSB	Middle States	NACE
Critical Thinking	✓	✓	✓	✓	✓
Deduction/Reasoning	✓	✓	✓	✓	✓
Problem Solving	✓	✓	✓		✓
Teamwork and Collaboration	✓	✓			✓
Inclusive Mindset	✓				✓
Communication and Presentations	✓	✓		✓	✓
Writing	✓	✓		✓	✓
Professionalism	✓	✓	✓		✓
Ethical Reasoning	✓	✓	✓	✓	
Provide/Receive Constructive Criticism	✓				

Table 2. Top 5 states of licensure and accounting accreditation schools

	New York	California	Texas	Florida	Illinois	Total
Total Schools	7	5	14	8	11	45
Total Public	4	2	12	6	8	32
Skills Yes	0	0	1	1	3	5
Skills No	4	2	11	5	5	27
Total Private	3	3	2	2	3	13
Skills Yes	0	0	1	0	1	2
Skills No	3	3	1	2	2	11
Total Skills Yes	0	0	2	1	4	7
Total Skills No	7	5	16	7	7	42

Employers and the profession have argued that it is the ES that are important to their determination of whether to hire someone. Anecdotal evidence from employers have suggested that they can train any individual to be an accountant or an auditor if they have the ES. This is evident by the profession hiring students that are non-accounting majors to do audits or even hiring students with only a high school degree (PwC 2023). Albeit these employees cannot sign an audit opinion without further education and the CPA license. Otherwise, anyone with a general business background can conduct an audit under the supervision of a CPA. Employers value the ES for success and therefore universities and colleges should prepare students with these skills. Under that approach, students will be engaged using cases and will exercise and be evaluated on using ES repeatedly throughout a course. The suggested approach is a more intensive preparation for instructors, but the students will engage in active learning. That approach is a far departure from teaching technical knowledge that does not encourage active learning.

We propose to flip the discipline driven approach into an ES driven approach. That approach involves courses devoted to ES with discipline based intertwined. An ES approach is contrary to a learning objectives approach, whose emphasis is placed on concepts and theories of a discipline (e.g. Internal Auditing). The ES driven approach has the course learning objectives structured around the ES. The students repeatedly learn, exercise, and apply the ES using case studies (eg, Harvard - case study approach). The case-based approach can enable students to experience (Experiential Learning – learn by doing) the practical activities that are used in practice. Therefore, upon graduation, a student will enter the profession with the desired ES.

The case studies can focus on conceptual topics or practical tasks related to the discipline but ideally, the topic or task is relevant and aligned to the accounting curriculum. For example, in an internal auditing, case topics and tasks can be scenarios involving risk assessment, control testing, substantive testing, communication with a client, and report writing or presentation. These learning objective concepts and theories will be intertwined into the specific ES: critical thinking, deduction, problem solving, teamwork and collaboration, inclusive mindset, effective communication and presentations, articulate writing, professionalism, ethical reasoning, and the ability to provide/receive constructive criticism. Cases will drive the topics or tasks in every course while applying the ES. Table 3 provides an example course outline for an internal audit course.

The risk management course topic (Week 4) in the example internal audit course outline above can have a problem-solving case that may involve the students performing data analytics on the accounts payable to determine the reasonableness of the transactions for inaccuracies or fraud. An organization would like to manage the risk of paying for invoices that are not owed or that are fraudulent in nature. The student must determine the relevant data, data sources, reliability of the data sources, and the analytical method to complete the case. The student then exercises judgment to determine what is reasonable and then investigate possible explanations for any unreasonable transactions.

The culmination of every case involves the students making a professional report and presentation about their findings and experience. Students may have different

Table 3. Example internal audit course outline

Course Outline		
Week	**ES**	**Course Topics**
1	Introduction to the course	Introduction to Internal Audit
2	Critical Thinking	Internal Audit Standards
3	Deduction	Governance
4	Problem Solving	Risk Management
5	Presentation 1	
6	Teamwork and Collaboration	Internal Controls
7	Inclusive Mindset	Planning the Assurance Engagement
8	Effective Communication and Presentation	Audit Evidence and Workpapers
9	Presentation 2	
10	Articulate Writing	Communicating Engagement Outcomes
11	Professionalism	Conducting the Assurance Engagement
12	Ethical Reasoning	Conducting the Consulting Engagement
13	Constructive Criticism	Managing the Internal Audit Function
14	Presentation 3	

results due to judgment but that is acceptable as every student can learn from each other. The instructor provides constructive criticism, and all the students learn from that experience too. The case-based approach enables the students to develop many ES as the primary benefit, while also allowing students to learn about the conceptual topic of risk management and to perform a practical task.

Challenges

Under ideal conditions, ES would be integrated into every course in an accounting curriculum. However, practical implementation may be more difficult. A piecemeal approach may be more feasible for some accounting programs and therefore the authors recommend as an alternative a single required course offering that is focused on honing the ES. We propose a required experiential learning accountancy course that will focus on the same ES and prepare a student for success in the professional environment: critical thinking, deduction, problem solving, teamwork and collaborative work, inclusive mindset, effective communication, presentations, articulate writing, ethical reasoning, and the ability to accept constructive criticism. The course topics will not be specific to a course but will provide a variety of business topics because the topic is not dedicated to a specific course domain. The course topics can be from any area in the accountancy curriculum or general business curriculum. The purpose of the course is to focus on the ES. Table 4 provides an example course outline for a course on ES.

Table 4. Example ES course outline

Course Outline		
Week	**ES**	**Course Topics**
1	Introduction to the course	Introduction to Course
2	Critical Thinking	Accounting
3	Deduction	Auditing
4	Problem Solving	Taxation
5	Presentation 1	
6	Teamwork and Collaboration	Information Systems
7	Inclusive Mindset	Finance
8	Effective Communication and Presentation	Management
9	Presentation 2	
10	Articulate Writing	Economics
11	Professionalism	Marketing
12	Ethical Reasoning	Human Resources
13	Constructive Criticism	Ethics
14	Presentation 3	

CONCLUSION

The current methodology of higher education is not sufficient to prepare students for the profession due to advancements in and the ever-increasing reliance on technologies in addition to the demand for ES. The ubiquitous availability of information and the automation of certain tasks once performed by accountants has made certain skills such as retention of discipline content and mechanical tasks become less relevant or even obsolete. Accounting programs generally focus on the delivery and retention of accounting technical knowledge and related mechanical tasks. We propose that accounting programs convert from a discipline driven approach to an ES driven approach. The ES include critical thinking, deduction, problem solving, teamwork and collaboration, inclusive mindset, effective communication and presentations, articulate writing, professionalism, ethical reasoning, and the ability to provide/ receive constructive criticism.

The adoption of the ES approach will prepare students with the desirable skills for the current workforce. Accounting program directors can holistically change the entire curriculum where the focus of each course will be on the ES and the accounting technical knowledge will be secondary. However, the authors recognize that implementation of an ES approach may be difficult or impossible for some programs. Therefore, offering a single course may be a viable approach, which can serve as the capstone of an accounting program. Regardless of the approach taken by an institution, it is important to recognize that the skills needed to succeed in the profession has changed and it is the fiduciary responsibility of accounting programs to evolve and prepare students to succeed in profession.

REFERENCES

AACSB. (2018). 2018 Standards For Accounting Accreditation. AACSB. https://www.aacsb.edu/-/media/documents/accreditation/accounting/standards-and-tables/accounting2018standards-july-1-2022.pdf

AACSB. (2020). 2020 GUIDING PRINCIPLES AND STANDARDS FOR BUSINESS ACCREDITATION. AACSB. https://www.aacsb.edu/-/media/documents/accreditation/2020-aacsb-business-accreditation-standards-jul-1-2022.pdf

AACSB. (2022). 2022 State of Accreditation Report. AACSB. https://www.aacsb.edu/insights/reports/2022-state-of-accreditation-report

AICPA. (2022). AICPA releases updated Foundational Competencies Framework for Aspiring CPAs. AICPA. https://www.aicpa.org/news/article/aicpa-releases-updated-foundational-competencies-framework-for-aspiring-cpas

AICPA/CIMA. (2022). The AICPA Foundational Competencies Framework for Aspiring CPAs. *This Way To CPA*. https://thiswaytocpa.com/collectedmedia/files/foundational-competencies-framework-pdf.pdf

IIA. (2022). The IIA's Global Model Internal Audit Curriculum. IIA. https://www.theiia.org/globalassets/documents/about-us/initiatives--awards/academic-relations/global-model-internal-audit-curriculum.pdf

IIA. (2022). *Internal Auditing Education Partnership (IAEP) Program Program Guidelines and Operating Framework.* IIA. https://www.theiia.org/globalassets/documents/about-us/initiatives--awards/academic-relations/iaep-program-requirements-and-operating-framework.pdf

Middle States Commission on Higher Education. (2015). *Standards for Accreditation and Requirements of Affiliation*. MSCHE. https://msche.box.com/shared/static/6upfla8coxha663p0j10u3gatow38jel.pdf

NACE. (2021). *Competencies for a Career-Ready Workforce*. NACE Web. https://www.naceweb.org/uploadedfiles/files/2021/resources/nace-career-readiness-competencies-revised-apr-2021.pdf

NASBA. (2020). *Candidate Performance on the Uniform CPA Examination*. NASBA. https://nasbareport.com/

NASBA. (2020). *Uniform Accountancy Act Model Rules*. NASBA. https://nasba.org/wp-content/uploads/2021/03/REV-Mar-2021-Nov-2020-Model-Rules-FINAL-edited.pdf

NYSED. (2022). Registration of Curricula, Part 52.13 Accountancy. NYSED. https://www.op.nysed.gov/professions/certified-public-accountants/laws-rules-regulations/part-52

PwC. (2023). Higher Apprenticeship Program. PwC. https://jobs-au.pwc.com/au/en/higher-apprenticeship

ENDNOTES

1 Middle States is a regional accreditor recognized by the United States Department of Education.

2 See https://www.aicpa.org/news/article/aicpa-releases-updated-foundational-competencies-framework-for-aspiring-cpas

3 Although NASBA last publication was for 2019 performance, based on review of licensing jurisdictions, the top five in 2019 are still applicable for 2022.

4 https://www.op.nysed.gov/professions/certified-public-accountants/laws-rules-regulations/part-52

Chapter 2
The Opportunity for Growth of Sustainability Accounting and Reporting in the College Accounting Curriculum

Timothy G. Coville
St. John's University, USA

ABSTRACT

This chapter provides the reader with the following: 1) background on the numerous calls for the incorporation of sustainability topics into the college level accounting curriculums; 2) evidence that these calls have been largely neglected; and 3) further evidence for how the business community, regulators, and other professional organizations are demonstrating both the desire, and the need for, sustainability knowledge in our graduates. The intent is to support the belief that more higher education institutions (HEI) will indeed increase their incorporation of sustainability topics into their accounting curriculum.

INTRODUCTION

This chapter provides the reader with the following: 1) background on the numerous calls for the incorporation of sustainability topics into the college level accounting curriculums; 2) evidence that these calls have been largely neglected; and 3) further evidence for how the business community, regulators, and other professional organizations are demonstrating both the desire, and the need for, sustainability knowledge in our graduates. The intent is to support the belief that more higher

DOI: 10.4018/978-1-6684-5483-1.ch002

Copyright © 2023, IGI Global. Copying or distributing in print or electronic forms without written permission of IGI Global is prohibited.

education institutions (HEI) will indeed increase their incorporation of sustainability topics into their accounting curriculum.

The next section covering previous literature, provides a review some of the earlier calls to add sustainability into the accounting curriculum from the 1990s, i.e., Gray et. al. (1994), Bebbington (1997) and Gordon (1998), continuing through and into the present. The United Nations' Principles for Responsible Management Education (UN PRME) a 2007 initiative to ensure future business leaders would have the skills needed to balance economic and sustainability goals added still another high-profile voice to the various calls for sustainability's inclusion into accounting and business curriculums. Just in this past decade, in 2013, the American Institute of Certified Public Accountants (AICPA) issued a paper that encouraged accountants to use their expertise and skills to "help an organization link sustainability activity to strategies using accounting measures, tools, theories, and techniques" AICPA (Oct. 2013 page 6). Later that same year, the Association to Advance Collegiate Schools of Business (AACSB) added "diversity, sustainable development, environmental sustainability, and other emerging corporate and social responsibility issues" to its accreditation standards for accounting programs. (AACSB 2013) These various organizations didn't arrive at these similar calls by coincidence. They were responding to decades of suggested additions of sustainability in business education, and in practice (Mathews, 1997; Gray & Collison, 2002; America & Craig, 2004; Collison et al. 2007) to incorporate environmental and social dimensions into traditional financial reporting, management accounting and auditing courses that allow students the opportunity to consider accounting's real and potential impacts more broadly on society.

This chapter's third section will provide evidence of neglect from both the American Accounting Association's "Hasselback Accounting Faculty Directory" provided through their "Membership" link, http://www.accountingfacultydirectory.org/. This is the same data employed by Wertheim, P. et. al. (2022). Further evidence of sustainability's neglect is provided from a review of the course offerings at each of the 179 AACSB dual accredited accounting programs.

The fourth section will focus on current developments from both business and regulatory bodies, all of which provide evidence that sustainability accounting and reporting will continue to grow in importance over the coming decades.

The fifth and final section will share some observations from the chapter's author's work and express some conclusions drawn from the evidence provided in the earlier sections.

PREVIOUS LITERATURE CONCERNING SUSTAINABILITY ACCOUNTING AND REPORTING EDUCATION

By adding an accounting for sustainability course, we are responding to calls to introduce businesses' responsibility for sustainability into our curriculums, as called for by others, UN PRME (2007), AICPA (2013), AACSB (2013) and the numerous authors cited below. Some of those calls were inspired by the global credit crisis 2007 – 2009 and still others by the increasing concerns over the threats posed by climate-change. The hope is that students will come to better appreciate the limitations that are part of business transactions, in general, and specifically in traditional accounting journal entry formats. As stated by McPhail (2001) these objectives will allow us to rehumanize accounting by: (a) changing a student's view of their profession, themselves and the potential impact of their choices as accountants; (b) developing a broad vision of the profession through exposure to injustices and inequalities that exist within our economic system, and (c) allowing for the development of ethical and moral awareness of the others impacted by an organization, beyond its investors, each time decisions are made.

Current accounting curriculum are criticized for not being useful in developing these appreciations, in large part because they are still based on the paramount importance of the investor's needs. This reinforces the notion that it is only the shareholder's needs that must be met, leaving externalities as a sidenote. Also, accounting is often presented as a collection of accounting techniques, i.e., depreciation methods or inventory cost-flow assumptions. Each of these techniques translate business situations into a business language that fails to consider impacts on others (McPhail, 2001) Accounting is, in this regard, only seen as related to the financial management of a business.

Some have pointed to these limitations as promoting a value system for students that fails to consider the needs of other stakeholders. Consistent with Gray et al. (1994) accounting for sustainability is proposed to enhance a student's ability to think critically about the limitations of a view based only on the financial management of a firm. This not only allows for the students' greater intellectual development, but also prepares them to concern themselves with the interests of different stakeholders in their organization.

Gordon (1998) described the use of a module on sustainability accounting in an accounting theory course. There, the students were given selected reading assignments, for subsequent discussion in class. This was done, in part, to see whether the students' perceptions had changed. The author concluded that this way of teaching was an opportunity for instructors to contribute to engagement with values changes.

Gray and Collison (2002 page 813) make the observation that: "Accounting education encourages insufficient intellectual and/or ethical development together with a lack of critical intellectual independence: Teaching to be really educational should, therefore, aim to provide such stimuli for the student that they go forward seeking an understanding of the principles of their subject rather than sitting back smug in the knowledge that they learned the correct material for their examination."

In Australia, Mangion (2006) found that sustainability accounting is gaining acceptance in undergraduate curricula. Her conclusions affirmed that the principal reason for teaching sustainability accounting is to enhance students' awareness of the social and environmental obligations relevant in corporate decision making. She also listed options that have been proposed for inclusion of education in sustainability for accounting: (a) include sustainability accounting in traditional accounting-finance courses; (b) offer sustainability accounting as an independent study module (normally in the final study modules of the syllabus); (c) create a specialized curricular route in sustainability accounting (noting that was unusual); and (d) including sustainability accounting in a general study module on accounting theory.

Coulson and Thomson's (2006) involves an independent sustainability accounting course using dialogic pedagogy. These authors present the course content in detail and their stated intention is to show the benefits of the dialogic approach with the instructor as facilitator. This chapter's author used a similar approached, inspired to a degree by their study.

Collison et al. (2007) shared the results of interviews with numerous members from different European accounting associations (now part of the International Federation of Accountants). Many of those interviewed stated that social and environmental concerns are important for the profession and that too many accountants and auditors continue to underestimate their significance.

Hazelton and Haigh (2010) speak to the predominantly vocational orientation of student cohorts; the traditionally technical focus of the professional bodies; and competing educational reform agendas (such as technological skills), as barriers to sustainability "penetrating an already overcrowded curricula."

Gray (2013) contends that a fundamental difficulty for instructors bringing these sustainability ideas into their classrooms is that unless sustainability is 'keeping you awake at night', you do not understand it, and yet at the same time, we do not want our students "to be frightened into immobility." He goes on to support this contention and offers an example of one undergraduate course that was explicitly designed to make students uncomfortable. He shares a quote from Kelly and Allam (2009) page 32, who themselves quoted approvingly from the New Zealand Parliamentary Commission for the Environment:

"Ultimately, education for sustainability requires people to critically think about and reflect on their own values and the values embedded in the institutions that surround them."

His overarching point being that "new views and new insights will be most easily examined when there is serious intellectual discomfort." page 320.

Haskin and Burke (2016) provide readers with a suggested outline for including sustainability reporting in a financial accounting course. Their outline makes significant use of materials developed by the Sustainability Accounting Standards Board (SASB). They also present the argument that, modern capital allocation decision making suggests that sustainability reporting needs to be incorporated into the financial accounting curriculum.

Hart (2018) mentions a Leeds School of Business, University of Colorado Boulder course titled, "Integrated Reporting for Social Responsibility Strategies" that regularly has a waitlist. She quotes the instructor as saying, "We saw this as an emerging issue, and thought it would be a good elective for students wanting to get away from the intense, quantitative courses," and "The students like it because they think it's part of the future."

Creel and Paz (2018) provide examples, from their own years of experience, of where and how to incorporate sustainability concepts across several traditional accounting courses, e.g., managerial accounting, intermediate financial accounting, and auditing. Their article provides support for the growing importance of sustainability concepts for society, businesses, and the accounting profession. As they express in their conclusion, "By teaching them the importance of sustainability, we not only teach them accounting but also show them how to be responsible citizens and thrive in a more sustainable future economy." page 83. Much like Haskin & Burke 2016 and Porco & Hedley (2019), their paper is designed to assist and encourage other accounting faculty, to integrate sustainability into the accounting curriculum.

Business leaders are also calling for comprehensive, comparable, and consistent sustainability metrics reporting. Two high profile instances of this include:

- The World Economic Forum's – International Business Council's (WEF-IBC) September 2020 whitepaper titled, "Measuring Stakeholder Capitalism Towards Common Metrics and Consistent Reporting of Sustainable Value Creation" These are the Davos conference's titans of industry and the whitepaper's title speaks for itself.

- The CEO of BlackRock's annual letters to fellow CEOs calling on them to both improve their sustainability reporting and their sustainability performance. BlackRock is the world's largest asset manager, with over $10 trillion under management in January 2022.

Another group of articles, ranging from 1997 through 2021, are all focused on investigating the lack of coverage of sustainability in the accounting curriculum.

Bebbington (1997) reported that few were providing sustainability accounting courses, and that those that did exist were more due to individual than institutional initiatives. Almost twenty years later, still more evidence of its limited coverage is provided by Pippen et al. (2016). Those authors found that only 2%, 17 of 900, U.S. Colleges and Universities had sustainability courses within their accounting curriculum. Combs and Matti (2021) paper states that the literature has been conflicting as to whether sustainability is being addressed or not in higher education's business curriculum. However, their references are from 2012, farther back than the starkly clear Pippin, et al. (June 2016) findings. As Pippin et al. (November 2021) state, "Despite the calls from the business community and the AACSB, relatively few educators have taken actions to integrate sustainability into the business and accounting curricula." They go on to mention Porco and Hedley (2019) and a YouTube video by Porco (2018) of Fordham University as an exception to this neglect of the topic.

Coville's (2023) study showed that after taking a course in sustainability accounting and reporting, most students expressed a broader appreciation for the role of accounting and the business organizations it supports. The course in that study appears to have enhanced their willingness to consider new ways of doing business and to question some beliefs gained during earlier accounting courses in the curriculum. Therefore, those results were supportive of the idea that students will benefit from the study of a subject, like sustainability accounting, that promotes a broader view beyond the financial management of a firm.

Summary points from the above literature review:

- Several authors hope that adding a course(s) on sustainability accounting will provide students the intellectual development necessary for critical thinking and questioning of their roles as accountants in society and the natural environment.
- Providing students with this sort of instruction requires a commitment on the part of their instructor(s) to broaden their exposure beyond simply what is already done in commercial organizations to what could possibly be done in the future. By doing so they can prepare these future professionals to not only accept what is done, but to also ask what alternatives could be done to better serve both their firms and society.
- Several articles provide examples and guidance on how to incorporate sustainability into the accounting curriculum, whether as standalone course(s) or through integration into existing courses, to help and encourage other instructors and programs.
- Several studies, from 1997 through to 2021, have provided evidence of the lack of coverage of sustainability in HEI's accounting curriculum.

- The business community, governments, regulatory bodies, and others are also calling out for improved sustainability accounting and reporting, that will require knowledgeable, educated, professionals. This chapter will present a number of these statements in its fourth section.

CURRENT EVIDENCE OF NEGLECT

To obtain fresh evidence as to what extent highly accredited universities have begun to offer sustainability related courses in their accounting programs (because sustainability courses in the accounting curriculums were as small as the 2% found by Pippen et al. (June 2016) this author undertook a fresh review, during the 2022 spring semester. Here the focus was narrowed to the 179 highly accredited, AACSB dual accredited, accounting programs, in the U.S.A.

See https://www.aacsb.edu/accredited?accreditations=business-accounting&regions=americas

The course catalogs of all these highly accredited colleges and universities in the United States that have undergraduate or graduate accounting degree programs were searched for a stand-alone course in sustainability, at either the undergraduate or graduate levels. This search allowed for similar terms, often used interchangeably with sustainability, such as: Corporate Responsibility; Environmental, Social & Governance (ESG) and Social Responsibility. Of these 179 colleges and universities only 19, or 10.6%, had at least 1 one course devoted to sustainability.

While 10.6% is a big improvement over 2%, it still feels insufficient given the earlier mentioned calls from the U.N., the AICPA, and the AACSB, let alone how topical Social and Environmental concerns have become and threaten to remain.

For still another view into what coverage of sustainability is being provided by accounting faculty, this investigation used the same data employed by Wertheim et al. (2022) abstracted from the American Accounting Association's "Hasselback Accounting Faculty Directory" provided through their "Membership" link, http://www.accountingfacultydirectory.org/. In their data covering 7,445 faculties' self-reported subject coverage, the closest term to sustainability used was "social" and it ranked 25th among the 27 topics reported, with just 40 faculty, 0.3%. The top ranked subjects were: Financial, Managerial, Auditing, Tax, followed by Systems, these all seem intuitively reasonable.

Assured from the above evidence of current neglect, despite decades of literature pushing inclusion of sustainability in an accounting curriculum, there remains substantial room for growth in the number of colleges and universities accounting programs that offer sustainability related courses and/or topic coverage, this chapter's focus now shifts to how businesses, governments, regulators, and non-governmental organizations are pulling for that neglect to be corrected.

CURRENT EVIDENCE OF DEMAND

Statements and Developments from Sustainability Reporting Framework Providers

The International Sustainability Standards Board **(ISSB)** is a relatively new organization and has yet to make any public statements, as a board, about adding sustainability to college accounting programs. However, the ISSB's mission is to develop sustainability reporting standards for companies that are globally applicable and consistent. The ISSB believes that sustainability reporting can help companies better understand and manage their environmental, social, and governance (ESG) risks and opportunities. As the ISSB develops its sustainability reporting standards it is likely, it will also consider the role of accounting education in promoting the integration of sustainability into corporate reporting. One of the ISSB board members, Jeffrey Hales, did say when asked, speaking on his own behalf and not for the board,

"In my view, the shifting landscape of sustainability represents the biggest growth opportunity for the accounting profession that we've seen since at least Sarbanes-Oxley. As sustainability issues have become more integrated into corporate strategy, we are seeing businesses create new sustainability roles and functions, elevate the responsibilities of existing sustainability roles, and work to extend an improved understanding of sustainability to employees throughout their organizations."

"A similar shift needs to happen in the way we teach accounting. We need new courses to meet growing interest from students who want to develop sustainability expertise. But, even more, we need to improve our existing courses. At the end of the day, sustainability issues are business issues. They permeate business activities and so should be an integral part of how we teach any functional area of accounting, whether managerial, financial, audit/assurance, or tax."

The Global Reporting Initiative **(GRI)** has emphasized the importance of incorporating sustainability into college accounting programs to promote sustainability reporting and accountability. In a 2019 report titled "Education for Sustainability Reporting: A Curriculum Framework," GRI outlined a framework for incorporating sustainability reporting into accounting and business programs. The framework includes four modules: Introduction to Sustainability Reporting,

Sustainability Context and Strategy, Materiality and Stakeholder Engagement, and Reporting Quality and Verification. The report notes that "accounting and finance professionals have a critical role to play in supporting sustainability reporting" and that incorporating sustainability into college curricula can help develop the knowledge and skills needed for sustainability reporting. Additionally, GRI has developed a Sustainability Disclosure Database, which provides access to sustainability reports from companies around the world. This database can be used as a resource for college accounting programs to teach students about sustainability reporting and to provide examples of best practices.

The Task Force on Climate-related Financial Disclosures **(TCFD)**, in its 2017 report, "Recommendations of the Task Force on Climate-related Financial Disclosures," called for companies to disclose information about their climate-related financial risks and opportunities in their financial reporting. The report also noted that companies may need to enhance their internal processes to identify and assess climate-related financial risks and opportunities, and that this may require additional expertise in areas such as climate science and policy. To support the integration of climate-related financial risks into accounting education, TCFD has worked with academic institutions and organizations to develop guidance and resources. For example, TCFD has partnered with the U.N. supported international network Principles for Responsible Investment (PRI) to develop guidance for investment professionals on integrating climate-related considerations into investment decision-making. Additionally, TCFD worked with the University of Cambridge Institute for Sustainability Leadership to develop a curriculum framework for integrating climate-related financial risks into business and finance programs.

The United Nations **(UN)** has emphasized the importance of incorporating sustainability into college accounting programs as a means to promote sustainable development and achieve the United Nations' Sustainable Development Goals (SDGs). In a 2017 report titled "Education for Sustainable Development Goals: Learning Objectives," the United Nations highlighted the need for education to address sustainable development challenges, stating that "education is critical to achieving sustainable development and is an essential tool for empowering people, preserving the planet, and building peaceful, just, and inclusive societies."

The United Nations has also taken steps to support sustainability education through its initiatives, such as the Global Compact's Principles for Responsible Management Education (PRME) initiative. The PRME initiative promotes sustainability education in business and management programs, including accounting programs, by providing guidance to academic institutions on integrating sustainability into their curricula. Additionally, the United Nations has established the SDG Academy, which provides free online courses on the SDGs and sustainability-related topics to promote education and awareness.

Statements From Governments and Their Regulatory Bodies

The U.S. Securities and Exchange Commission **(SEC)** has recognized the growth in sustainability reporting and assurance and has taken steps to promote greater transparency and consistency in this area. In March 2021, the SEC announced the establishment of a Climate and ESG Task Force to identify potential violations of securities laws related to climate and ESG disclosures. The task force will analyze data to identify disclosure gaps and inconsistencies and will work closely with the SEC's Division of Corporation Finance to review public company filings.

The SEC has also issued guidance related to sustainability reporting. In 2010, the SEC issued guidance on climate change disclosures, which encouraged companies to consider the potential impact of climate change on their business and disclose material risks and opportunities related to climate change. In 2020, the SEC issued new guidance related to human capital disclosure, which encouraged companies to provide information on their workforce, including information related to diversity and inclusion. In March 2022, the SEC issued a proposal titled "The Enhancement and Standardization of Climate-Related Disclosures for Investors."

E.U.'s European Securities and Markets Authority **(ESMA),** has recognized the growth in sustainability reporting and assurance and has taken steps to promote greater transparency and consistency in this area. ESMA has been active in promoting the use of the Non-Financial Reporting Directive (NFRD), which requires large companies in the EU to disclose information on their environmental, ESG performance. In 2019, ESMA issued guidance on the disclosure of climate-related information under the NFRD, which provided practical recommendations for companies on how to report on climate-related risks and opportunities. ESMA has also been active in promoting the use of sustainability reporting standards, such as those developed by the Global Reporting Initiative (GRI) and the SASB.

ESMA has been active in promoting greater assurance of sustainability reporting. In June 2020, ESMA issued a report titled, Strategy on Sustainable Finance on the state of sustainability reporting in the EU. That report noted that while there had been progress in the quality and quantity of sustainability reporting, there was a need for greater assurance and standardization in this area. The report called for the development of common assurance standards for sustainability reporting.

EU law requires all large companies and all listed companies to disclose information on their risks and opportunities arising from social and environmental issues, and on the impacts of their activities on people and the environment. On 5 January 2023 the Corporate Sustainability Reporting Directive entered into force, modifying, and adding to the NFRD. Companies subject to the CSRD will have to report according to European Sustainability Reporting Standards (ESRS). The

CSRD also makes it mandatory for companies to have an audit of the sustainability information that they report.

U.K.'s financial services regulatory body Fed Equivalent, The Prudential Regulation Authority **(PRA)** does not have a direct role in shaping college accounting curricula, and yet has been active in encouraging financial institutions to consider sustainability risks in their operations and decision-making. For example, the PRA has issued guidance to banks and insurers on how to integrate climate-related risks into their risk management frameworks, stress testing, and disclosure practices.

Moreover, in June 2021, the PRA published a consultation paper that proposes to introduce new requirements for banks and insurers to manage the financial risks from climate change. The paper acknowledges that climate change and the transition to a low-carbon economy pose significant financial risks that must be managed by financial institutions. The paper sets out expectations for firms' approaches to managing climate-related financial risks, including the integration of climate risk considerations into their governance, risk management, and strategic planning processes. It also highlights the importance of high-quality data and disclosure in managing climate-related financial risks, which may include sustainability accounting and assurance. The PRA notes that there is a growing demand for sustainability-related data and disclosures from investors, regulators, and other stakeholders. Therefore, financial institutions are encouraged to develop robust data and reporting capabilities to effectively manage climate-related financial risks.

UK's SEC equivalent the Financial Conduct Authority **(FCA)**, the financial regulator in the United Kingdom, has made several statements in support of the growth of sustainability accounting and reporting. In March 2021, the FCA published a consultation paper on climate-related financial disclosures, which proposed new rules to enhance climate-related disclosures by issuers, including listed companies and asset managers. The proposals aim to improve the quality, consistency, and comparability of climate-related financial information, which could support the growth of sustainability accounting and reporting.

The FCA has also been active in promoting sustainable finance and encouraging financial institutions to consider environmental, social, and governance (ESG) factors in their decision-making. In September 2020, the FCA launched a consultation on proposals to require asset managers to disclose how they integrate ESG factors into their investment decisions and processes. That proposal's aim was to improve transparency and encourage asset managers to consider the long-term sustainability of their investments.

Furthermore, the FCA is a member of the UK government's Green Finance Strategy, which aims to mobilize capital towards a greener and more sustainable economy. The strategy includes a range of initiatives, such as the establishment of a Green Finance Institute, the issuance of green bonds, and the development of a taxonomy for sustainable finance. These initiatives could help to raise awareness of sustainability issues and support the growth of sustainability accounting and reporting.

International Organization of Securities Commissions' **(IOSCO)** Principle 16 states that issuers should provide "full, accurate, and timely disclosure of financial results, risk, and other information which is material to investors' decisions." With regard to this Principle, IOSCO emphasizes that ESG matters, though sometimes characterized as non-financial, may have a material short-term and long-term impact on the business operations of the issuers as well as on risks and returns for investors and their investment and voting decisions." (IOSCO Jan. 2019)

International Ethics Standards Board for Accountants **(IESBA)** stated the "Market demand for sustainability information has risen substantially and rapidly in recent years as there is a growing public expectation that corporate citizens must play their part in securing a sustainable future. As such, sustainability information is increasingly being used to support capital allocation or other decisions by investors, customers, workers, government agencies and other stakeholders." (IESBA Dec. 2022)

Statements From Individual Businesses

KPMG

In a 2020 report titled "The Role of the Accounting Profession in Achieving a Sustainable Future," KPMG stated that "the accounting profession plays a critical role in supporting the transition to a sustainable future, and it is therefore essential that sustainability and environmental, social and governance (ESG) considerations be integrated into accounting education." The report noted that accounting professionals need to have a thorough understanding of sustainability issues, and that colleges and universities have a key role to play in providing this education.

PwC

In a 2019 report titled "Preparing the next generation of accountants for a sustainable future," PwC emphasized the importance of sustainability in accounting education, stating that "today's accountants must be prepared to address the evolving demands of investors, regulators, customers, and other stakeholders who expect organizations to address a range of environmental, social, and governance issues." The report also noted that accounting students should receive training in sustainability-related skills, including data analytics, risk management, and stakeholder engagement. PwC has also taken steps to support sustainability education through its PwC Foundation, which has provided funding for programs aimed at integrating sustainability into accounting and business curricula.

Deloitte

In a 2018 report titled "The Fourth Industrial Revolution and the Future of Sustainability," Deloitte highlighted the need for sustainability education in accounting programs, stating that "tomorrow's accountants will need to be equipped with new skills and knowledge to help their clients and organizations navigate the rapidly changing landscape of the Fourth Industrial Revolution." The report emphasized the importance of integrating sustainability-related skills, such as data analytics, risk management, and stakeholder engagement, into accounting curricula.

EY

In a 2020 report titled "Navigating Disruption: EY Megatrends in Accounting Education," EY emphasized the need for sustainability education in accounting programs, stating that "today's accounting graduates must have the skills to work in a rapidly changing, digitally enabled, and increasingly sustainable world." The report noted that accounting students should receive training in sustainability-related skills, such as data analytics, risk management, and stakeholder engagement.

All of these "Big 4" Public Accounting Firms have supported sustainability education through their Foundations, which has provided funding for programs aimed at integrating sustainability into accounting and business curricula.

State Street Asset Management

In a 2019 report titled "Accounting for Sustainability: Asia-Pacific Insights," State Street Asset Management emphasized the importance of sustainability education in accounting programs, stating that "integrating ESG (environmental, social, and governance) considerations into accounting and finance courses can help cultivate future business leaders who are well equipped to navigate complex sustainability issues." The report also noted that accounting students should receive training in sustainability-related skills, such as data analytics and risk management.

BlackRock Asset Management

In a 2019 report titled "Sustainable Investing: The Education Advantage," BlackRock Asset Management emphasized the importance of sustainability education in accounting and business programs, stating that "sustainability must be incorporated into the curriculum if we are to build the future workforce that will be needed to drive sustainable investing forward." Their report also encouraged accounting and business students receiving training in sustainability-related skills, e.g., data analytics, risk management, and stakeholder engagement. The CEO, Larry Fink, of BlackRock's annual letters to fellow CEOs has for the past several years called on them to both improve their sustainability reporting and their sustainability performance.

Statements From Business Organizations

The Business Roundtable, in a 2019 statement titled "Statement on the Purpose of a Corporation," emphasized the importance of sustainability in corporate decision-making, stating that "we commit to delivering value to all of our stakeholders, and we acknowledge the integral role we play in the broader societal framework." The statement noted that companies should invest in their employees, support their communities, and protect the environment.

The Business Roundtable has also advocated for the incorporation of sustainability into business education. In a 2018 report titled "Investing in America's Workforce: Improving Outcomes for Workers and Employers," The Business Roundtable emphasized the need for business schools to incorporate sustainability into their curricula, stating that "business schools should provide students with the skills and knowledge needed to advance sustainable practices in the corporate world."

The World Economic Forum's – International Business Council's in a 2020 report titled "Measuring Stakeholder Capitalism: Towards Common Metrics and Consistent Reporting of Sustainable Value Creation," emphasized the need for sustainability education in accounting and business programs, stating that "the world needs to develop the right skills and capabilities to deliver sustainable value creation." They have also taken steps to support sustainability education through its initiatives, such as the "4IR for Sustainable Development" initiative, which aims to prepare students for the Fourth Industrial Revolution by incorporating sustainability into their curricula. These are the annual Davos conference's titans of industry, and these whitepaper titles speak for themselves.

The AICPA in a 2020 report titled "The State of Sustainability in the Accounting Profession," emphasized the importance of sustainability education in accounting programs. They stated that "accountants have a critical role to play in addressing sustainability challenges, and accounting programs must integrate sustainability into their curricula to prepare future professionals."

The AICPA has taken other steps to support sustainability education through its resources and initiatives. For example, the AICPA has developed a Sustainability Task Force to identify and develop sustainability-related resources for the accounting profession. Additionally, the AICPA has partnered with the SASB, which has now been acquired by the International Financial Reporting Standards – Foundation, to develop a credential program focused on sustainability reporting.

The AICPA's Practice Analysis (December 2022) that serves to guide both educators and students as to what knowledge is expected on future CPA exams, points to the importance of not only the COSO's Internal Controls Framework, but also COSO's Enterprise Risk Management (ERM) Framework. This COSO ERM framework is particularly important for the current "Business Environment and Concepts" (BEC) section of the CPA four section exam[1]. That is relevant in this chapter because the COSO ERM framework points to the importance of "communicating with stakeholders." Consideration of stakeholders, beyond investors and creditors, is the basis for sustainability accounting and reporting emphasized by GRI, the Business Roundtable and others, above.

The International Federation of Accountants **(IFAC)**, in a 2020 report titled "Enhancing the Role of the Accountancy Profession in Supporting the Achievement of the Sustainable Development Goals," the IFAC emphasized the importance of sustainability education in accounting programs, stating that "accountants must be equipped with the knowledge, skills, and mindset to identify, measure, and report on sustainable value creation." IFAC has also partnered with other organizations, such as the World Business Council for Sustainable Development (WBCSD) and the United Nations Environment Programme Finance Initiative (UNEP FI), to promote sustainability education and reporting.

In its 2021 report titled "SMPs and the Sustainable Development Goals," IFAC notes that the demand for sustainability and assurance services is growing rapidly, and that small- and medium-sized practices (SMPs) have an important role to play in meeting this demand. The report notes that SMPs can provide assurance on sustainability reporting and help clients integrate sustainability into their business strategies.

To support the growth of sustainability and assurance work, IFAC has developed guidance for accountants on sustainability reporting and assurance, including the "International Framework for Assurance Engagements (IAASB) Proposed International Standard on Assurance Engagements (ISAE) 3410" which provides guidance on assurance engagements related to sustainability information.

IFAC (2023) reports that: 95% of global companies, reviewed, reported some level of sustainability information; 64% of companies that report sustainability information provide some level of assurance on it, and 57% of these assurance engagements were conducted by audit or audit-affiliated firms, again looked at globally. In the U.S. only about 15% of these assurance engagements were performed by audit or audit-affiliated firms.

The Committee of Sponsoring Organizations of the Treadway Commission (COSO) has not made any specific statements about adding sustainability to college accounting programs. However, COSO has emphasized the importance of integrating sustainability into an organization's overall risk management framework. In its 2017 publication "Enterprise Risk Management - Integrating with Strategy and Performance," COSO stated that "sustainability risk, including environmental and social risks, should be considered within an organization's overall ERM framework." The publication noted that organizations should identify and assess sustainability risks as part of their overall risk management process and integrate sustainability considerations into their decision-making and performance management processes. As noted earlier the AICPA has stated that knowledge of this COSO material is relevant for those aspiring to become Certified Public Accountants.

CLOSING OBSERVATIONS AND CONCLUSION

The author of this chapter is a member of the first cohort of less than 100 individuals internationally to successfully complete both exams required for the SASB's FSA Credential, back in 2017. The number of such credential holders has grown to nearly 1,600 by February 2023. This dramatic growth is evidence of demand in the market for sustainability accounting and reporting knowledge.

From my research, I have observed that 96% of S&P500 listed firms issued an annual Sustainability Report (SR) in 2021, up from the 78% reported in an Investor Responsibility Research Center Institute (IRRC) 2018 report. Of those 2021 reports, 53%, or 251 of the 478, obtained assurance on at least one of their metrics., which was another significant increase from just 38% in IRRC's 2018 report. My observations are consistent with the current levels noted in the IFAC (2023). The growth in assurance engagements trend is highly likely to continue as more sustainability metrics become mandatory in required regulatory filings. CPA firms are also expected to provide more of these engagements in the U.S., given their existing audit work with these same mandatory filings.

My university, has 3 courses with sustainability in their titles at both the undergraduate and graduate levels, corresponding to three primary accounting disciplines: reporting, auditing, and managerial accounting. From my teaching, I have observed consistent appreciation and broadened perspectives from students in my sustainability accounting and reporting courses. This is evidenced by some representative quotes below, from the anonymous semester-end course evaluations students submitted:

- "By far the most interesting accounting course I have taken at St. John's. The course in its entirety was beneficial."

- "I think the discussions really help to explain what we are learning and reinforce how it applies to the real world."
- "Teaches about a newer sector of accounting and addresses real world issues through current events."
- "The open discussions at the beginning when we analyzed an article. The class interaction was very beneficial. I think it's great this topic is offered, we will be seeing a lot of it in the near future I'm sure and as far as accounting classes go it is more applicable to our lives."

This chapter has described the multitude of calls for college level sustainability accounting and reporting courses. It has also provided evidence of the limited number of such courses currently being offered by accredited accounting programs at either the undergraduate or graduate levels. In contrast with the limited number of such courses currently provided, the chapter provides evidence that the current business community is expressing a need for college graduates to possess knowledge and understanding of this growth area referred to as Sustainability Accounting & Reporting. It also gives a glimpse into how much the students themselves appreciate this material, when it is offered.

A reader of this chapter may then wonder how they may help increase the amount of coverage the subject of sustainability accounting and reporting (SAR) receives in their university's accounting programs. To fully address this question, of how, could easily require another full chapter. Still, some suggestions for this include:

- Understand that as Hazelton and Haigh (2010) mentioned above wrote, there are barriers to SAR "penetrating an already overcrowded curricula." Therefore, for now, it is likely that an elective course is the most that can be justified, at least while SAR remains voluntary and market driven, as opposed to a regulatory mandate. There is no reason that such an elective could not be offered at both the undergraduate and graduate levels.
- Keep the scope of your initiative consistent with your program's vision and mission, i.e., if your school is a UN PRME signatory, then such a standalone elective course would likely find support; if your school is not aligned with UN PRME, then you may need to settle for integrating the subject into existing courses.
- Take time to fully read a number of the articles mentioned in this chapter's literature review that focused on <u>how</u> to bring SAR, i.e., Haskin and Burke (2016), Creel and Paz (2018), and Porco & Hedley (2019).
- Consider earning the SASB FSA Credential, now offered with 27.5 CPE credits, from the AICPA see https://www.aicpa-cima.com/cpe-learning/course/fundamentals-of-sustainability-accounting-fsa-credential. The training offered

by this program not only provides a potential SAR instructor knowledge appropriate for such a course, SASB, now as part of IFRS Foundation, has been willing to allow college faculty to share these same training materials with their students free of charge.

- Speaking of training materials that are free of charge, explore the wealth of materials offered for free by many relevant organizations, over the internet, i.e., IFRS Foundation, TCFD, GRI, and the UN SDGs to name a few. They easily constitute more than a semester's worth of reading materials and they are all highly regarded in the SAR space.
- Know that most faculty, this author included, with experience teaching SAR materials, would happily answer questions and share additional ideas to help either integrate these materials into existing courses or to launch a standalone elective course.

This chapter's author fully expects that more college level accounting programs will seize the opportunity to provide SAR materials either via low impact integration into existing courses or via standalone dedicated SAR elective courses in their curriculums, at both the undergraduate and graduate levels.

REFERENCES

AACSB International – The Association to Advance Collegiate Schools of Business. (n.d.) *2013 Eligibility Procedures and Accreditation Standards for Business Accreditation.* AACSB. https://www.aacsb.edu/-/media/documents/accreditation/2018-business-standards.pdf?la=en&hash=B9AF18F3FA0DF19B352B605CBCE17959E32445D9

AICPA. (2013, October). *Accounting for the sustainability cycle: how the accounting profession can add value to sustainability-oriented activities.* AICPA. https://documents.pub/document/accounting-for-the-sustainability-cycle-dcclean-for-the-sustainability-cycle.html?page=1

AICPA. (December, 2022). *Maintaining the Relevance of the Uniform CPA Examination –Aligning the Exam with the CPA Evolution Licensure Model: Practice Analysis Final Report Practice Analysis.* AICPA. https://www.aicpa.org/resources/download/learn-what-is-tested-on-the-cpa-exam

Amernic, J., & Craig, R. (2004). Reform of accounting education in the post-Enron era: Moving accounting 'out of the shadows.'. *Abacus, 40*(3), 342–378. doi:10.1111/j.1467-6281.2004.00162.x

Bebbington, J. (1997). Engagement, education, and sustainability. A review essay on environmental accounting. *Accounting, Auditing & Accountability Journal, 10*(3), 365–381. doi:10.1108/09513579710178115

Collison, D., Ferguson, J., & Stevenson, L. (2007). Sustainability accounting education. In J. Unerman, J. Bebbington, & B. O'Dwyer (Eds.), *Sustainability accounting and accountability* (pp. 327–344). Routledge.

Combs, D. G., & Mattix, C. (2021). Sustainability Accounting in the United States Higher Education System. *Quarterly Review of Business Disciplines, 8*(1), 19–40.

Coulson, A., & Thomson, I. (2006). Accounting and sustainability, encouraging a dialogical approach; integrating learning activities, delivery mechanisms and assessment strategies. *Accounting Education, 15*(3), 261–273. doi:10.1080/09639280600850695

Coville, T. (2023). *The Neglected Need for and the Effects of Sustainability in Accounting Curriculum.* Journal of Global Awareness.

Creel, T., & Paz, V. (2018). Teaching Sustainability in an Accounting Classroom. In Discourse and Communication for Sustainable Education, 9(1) 79-85. doi:10.2478/dcse-2018-0006

Gordon, I. M. (1998). Enhancing students' knowledge of social responsibility accounting. *Issues in Accounting Education, 13*(1), 31–46.

Gray, R. (2013). Sustainability + Accounting Education: The Elephant in the Classroom. *Accounting Education, 22*(4), 308–332. doi:10.1080/09639284.2013.817795

Gray, R., Bebbington, J., & McPhail, K. (1994). Teaching ethics in accounting and the ethics of accounting teaching: Educating for immorality and a possible case for social and environmental accounting education. *Accounting Education, 3*(1), 51–75. doi:10.1080/09639289400000005

Gray, R., & Collison, D. (2002). Can't see the wood for the trees, can't see the trees for the numbers? Accounting education, sustainability and the public interest. *Critical Perspectives on Accounting, 13*(5-6), 797–836. doi:10.1006/cpac.2002.0554

Hart, L. (July 2018). Should students learn sustainability accounting? *Journal of Accountancy.* https://www.journalofaccountancy.com/newsletters/extra-credit/sustainability-accounting-education.html

Haskin, D. L., & Burke, M. M. (2016). Incorporating Sustainability Issues Into the Financial Accounting Curriculum [AJBE]. *American Journal of Business Education, 9*(2), 49–56. doi:10.19030/ajbe.v9i2.9611

Hazelton, J., & Haigh, M. (2010). Incorporating sustainability into accounting curricula: Lessons learnt from an action research study. *Accounting Education, 19*(1-2), 159–178. doi:10.1080/09639280802044451

IESBA. (Dec. 2022). *December 2022 Sustainability Update.* IESBA. https://www.ifac.org/system/files/publications/files/IESBA-December-2022- Sustainability-Update.pdf

IFAC. (2023). *The State of Play in Sustainability Assurance.* IFAC. https://www.ifac.org/knowledge-gateway/contributing-global-economy/discussion/state-play-sustainability-assurance

Investor Responsibility Research Center Institute (IRRC). (2018). *State of Sustainability & Integrated Reporting 2018.* CPB. https://cpb-us-w2.wpmucdn.com/sites.udel.edu/dist/8/12944/files/2022/07/2018-SP-500-Integrated-Reporting-FINAL-November-20181.pdf#:~:text=State%20of%20Sustainability%20%26%20Integrated%20Reporting%202018%204,their%20corporate%20identities%20and%20approach%20business%20in%20general

IOSCO. (Jan. 2019) https://www.iosco.org/library/pubdocs/pdf/IOSCOPD619.pdf

Mangion, D. (2006). Undergraduate education in social and environmental accounting in Australian universities. *Accounting Education, 15*(3), 335–348. doi:10.1080/09639280600850844

Mathews, M. R. (1997). Twenty-five years of social and environmental accounting research. Is there a silver jubilee to celebrate? *Accounting, Auditing & Accountability Journal, 10*(4), 481–531. doi:10.1108/EUM0000000004417

McPhail, K. (2001). The other objective of ethics education: Re-humanising the accounting profession – a study of ethics education in law, engineering, medicine, and accountancy. *Journal of Business Ethics, 34*(3/4), 279–298. doi:10.1023/A:1012576631990

Pippin, S. E., Stallings, M. A., Weber, J. L., & Wong, J. A. (November 2021). Integrating Sustainability into the Accounting Curriculum: Meeting an Emerging Student Demand. *CPA Journal.* https://www.cpajournal.com/2021/11/12/integrating-sustainability-into-the-accounting-curriculum/

Pippin, S. E., Weber, J. L., Wong, J. A., & Bergner, J. (June 2016). The Inclusion of Sustainability in the Accounting Curriculum. *CPA Journal.* https://www.cpajournal.com/2016/06/17/inclusion-sustainability-accounting-curriculum/

Porco, B. (2018). *Importance of Sustainability Reporting*. [Video]. Youtube. https://www.youtube.com/watch?v=tonVGMZ8guo

Porco, B. M., & Hedley, T. P. (2019). Seven Easy Ways to Introduce Sustainability Reporting into Existing Accounting Curricula. *CPA Journal*. https://www.cpajournal.com/2019/10/11/seven-easy-ways-to-introduce-sustainability-reporting-into-existing-accounting-curricula/

Wertheim, P., Clements, C., & Stovall, O. (2022). *School Characteristics, Teaching Areas, and Other Factors Affecting the Impact from Pending Retirements of Accounting Faculty*. (Working paper presented at the Academy of Business Research, San Antonio, Texas).

World Economic Forum – International Business Council's. (2020). Measuring Stakeholder Capitalism: Towards Common Metrics and Consistent Reporting of Sustainable Value Creation. WEF. https://www.weforum.org/reports/measuring-stakeholder-capitalism-towards-common-metrics- and-consistent-reporting-of-sustainable-value-creation .

ENDNOTES

1 With the introduction of the CPA Evolution exam in January 2024, BEC section is no longer a separate section. However, BEC content, including COSO ERM, remains testable within the CPA Evolution exam

Chapter 3
Gamification as a New Approach in International Accounting Education in the Digitalizing World:
Gamification Application in Teaching the International Measurement Principles

Feden Koç
https://orcid.org/0000-0003-4413-5188
Uşak Üniversity, Turkey

ABSTRACT

In the study, gamification method is suggested as an alternative or supportive learning method to traditional theoretical and applied courses in training the accounting staff needed by businesses in higher education institutions in the digitalized world. In this context, it is aimed to teach the measurement principles within the scope of IAS/IFRS to a total of 108 students studying at Uşak University, a state university in Turkey, and taking accounting courses, by gamification method. For this purpose, first of all, a theoretical lesson on the measurement principles within the scope of "IAS/IFRS" was taught with the students, and then a written test on each valuation basis was administered to the students. Afterwards, students were allowed to play the digital game "Let's Measure Its Value," which the authors created in line with a scenario in the digital environment and where each measurement basis was exemplified with visuals. The answers given by the students regarding the measurement principles with both methods were compared.

DOI: 10.4018/978-1-6684-5483-1.ch003

Copyright © 2023, IGI Global. Copying or distributing in print or electronic forms without written permission of IGI Global is prohibited.

INTRODUCTION

In the digitalizing world, developments in information and communication technologies appear in many areas of daily life. The reflection of digitalization on the education sector has led to the development of many learning methods in addition to traditional learning methods. In this context, with the reflection of digitalization in the education sector, alternative or supportive new learning methods have been developed to the traditional learning method, which is based on learning with paper, pencil, book, which provides one-way information flow. The gamification method in education developed in this context is based on ensuring that students play an active role in the learning process by improving their thinking skills, rather than the learning approach in which the instructors provide one-way information in the classroom (Fratto, 2011:3). As a matter of fact, with the technological developments at the end of the 1980s, the views of the Accounting Education Change Commission (AECC) and the American Institute of Certified Public Accountants (AICPA) on providing active learning by using technology in accounting education at universities and the Institute-wide Task Force on the Future of MIT Education In line with the recommendations presented in the final report prepared by. Along with these developments, The Landlord's Game home game, which is based on the teaching of accounting information and accounting techniques, which Elizabeth Magie patented in 1904, formed the basis of gamification in accounting education. In the following years, Easy Money, derived from Elizabeth Magie's The Landlord's Game, Finance and Fortune created by Parker Brothers Company and Finance Game Co. Finance games created by the company were used as home games related to accounting-finance (Abbasi, 2014: 1-15; Hocking & Hockng: 1-15; Koç, 2021: 162-180). Today, Working Capital Simulation: Managing Growth V2, Marty Raygun's Fistful of Dollars, Globalsym Euro Simulation, Bank on It are among the games that can be played digitally in the field of accounting and finance.

Today, in higher education institutions, accounting courses are generally offered with traditional methods to train the accounting staff that businesses need. Books, lecture notes and power point presentations are used as educational materials in these teaching staff-centered traditional methods in which one-way information flow is provided in accounting education. However, this learning method, in which students are not actively involved, may cause lack of motivation and focusing problems. Gamification in accounting education provides a student-centered education method, but it is an effective tool for students to learn accounting information with a high motivation and on an entertaining platform. In this context, there is a very limited number of studies on gamification in accounting education compared to the research in the literature on gamification in education. In addition, most research on gamification focuses on children and adolescents. Research on gamification for undergraduate and graduate students is very limited. Therefore, in this study, it is aimed to teach the measurement principles within the scope of International Accounting Standards / International Financial Reporting Standards (IAS / IFRS), which entered the literature as a result of the need to establish a common language in accounting at the global level, to students who receive accounting education in higher education institutions through gamification. In addition, within the scope of the study, the evaluation of students' views on this teaching method and the evaluation of the relationship between students' interactions with video games and gamification in accounting education have contributed to the literature.

BACKGROUND

Various theories such as Landers' Theory of Gamified Learning, Self Determination Theory, Flow Theory and Planned Behavior have been used and correlated with each other, with the studies of Silva, Rodrigues and Leal (2021), which deal with game-based learning in accounting education. The study also aims to determine how the dimensions of motivation, flow and attitude affect the game-based learning process. In this context, 816 university students were enabled to use an accounting game and how the game affected students were examined. As a result of the study, a contribution has been made to the literature on game-based learning in accounting education. In addition, the findings obtained from the study reveal that after using accounting Game together with the content they learn in the lessons, the motivation, and attitudes of the university students, unlike the flow, affect the perceived learning (Silva, Rodrigues, and Leal, 2021: 159-187). Queiro, Carmen, Marti-Parreño Seguí-Más, and Lynn (2019) aimed to examine academic literature on gamification methods in accounting education in depth with their studies. In this context, the methodologies used in the research were determined and the types of games used by the researchers were examined. The results obtained from the study have been evaluated as an area where more research can be done on gamification in accounting education and there are limited studies. Queiro, Carmen, Marti-Parreño Seguí-Más, and Lynn, 2019: 7662-7667).

Another study aimed to reveal the effect of gamification on students in accounting education. For this purpose, a gamified course was offered to 118 undergraduate students studying accounting at a large public university in Brazil and a questionnaire was applied to the students about gamification in accounting education. The results obtained from the study reveal that with gamification in accounting education, students consider many skills such as curiosity, leadership, initiative, persistence, cooperation, and critical thinking. In addition, it was determined that familiarity with the tools available in the online game and game experience were significantly related to the perception of gamification on students. However, some students did not like the complexity of the game. (Durso, Reginato, and Cornacchione, 2019: 79-100).

In another study, it has been tried to determine when gamification is most appropriate in teaching financial accounting to students who have not yet taken an accounting course in Cawangan Pahang, Campus Raub in Malaysia. Quantitative research method was used in the study and the data were collected and analyzed through the final exam of the students. In addition, as a gamification pedagogy, first-year students were allowed to play the game Accounting on the block's board game (AOTB) so that they could prepare financial statements (Nias, Jamaluddin, Norlaila, Fadzillah, Syazwani and Faizan, 2017: 1-4). In another study, in which the first mobile game application, Accounting Challenge (ACE) was introduced in the development of accounting education and the use of the game was explained, it was revealed that the mobile game had been downloaded 23,230 times until 2016 and won three international teaching awards. In addition, it was stated that the Accounting Challenge (ACE) mobile game, which was presented at various local and international events and received positive feedback, can be used free of charge on iPhone/iPad and Android versions (Seow and Wong, 2016: 434-439). In another study in the literature, which aims to draw attention to the importance of gamification in education as an alternative learning method to the traditional accounting lesson, it has been revealed that gamification in accounting education can be an alternative learning method to traditional accounting lessons or that it can be carried out in cooperation with traditional accounting lessons, thus increasing the effectiveness in accounting education. (Moncada and Moncada, 2014: 9-19).

When the literature examined above is evaluated, it is seen that gamification in accounting education is handled in a multifaceted way. However, in determining the effect and success of gamification in accounting education, no study has been found in which any accounting subject has been tried to be taught face-to-face, then with an online game, and then the results have been evaluated. Study is important in this respect and will make a significant contribution to literature. In this context this study, in which the gamification method in accounting education is discussed within the scope of a digital game designed and the results obtained are evaluated, and its contributions to the literature are presented below.

- The literature on gamification methods as an alternative to traditional theoretical and applied courses in accounting education in the digitalized world has been examined. The purpose of gamification, its contribution to the learning process and examples of gamification used in accounting education from past to present are discussed.
- The measurement principles within the scope of IAS/IFRS were taught to the students who receive accounting education in higher education institutions

with traditional theoretical-practical courses and gamification method, and it was determined which method was more successful on the students.

- The opinions of students who receive accounting education in higher education institutions about gamification in accounting education were evaluated.
- Whether the effectiveness of gamification in accounting education is related to the digital game experience and the frequency of playing digital games has been determined within the scope of the study.

Research Methodology

Under this title, the purpose of the study, the research method used in the study and the importance of the study are discussed.

a. Purpose of the Research

In this study, it is aimed to teach the students studying accounting in higher education institutions with the gamification method, the historical cost, current cost, value in use and performance value and fair value measurement principles within the scope of IAS / IFRS. For this purpose, students studying at Uşak University, one of the higher education institutions in Turkey, are asked to play the digital game "Let's measure its value", which is developed in the digital environment and exemplified on the basis of each measurement, in the game environment. Scope of teaching measurement principles under IAS/IFRS through gamification. Then, a questionnaire was applied to the participating students. Thus, the effectiveness of gamification in accounting education can be measured practically and students' views on gamification in accounting education can be evaluated.

b. Research Method

In the study, gamification method in accounting education has been proposed as an alternative to traditional accounting education, which is given with theoretical and applied courses in higher education institutions in the digitalized world. In this context, it is aimed to teach the measurement principles within the scope of IAS/IFRS to students who take accounting courses at Uşak University, one of the higher education institutions in Turkey, by the gamification method. In the study, a total of one hundred and eight students studying accounting education were selected by random sampling method among 395 students studying at Uşak University in 2022. A written test was applied to a total of one hundred and eight students, who formed the sample of the research, after the theoretical course on the measurement principles within the scope of IAS/IFRS, which they had knowledge of from accounting courses before. In the test, explanations regarding the measurement principles within the scope of IAS/IFRS were presented, and the students were asked questions consisting of four options about which valuation basis these explanations were related to, and the students were asked to answer these questions. Thus, students' knowledge of each measurement basis was evaluated in writing.

Then, in my work titled "Role play in accounting training: Turkish accounting standards/Turkish financial reporting standards (TAS/TFRS) in accordance with teach the basis of valuation" (Koç, 2021: 162-180), I developed the digital game "Let's Measure Your Value", which I developed in line with a scenario, and students were allowed to play voluntarily. (https://docs.google.com/forms/d/1UCvhPhHlKzUS3O8JSDD6JW7ri6I-TBkG_i5Ifw7FH6U/edit) The digital game, which can be accessed through the classroom system, contains visual examples of teaching the measurement principles within the scope of IAS/IFRS. When the game is clicked, short images about the scenario of the game will meet with the students and the rules of the game will appear on the screen. Then a visual will come from the students where they have to name their characters in order to start the game. After the character was named, the students were asked questions consisting of four options about which measurement basis should be associated with the visually presented examples of each measurement basis within the scope of IAS/IFRS. If the answers given by the students are correct, information about the correct answer will be displayed on the screen of the student and the student will be able to move on to the next question. If the answer given by the student is wrong, the student's screen will receive feedback that the answer is wrong. In addition, if the relevant question is answered incorrectly, a link to the documents related to the IAS/IFRS conceptual framework will be presented to the players in the attachment of the feedback message, along with explanations on the measurement principles. Then you can move on to the next question. The game will end with the answering of the visual samples prepared on the basis of each valuation. At the end of the game, students will earn 25 points for each correct answer and will not lose points for their incorrect answers. At the end of the game, the student who collects 100 points will win the gold medal, and the student who collects 75 points will win the bronze medal. Students who score below 75 points, that is, who correctly answer at most two questions on the basis of evaluation, will be directed to start the game again. After the completion of the digital game called "let's measure its value", the differences between the answers given by the students to the test questions applied to them before the game and the answers given about the principles of valuation in the digital game will be determined and the effect of gamification on learning will be determined.

In addition, after the completion of the digital game, a questionnaire was applied to the students within the scope of the quantitative research method in order to evaluate the effectiveness of the "let's measure its value" digital game, its contribution to the learning process and the effectiveness of the gamification method in accounting education. The data obtained with the questionnaire applied to the participants within the scope of the research were analyzed with the IBM SPSS Statistics 26 program. Frequency distribution, crosstabs, correlate, and regression analyzes were used in the analysis of the obtained data.

c. Importance of Research

This study is important in that it is based on teaching the measurement principles within the scope of IAS/IFRS to the students taking accounting courses in higher education institutions within the scope of a digital game called "let's measure its value" developed online. In this study, in order to measure the effectiveness of gamification in accounting education, to compare gamification with traditional learning methods, to evaluate students' views on the use of gamification in accounting education, and to evaluate the relationship between the effectiveness of gamification in accounting education and the frequency of playing video games, the participants in the digital game "let's measure its value", which was developed online. A questionnaire was applied to the participants. In this context, it is important that the effectiveness of the gamification method in accounting education is based on data collection with two different methods, a digital game played to the participants and a survey method applied to the participants, in order to make healthier evaluations about the results of gamification in accounting education.

THE IMPORTANCE OF GAMIFICATION IN ACCOUNTING EDUCATION AND THE BENEFITS OF DIGITAL GAMES FROM PAST TO PRESENT

Gamification in accounting education is based on presenting accounting information and accounting techniques to students through games. Thanks to the information transferred by this method, students are not passive recipients of information, but active participants in the learning process, and the learning process can become more enjoyable. Especially with the development of information and communication technologies, it can be shown that games can motivate students more effectively as the most important factor that directs students to computer games in the learning process. In this context, it is important to use games and computer games as a tool in order to encourage and motivate students in the learning process.

The first records of the use of games in education were recorded more than 4,000 years ago in China. With the development of computer technology over time, the use of games for education has gained importance, based on both anecdotal and observational evidence supporting computer games for teaching (Sigmund et al., 2011, p. 127-221; Tobias, Fletcher, Dai, Wind, & Fletcher, 2011, p. 127-221). In this context, the application of different methods as an alternative to the traditional education in which textbooks and power point presentations are used as course materials, which are offered with theoretical and applied courses from the past to the present, within the scope of accounting education, and enabling students to interact with computer-based education are a necessity today.

As a matter of fact, along with the digitalization process, the learning process should also be transformed in line with the needs of the digital generation youth. In this context, in order to transform accounting education in the digitalized world and to encourage the application of different learning methods in addition to theoretical and applied courses, the Accounting Education Exchange Commission (AECC) stated that "Lessons should focus on both basic concepts" and "students learn from unstructured problems and solve problems." (AECC Global; Yaşar and Alkan, 2019). In addition, in a report prepared at Massachusetts Institute of Technology (MIT) in which institutional views on the higher education process were presented, the necessity of transforming education was emphasized and some suggestions were presented. Among these suggestions, it was stated that the effect of games on students in the higher education process should be investigated and the use of game-based learning should be encouraged in this direction (MIT, 2014). In this context, in parallel with the developments in information and communication technologies and in line with the opinions of the Accounting Education Amendment Commission, the gamification method has begun to be used in accounting education in the digital world.

Teaching accounting techniques to students through gamification is based on The Landlord's Game, which was patented by Elizabeth Magie in 1904 and was the forerunner of Monopoly. An adaptation of this game has also been used to teach economics to students in some schools, including Columbia University. Also, in 1936, Finance Game Co. Firm's Finance and Fortune games and Milton Bradley's Easy Money games are among the first home games related to accounting-finance (Whitehill, 1999, p. 131-132). Apart from these games, other games that are used in the field of accounting and finance from past to present and based on teaching accounting knowledge and techniques to the players apart from these games, jeopardy, marty raygun's fistful of Dollars, globalsym euro simulation, working capital, simulation: managing growth V2, on top of that, bank, wordwall, learning applications, quiz and counting Platonsim games are possible (Koç, 2021, p. 162-180). The use of such games as teaching material in accounting education and in education in general makes it possible for students to focus on both words and pictures. In addition, it is possible to say that such games, which are used for educational purposes, appeal to both visual sensory memory and auditory sensory memory of students. In this context, in Figure 1 below, a visual about the effect of games, which are generally

Figure 1. The study of the learning process in the case of using games as learning materials
(Adapted from Mayer, 2019, p. 531-549)

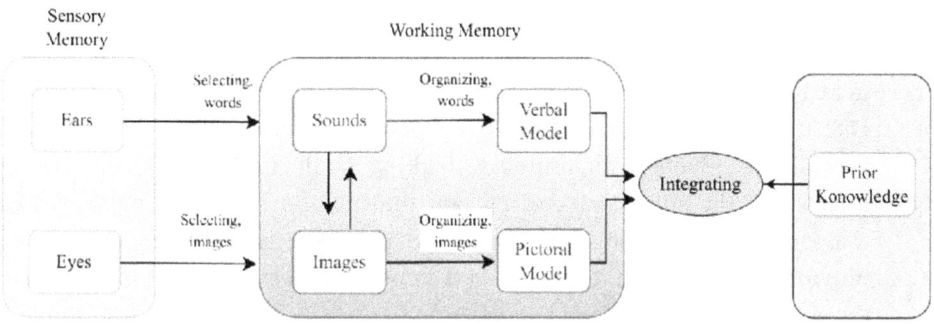

used as teaching materials, on the learning process and the processing process in the minds of the students is presented.

According to Figure 1, when a computer game is used within the scope of the instructional material, it is seen that the short information that affects the memory of the students quickly disappears from the time the expressions and pictures used in this game enter the students' visual sensory memory and auditory sensory memory. However, if the student pays attention to this short information, these expressions and images chosen by the student are transferred to the working memory. The expressions and images transferred to the working memory are arranged in a verbal model and the images are arranged in a pictorial model. They can then relate these verbal and pictorial models to each other. Subsequently, the resulting information is transferred to the long-term memory for storage (Mayer, 2019, p. 531-549).

In the learning process with gamification, which is related to students' visual sensory memory, auditory sensory memory, and their skills in using information communication technologies, students communicate with other students, work together, share resources, be open to discussion, creative thinking, strategy development, questioning, actions in order to complete the games. evaluation, rational decision making, etc. they are also improving themselves. To ensure the continuity of these motivating elements provided by the use of computer games in the learning process, the development of cooperation between game designers, educational researchers and game evaluation institutions should also be focused on, and this situation should not be ignored in order to get the highest efficiency from computer games in accounting education (Facer, 2002).

Generally, when active learning methods based on playing games are compared with passive learning methods, it has been revealed that accounting information learned with active learning methods based on playing games can be remembered more easily and has a positive effect on student performance (Kapp, 2012). In this respect, the benefits of digital games to students in accounting education are presented below.

- The fact that the visual perceptions of the young people in the digital generation are quite sharp, combining the accounting information presented in text with the visuals, can increase the success of gamification in education.
- Due to the high awareness of young people in today's digital generation, providing students with multiple thinking skills in digital games, being directed to the source of the relevant information in the wrong moves in the games or the wrong answers to the questions asked in the games, and providing feedback on the scores at the end of the game can positively affect the success of gamification in education.
- The fact that digital games are based on the use of technological tools such as computers, keyboards, and mice provide an interdisciplinary learning environment for today's digital generation young people and makes the learning process more enjoyable.
- Digital games enable students to take an active role in the learning process.
- As digital games enable students to think of many moves at the same time, they encourage students to think creatively and improve their problem-solving skills.
- Digital games enable players to develop their skills of discovering rules with observation, trial and error and hypothesis tests. As a matter of fact, Greenfield (1984) used the following statements on the subject: "The process of observing, formulating hypotheses, and finding the rules that regulate the behavior of a dynamic representation is basically the cognitive process of induction. This process constitutes the thought process behind scientific thought" (Greenfield, 2014).

Measurement Principles Under IAS/IFRS

Under this title, definitions regarding the measurement principles within the scope of IAS/IFRS, which will be taught to students studying at Uşak University within the scope of the study, and which allow the accounting systems of countries to be expressed in a common language, are presented. In addition, visualized examples of teaching each measurement basis are presented in the digital game "let's measure its value".

a. Historical Cost

The historical cost measurement basis, which provides monetary information about assets, liabilities, transactions that give rise to income and expenses, expresses the value of the costs incurred in the process of acquiring or creating an asset (IFRS Foundation, Conceptual Framework for Financial Reporting, Paragraph 6.4- 6.5). According to the historical cost measurement basis, this value is formed by adding the transaction costs to the price paid for the acquisition or creation of an asset. When evaluated in terms of liabilities, historical cost consists of the value of the price received to bear the related obligation or to undertake the obligation, less the transaction costs. One way to apply the historical cost measurement basis to financial assets and financial liabilities is to measure them at amortized cost. In this context, the amortized cost of a financial asset or liability reflects estimates of future cash flows discounted at a rate determined at recognition (Conceptual Framework for Financial Reporting, Paragraph 6.9). However, the historical cost measurement basis, unlike the current value measurement basis, does not reflect the changes in value of assets or liabilities unless they are related to the loss of value of an asset or liability that has become economically disadvantaged (Akgün, 2016, p. 12-153; Conceptual Framework for Financial Reporting, Paragraph 6.4).

A visualized example of the historical cost measurement basis in the digital game "let's measure its value" is presented in Figure 2 below.

b. Current Value

The current value measurement basis, which provides monetary information about assets, liabilities, income, and expenses, reflects changes in cash flow estimates and current values since the previous measurement date of assets and liabilities using updated information to reflect conditions at the measurement date. This measurement basis, unlike the historical cost measurement basis, cannot be derived from the current value of the asset or liability and the price of the transactions or other events that create the asset or liability (Akintoye and Fitzgerald, 2010, p. 161-171; Conceptual Framework for Financial Reporting, Paragraph 6.10). The current value measurement basis includes fair value, value in use for assets and fulfillment value and current cost for liabilities.

c. Fair Value

Fair value is a valuation basis that reflects market participants' current expectations about the amount, timing and uncertainty of future cash flows from assets and liabilities. In this context, expectations regarding assets and liabilities are priced to reflect the current risk preferences of market participants. In addition, this information can have validation value by providing feedback on previous expectations (Conceptual Framework for Financial Reporting, Paragraph 6.32). If the entity can determine the fair value of an asset acquired from a market using prices in a different market,

Figure 2. Visualized example of historical cost measurement basis in the digital game "Let's Measure Its Value"

the difference between the prices in these two markets is reflected in the financial statements when the fair value is first determined (Conceptual Framework for Financial Reporting, Paragraph 6.35; Graham, Lefanowicz and Petroni, 2003, p. 165-288). However, in the event of the sale of an asset or the transfer of a liability, if the asset or liability is measured at fair value, the net income or net expenses from that sale or transfer are low unless the effect of the transaction cost is material (Conceptual Framework for Financial Reporting, Paragraph 6.36).

A visualized example of the fair value measurement basis in the digital game "let's measure its value" is presented in Figure 3 below.

d. Value in Use and Fulfilment Value

Value in use represents the estimated present value of the net cash flows from the use or disposal of an asset (Conceptual Framework for Financial Reporting, Paragraph 6.37). The settlement value represents the present value of the estimated cash flows required to settle the obligation. In this context, performance value may have an estimated value in the event that an obligation is fulfilled, other than being settled or transferred through negotiation (Conceptual Framework for Financial Reporting, Paragraph 6.38). In addition, information about the amount, timing, and uncertainty of future expectations can have validation value, as updated estimates provide feedback on previous estimates of value in use or performance value (Akgün, 2016, p. 12-153; Conceptual Framework for Financial Reporting, Paragraph 6.39).

A visualized example of the measurement basis of value in use and fulfilment value in the digital game "let's measure its value" is presented in Figure 4 below.

e. Current Cost

This measurement basis reflects the cost of acquiring or creating a similar asset at the measurement date, and the consideration that would be received if a similar liability were incurred or acquired (Conceptual Framework for Financial Reporting, Paragraph 6.41). In addition, the current cost measurement basis also provides information about the cost value of an asset consumed or the income arising from the fulfillment of liabilities, such as historical cost. This information can be used as an input in deriving current margins or estimating future margins. In addition, a current cost measurement basis may be more useful than historical cost-based margins in estimating current cost-based margins for future periods when price changes are significant. In addition, the current cost measurement basis also reflects the prices at the consumption date, unlike historical cost (Conceptual Framework for Financial Reporting, Paragraph 6.42; Koç, 2021, p. 162-180).

Figure 3. Visualized example of fair value measurement basis in the digital game "Let's Measure Its Value"

Figure 4. Visualized example of value in use and fulfilment value measurement basis in the digital game "Let's Measure Its Value"

A visualized example of the relevant measurement basis in the digital game "let's measure its value" is presented in Figure 5 below.

Research Findings

Under this heading, the answers given by the participants to the questions about the relevant measurement principles were evaluated from the theoretical course on the measurement principles within the scope of IAS/IFRS for a total of 108 students

Figure 5. Visualized example of current cost measurement basis in the digital game "Let's Measure Its Value"

studying at Uşak University in Turkey and taking accounting courses. In addition, as a result of the participants playing the digital game "Let's Measure its Value", the answers given by the participants in the game regarding the measurement principles within the scope of IAS/IFRS were evaluated and the data obtained by both methods were compared.

Demographic data of the students participating in the research are presented in Table 1 below.

Table 1. Demographic data of the participants of the study

		Age					
		20-22	**23-25**	**26-28**	**29-31**	**32-34**	**Total**
Gender	Female	30	14	0	1	0	45
	Male	26	22	6	6	3	63
Total		56	36	6	7	3	108

According to the data presented in Table 1, 45 of the 108 participants included in the study consisted of female students and 63 of them were male students. In addition, most of the participants in both genders are between the ages of 20-22.

In Table 2 below, the questions of "Do you play video game?" Data on their answers to the question is presented.

Table 2. Data on video game and non-video game participants

		Female	**Male**	**Total**
Do you play video game?	Yes	26	63	89
	No	19	0	19
Total		45	63	108

According to the data presented in Table 2, it is seen that 26 of the 45 female students and all 63 male students play video games. In line with the data obtained from the table, it can be concluded that male students are more interested in video games.

Table 3 below shows the data on how many hours a day the video game participants spend on video games.

According to the data presented in Table 3, 30 percent of the participants played video games for less than 1 hour during the day, while 31 percent of the participants played for 1-2 hours, 23 of the participants for 3-4 hours, 8 of the participants for

Table 3. The time participants spent playing video games

The time (hours) participants spent playing video games						
	under 1 hour	1-2 hour	3-4 hour	5-6 hour	9-10 hour	Total
Total	27	28	20	7	7	89
Total (%)	30	31	23	8	8	% 100

5-6 hours. 8 of them spend 9-10 hours. Therefore, according to these data, it is seen that the participants mostly spend less than 1 hour and 1-2 hours during the day playing video games.

In Table 4 below, the data regarding the correct answers given by the participants who play video games and those who do not play video games, to the questions about the measurement principles, as a result of the theoretical lesson on the measurement principles within the scope of IAS/IFRS are presented.

Table 4. Number of correct answers given by participants who play video games and those who do not, as a result of the theoretical course on the measurement principles within the scope of IAS/IFRS

		The number of questions answered correctly by the participants after the presentation made to the participants about the measurement principles within the scope of TMS / TFRS					
		Number of participants who did not answer any question correctly	**Number of participants who answered one question correctly**	**Number of participants who answered correctly to two questions**	**Number of participants who answered three questions correctly**	Number of participants who answered correctly four questions	**Total**
Do you play video games?	Yes	4	35	12	29	9	89
	No	5	7	5	2	0	19
Total		4	42	17	31	9	108
Do you play video games? (%)	Yes	5	39	13	33	10	%100
	No	26	37	26	11	0	%100

According to the data presented in Table 4, as a result of the theoretical course held with the participants on the measurement principles within the scope of IAS/

IFRS, it is seen that the participants who played video games gave correct answers to more questions than the participants who did not play video games. A total of 43 percent of the participants who played video games answered three and four questions correctly, while a total of 11 percent of those who did not play video games answered three questions correctly. It is also noteworthy that none of the participants who did not play video games could answer all four questions correctly.

Table 5 below presents data on the correct answers given by the participants who play video games and those who do not, to the questions about the measurement principles within the scope of IAS/IFRS in the digital game named "Let's Measure Its Value".

Table 5. Number of correct answers given by participants who play video games and those who do not, regarding the measurement principles within the scope of IAS/IFRS in the digital game "Let's Measure Its Value"

		The question answered correctly by the participants in the digital game "Let's Measure its Value"				
		Number of participants who answered one question correctly	Number of participants who answered correctly to two questions	Number of participants who answered three questions correctly	Number of participants who answered correctly four questions	Total
Do you play video game?	Yes	10	3	19	57	89
	No	2	9	8	0	19
Total		12	12	27	57	108
Do you play video game? (%)	Yes	11	4	21	64	% 100
	No	11	47	42	0	% 100

According to the data presented in Table 5, a total of 85 percent of the participants who played video games in the digital game "Let's Measure Its Value" answered three and four questions correctly, while a total of 42 percent of the participants who did not play video games answered three questions correctly. In addition, it is noteworthy that none of the participants who did not play video games could answer all four questions correctly.

Table 6 below presents the data on the time spent by the video game participants for video games during the day and the correct answers they gave regarding the measurement principles in the digital game called "let's measure its value."

Table 6. The time spent by video game participants for video games and the number of correct answers they gave regarding the measurement principles in the "let's measure its value" digital game

		Number of participants who answered a question correctly				
		Number of participants who answered one question correctly	**Number of participants who answered correctly to two questions**	**Number of participants who answered three questions correctly**	**Number of participants who answered correctly four questions**	**Total**
If you play video games, how many hours per day do you play video games on average?	Under 1 hour	2	0	3	22	27
	1-2 hour	0	0	14	14	28
	3-4 hour	5	0	0	15	20
	5-6 hour	0	0	1	6	7
	9-10 hour	3	3	1	0	7
Total		10	3	19	57	89

According to the data presented in Table 6, it is seen that most of the participants who answered all the questions correctly in the video game played video games for less than an hour. On the other hand, the number of students who answered correctly to four questions decreased in participants who played video games for more than

Table 7. The correlation between the time spent by the participants for video games and the number of correct answers they gave regarding the measurement principles in the "Let's Measure Its Value" digital game

If you play video games, how many hours per day do you play video games on average?	**Pearson Correlation**	**If you play video games, how many hours per day do you play video games on average?**	**The number of questions answered correctly by the participants in the game "Let's measure its value"**
		1	**-.410****
	Sig. (2-tailed)		.000
	N	89	89
The number of questions answered correctly by the participants in the game "Let's measure its value"	Pearson Correlation	-.410	1
	Sig. (2-tailed)	.000	
	N	89	108

** Correlation is significant at the 0.01 level (2-tailed)

four hours. Therefore, according to the data presented in Table 7, it is possible to say that participants who play video games for less than an hour and between 1-2 hours are more successful than other participants who spend longer periods of time on video games.

Below, Table 7 presents the correlation table that deals with the relationship between the time spent by video game participants for video games and the number of correct answers they gave regarding the measurement principles in the "Let's Measure Its Value" digital game.

When the correlation table presented in Table 7 above is examined, it is seen that there is an inversely proportional relationship between the time spent by the participants for video games and the number of correct answers they gave regarding the measurement principles in the "let's measure its value" digital game. Pearson correlation coefficient is -0.410. A change in one of the variables affects the other variable by 41 percent in the opposite direction. Therefore, in the light of these data, it is possible to say that the number of correct answers given by the participants regarding the measurement principles in the "let's measure its value" digital game decreased by 41 percent in the opposite direction, as the time spent on video games increased.

In Table 8, Table 9 and Table 10 below, tables regarding the linear regression analysis that deal with the relationship between the time spent by the participants playing video games for video games and the number of correct answers in the "let's

Table 8. The regression model summary table between the time spent by the participants for video games and the number of correct answers they gave in the "Let's Measure Its Value" digital game

Model	R	R Square	Adjusted R Square	Std. Error of The Estimate
1	.410[a]	.168	.159	.91292

a. Predictors: (Constant), If you play video games, how many hours per day do you play video games on average?

measure its value" digital game regarding the measurement principles within the scope of IAS/IFRS are presented below.

H1: "The number of correct answers given by the students in the "Let's Measure Its Value" digital game is related to the video game playing time of the participants."

H0: "The number of correct answers given by the students in the "Let's Measure Its Value" digital game is not related to the video game playing time of the participants."

According to the data presented in Table 8 above, the value of R= 0.410 shows how well the model fits the variables.

Table 9. Analysis of variance (ANOVAa) between the time spent by the participants for video games and the number of correct answers to the measurement principles in the digital game "Let's Measure Its Value"

Model	Sum of Squares	df	Mean Square	F	Sig.
Regression	14.646	1	14.646	17.608	.000[b]
Residual	72.365	87	.832		
Total	87.011	88			

a. Dependent Variable: The number of questions answered correctly by the participants in the game "Let's measure its value"

b. Predictors: (Constant), If you play video games, how many hours per day do you play video games on average?

Table 10. Table of coefficients[a] between the time spent by the participants for video games and the number of correct answers they gave regarding the measurement principles in the digital game "let's measure its value"

Model		Unstandardized Coefficients		Standardized Coefficients Beta	t	Sig.
		B	Std. Error			
1	(Constant)	4.078	.192		21.244	.000
	If you play video games, how many hours per day do you play video games on average?	-.291	.069	-.410	-4.196	.000

According to the data presented in Table 9, since p= 0.000<0.025 (=0.050/2), the number of questions answered correctly by the participants in the game is needed to explain the dependent variable "Let's Measure Its Value".

According to the data presented in Table 10 above, since the t value calculated for the constant term α is 21,244 and the significance level of the test is p= 0.000<0.025 (=0.050/2), the constant term α must be present in the model. The t value calculated for the regression coefficient β is 4.196. Since the significance level of the test is p= 0.000<0.025, the regression coefficient β should also be included in the model. So, the simple linear equation is $y= 4.078 + (-0.291x)$. Therefore, in the regression analysis, Sig. since the value is less than 0.05 and 0.000, the H1 hypothesis is accepted. Therefore, it is possible to say that the number of correct answers given by the students in the "Let's measure the value" digital game is related to the video game playing time of the participants.

Table 11, Table 12, and Table 13 below contain tables for linear regression analysis that address the relationship between the time participants spend playing

Table 11. The regression model summary table between the time participants spent playing video games and the contribution of gamification to learning success in accounting education.

Model	R	R Square	Adjusted R Square	Std. Error of The Estimate
1	.403[a]	.162	.153	.58963

a. Predictors: (Constant), If you play video games, how many hours per day do you play video games on average?

Table 12. Analysis of variance between the time participants spent playing video games and the contribution of gamification to learning success in accounting education (ANOVAa)

Model	Sum of Squares	df	Mean Square	F	Sig.
Regression	5.865	1	5.865	16.871	.000[b]
Residual	30.247	87	.348		
Total	36.112	88			

a. Dependent Variable: The use of gamification method in accounting education increases the success of learning.

b. Predictors: (Constant), If you play video games, how many hours per day do you play video games on average? According to the data presented in Table 12, since p= 0.000<0.025 (=0.050/2), participants' answers regarding the contribution of gamification to the success of learning in accounting education are needed to explain the dependent variable.

Table 13. Table of the coefficients between the time spent by the participants on video games and the contribution of gamification to learning success in accounting education

Model		Unstandardized Coefficients		Standardized Coefficients Beta	t	Sig.
		B	Std. Error			
1	(Constant)	1.020	.124		8.221	.000
	If you play video games, how many hours per day do you play video games on average?	-.184	.045	.403	4.107	.000

video games for video games and the use of gamification method in accounting education increases learning achievement.

H1: "The duration of playing video games increases the success of learning when the gamification method is used in accounting education of the student."

H0: "The duration of playing video games does not increase the success of learning when the gamification method is used in accounting education of the student."

According to the data presented in Table 11 above, the value of R= 0.403 shows how well the model fits the variables.

According to the data presented in Table 13 above, since the t value calculated for the constant term α is 8,221 and the significance level of the test is p= 0.000<0.025 (=0.050/2), the constant term α must be present in the model. The t value calculated for the regression coefficient β is 4.107. Since the significance level of the test is p= 0.000<0.025, the regression coefficient β should also be included in the model. So the simple linear equation is y= 1.020 + (-0.184x).

Therefore, in the regression analysis, Sig. since the value is less than 0.05 and 0.000, the H1 hypothesis is accepted. Therefore, according to the regression analysis, it is possible to say that the duration of playing video games increases the success of learning when the gamification method is used in the accounting education of

Table 14. Number of participants who answered the questions about IAS/IFRS incorrectly in the "Let's Measure Its Value" digital game and clicked on the link to access the documents related to the IAS/IFRS framework as a result of the feedback on their screens.

	Number of Participants who gave incorrect answers to Questions on Measurement Basis within the scope of IAS/IFRS				**Total**
	Number of participants who answered the first question incorrectly (Historical cost question)	**Number of participants who answered the second question incorrectly (Current cost question)**	**Number of participants who answered the third question incorrectly (Value in use and fulfilment value question)**	**Number of participants who answered the fourth question incorrectly (Fair value question)**	
Number of participants who clicked on the link to access documents related to the IAS/IFRS conceptual framework	11	3	9	10	33
Number of participants who clicked on the link to access documents related to the IAS/IFRS conceptual framework (%)	30.33	9.10	27.27	30.30	%100

the student.

Table 14 below presents data on how many of the participants who gave incorrect answers to the questions about measurement principles in the digital game named

"Let's Measure its Value" clicked on the link to access documents related to the IAS/IFRS conceptual framework with the feedback on their screens.

According to the data presented in Table 14, it is seen that the most incorrect answers to the questions about the measurement principles in the "Let's Measure its Value" digital game were given about the fair value measurement basis. In addition, after the questions answered incorrectly in the digital game, it is seen that 30.33 percent of the participants who gave the wrong answer to the question about historical cost, clicked on the link to access the documents related to the IAS/IFRS conceptual framework. The least clicks on the link to access documents related to the IAS/IFRS conceptual framework were made by the participants who gave the wrong answer to the question about current cost, with a value of 9.10 percent. However, the measurement basis with the least wrong answer was the current cost

Table 15. Frequency table of participants' responses to different propositions about the use of the "Let's Measure Its Value" digital game in accounting education and the use of gamification method

	Absolutely I agree (%)	**I agree (%)**	**I'm undecided (%)**	**I do not agree (%)**	**I strongly disagree (%)**	**Total**
I think that the "Let's measure the value" game is effective in teaching the measurement principles within the scope of IAS/IFRS through the Google classroom system.	51.9	48.1	-	-	-	%100
The game called "Let's measure its value" contributed to my learning process in the scope of IAS/IFRS.	38.9	54.6	-	6.5	-	%100
The use of gamification method in accounting education increases the success of learning.	63	30.6	6.5	-	-	%100
The use of gamification method in accounting education increases the speed of learning.	44.4	55.6	-	-	-	%100
The use of gamification method in accounting education ensures that the learned knowledge is permanent.	38	49.1	13	-	-	%100
The use of gamification method in accounting education ensures that the learning process is fun.	69.4	18.5	5.6	6.5	-	%100
The use of gamification method in accounting education provides a more effective learning process compared to traditional theoretical and applied courses.	57.4	26.9	15.7	-	-	%100

measurement basis.

In Table 15 below, the frequency table of the participants' responses to different suggestions about the effectiveness of the "Let's Measure Its Value" digital game, its contribution to the learning process and the use of gamification method in accounting education is presented.

According to the data presented in Table 15, 51.9 percent of the participants strongly agree with the proposition that the "Let's measure the value" digital game is effective in teaching measurement principles within the scope of IAS/IFRS. 54.6 percent of the participants agree with the proposition that the "Let's measure value" digital game contributes to the learning process in teaching measurement principles within the scope of IAS/IFRS. 63 percent of the participants strongly agree with the proposition that the use of gamification method in accounting education increases the success of learning, 55.6 percent of the participants agree with the proposition that it increases the speed of learning, 49.1 percent of the participants agree with the proposition that the learned knowledge is permanent, and 69.4 percent of the participants agree with the proposition that it makes the learning process enjoyable. and 57.4 percent of the participants strongly agree with the proposition that it provides a more effective learning process compared to traditional theoretical and applied courses. 15.7 percent of the participants were undecided on the proposition that the use of gamification method in accounting education provides a more effective learning process compared to traditional theoretical and applied courses. In addition, the majority of the participants support the use of gamification methods in accounting education. 57.4 percent of the participants agree with the proposition that the use of gamification in accounting education provides a more effective learning process than traditional theoretical and applied courses.

SOLUTIONS AND RECOMMENDATIONS

With the gamification method in accounting education proposed within the scope of this study, students can take an active role in the learning process and improve their thinking skills rather than being a one-sided information receiver. In addition, gamification in accounting education enables students to process information faster and analyze information. In addition, the use of digital games in accounting education provides an interdisciplinary learning environment because students use technological tools such as computers, keyboards and mice. Learning accounting knowledge and techniques with digital games can also improve students' problem-solving skills, as they enable students to think of many moves at the same time. In this context, it is of great importance to transform accounting education in parallel with the digitalization process in the digital world, to use different materials in the education process, and to support the learning process with games, which are the most important means of entertainment for individuals.

FUTURE RESEARCH DIRECTIONS

Along with the digitalization process, it is necessary to transform accounting education and adapt to changing trends in accounting education. In this context, it is necessary to investigate the effects of presenting accounting information and techniques to students in higher education institutions with different tools in which information and communication technologies are predominantly used in accounting education in future studies. It is of great importance that academic research is carried out to investigate the effects of these methods on students and the learning process.

CONCLUSION

In the study, a gamification method based on a learner-centered education model in which students can take an active role in the learning process in training the accounting staff that businesses need in higher education institutions has been proposed. In this context, the data obtained from this research, in which the gamification method in accounting education is recommended in the digitalization process, reveals that among 108 participants, 26 of 45 female students and all 63 male students play video games. Therefore, based on this data, it can be concluded that male students are more interested in video games. In addition, 61 percent of the participants allocate less than 1 hour and 1-2 hours to video games during the day. However, after the theoretical lesson with the participants, 43 percent of the video game players answered three and four questions in total, and a total of 11 percent of those who did not play video games answered three questions correctly. While 85 percent of the participants who played video games in the digital game "Let's measure its value" answered three and four questions correctly, 42 percent of the participants who did not play video games answered only three questions correctly. In addition, none of the participants who did not play video games could answer all four questions correctly.

According to the findings of the research, the majority of the participants who answered all the questions correctly in the video game play video games for less than an hour. It was concluded that the success of the participants who spent more than 1-2 hours on video games decreased. Another of the findings obtained within the scope of the study reveals that there is an inversely proportional relationship between the time spent by the participants for video games and the number of correct answers they gave regarding the measurement principles in the "let's measure its value" digital game. Therefore, as the time spent by the participants for video games increased, it can be said that the number of correct answers they gave regarding the measurement principles in the "let's measure its value" digital game decreased by 41 percent in the opposite direction. According to the results obtained from the study, fair value was the measurement basis with the most wrong answers by the participants in the "Let's Measure its Value" digital game.

In addition, as a result of the feedback received on the screens of the participants in the questions that were answered incorrectly in the digital game, it was concluded that 30.33% of the participants who gave the wrong answer to the question about historical cost clicked on the link to access the documents related to the IAS/IFRS conceptual framework. The least clicks on the link to access documents related to the IAS/IFRS conceptual framework were made by the participants who gave the wrong answer to the question about current cost, with a value of 9.10 percent. When the data obtained from the questionnaire applied to the participants are analyzed, 51.9 percent of the participants strongly agree with the proposition that the "Let's measure the value" digital game is effective in teaching measurement principles, and 38.9 percent of the participants strongly agree with the proposition that the digital game contributes to the learning process in teaching measurement principles. 63 percent of the participants strongly agree with the proposition that the use of gamification method in accounting education increases the success of learning, 55.6 percent of the participants agree with the proposition that gamification increases the speed of learning, 49.1 percent of the participants agree with the proposition that gamification ensures the permanence of knowledge, 69.4 percent of the participants agree that gamification helps learning. and 57.4 percent of the participants stated that gamification is a more effective learning method compared to traditional theoretical applied lessons. It was concluded that they agreed with the proposition that it provided the process.

Generally, together with the digitalization process, it is possible to say that the use of gamification method in accounting education in higher education institutions can create many positive effects on students, including today's digital natives, so that students can take an active role in the learning process and the learning process can be more fun.

REFERENCES

Abbasi, N. (2014). Competency approach to accounting education: A global view. *Journal of Finance and Accountancy,* pp. 1-15. https://www.semanticscholar.org/paper/Competency-approach-to-accounting-education-%3A-A-Abbasi/ff8ffc3030ef5472c942898fcea4ba91369812b4

AECC Global. (2022). *International study overseas education consultants.* AECC Global. https://www.aeccglobal.com/

Akgün, A. İ. (2016). Towards from historical cost accounting to fair value in the turkish financial reporting standards. *Journal of Politics. Economics and Management Studies*, *4*(3), 127–153.

Akintoye, A., & Fitzgerald, E. (2010). A survey of current cost estimating practices in the UK. *Construction Management and Economics*, *18*(2), 161–172. doi:10.1080/014461900370799

Codish, D., & Gilad, R. (2014). *Personality based gamification – educational gamification for extroverts and introverts.* 9th Chais Conference for the Study of Innovation and Learning Technologies: Learning in the Technological EraAt, Ra'anana, IsraelRa'anana, Israel.

Durso, S. de O., Luciane, R., & Edgard, C. (2019). Gamificatıon in accounting and students' skillset. *Advances in Scientific and Applied Accounting*, *12*(3), 79–100.

Facer, K. (2002) *Interactive education: children's out of school uses of computers, Preliminary analysis of 2001 Survey.* Interactive Education. www.InterActiveEducation.ac.uk

Graham, R. C., Lefanowicz, C. E., Petroni, K. R. (2003). The value relevance of equitymethod fair value disclosures. *Journal of Business Finance & Accounting, 30*(7) & (8), 1065-1088.

Greenfield, P. M. (2014). *Mind and Media the Effects of Television, Video Games, and Computers.* Psychology Press. doi:10.4324/9781315735634

Hocking, D. E., & Hockng, R. T. (2008). An answer to the AICPA core competencies challenge. *Journal of Instructional Pedagogies,* pp. 1-15. https://files.eric.ed.gov/fulltext/EJ1056354.pdf

IFRS Foundation. (2022). *Conceptual framework for financial reporting.* IFRS. https://www.ifrs.org/content/dam/ifrs/publications/pdf-standards/english/2021/issued/part-a/conceptual-framework-for-financial-reporting.pdf

Kapp, K. M. (2012). *The Gamification of Learning and Instruction: Game-Based Methods and Strategies for Training and Education. 1 st.* John Wiley & Sons Inc.

Koç, F. (2021). Role play in accounting training: Turkish accounting standards/ Turkish financial reporting standards (TAS/ TFRS) in accordance teach the basis of valuation. *International Journal of Management Economics and Business*, *17*, 162–180.

Mayer, R. E. (2019). Computer games in education. *Annual Review of Psychology*, *70*(1), 531–549. doi:10.1146/annurev-psych-010418-102744 PMID:30231003

MIT (Masschusetts Institute of Technology). (2014). *Institute-wide task force on the future of mit education (final report).* MIT. https://future.mit.edu/final-report

Moncada, S. M., & Moncada, T. P. (2014). Gamification of learning in accounting education. *Journal of Higher Education Theory and Practice, 14*(3), 9–17.

Newzoo. (2022). *The destination for games market insights.* New Zoo. https://newzoo.com

Nias Ahmad, M. A. & Jamaluddin, J. & Mohd din, N. & Mohammad Fadzillah, N. S. & Abd Jabar, F. (2017). Gamification of introductory accounting course: when is the best time to implement it. *Business Management and Computing Research Colloquium.* UITM Cawangan Pahang Malaysia.

Proserpio, L., & Gioia, D. A. (2007). Teaching the virtual generation. *Academy of Management Learning & Education, 6*(1), 69–80. doi:10.5465/amle.2007.24401703

Queiro-Ameijeiras, C.-M., Marti-Parreño, J., Seguí-Más, E., & Summerfield, L. (2019). A literature review of the use of gamification in accounting education. *12th Annual International Conference of Education, Research and Innovation.* IATED, 7662-7667.10.21125/iceri.2019.1822

Seow, P., & Wong, S. P. (2016). Using a mobile gaming app to enhance accounting education. *Journal of Education for Business, 91*(8), 434–439. doi:10.1080/08832323.2016.1256264

Silva, R., Rodrigues, R., & Leal, C. (2021). Games based learning in accounting education - which dimensions are the most relevant? *Accounting Education, 30*(2), 159–187. doi:10.1080/09639284.2021.1891107

Squire, K. D. (2013). Video game-based learning: An emerging paradigm for instruction. *Performance Improvement Quarterly, 26*(1), 101–130. doi:10.1002/piq.21139

Tobias, S., Fletcher, J. D., Dai, D. Y., & Wind, A. P. (2011). Review of research on computer games. In S. Tobias & J. D. Fletcher (Eds.), *Computer games and instruction* (pp. 127–221). IAP Information Age Publishing.

KEY TERMS AND DEFINITIONS

Current Cost: It is the value at the measurement date of another asset equivalent to the related asset plus the transaction costs to be incurred.

Fair Value: The price that would be received to sell an asset or paid to settle a liability at the measurement date.

Gamification in Accounting Education: It is the presentation of accounting education to students with online or offline games.

Historical Cost: It represents the value of the costs incurred in the acquisition or creation of an asset.

International Accounting Standards/ International Financial Reporting Standards (IAS/IFRS): They are the standards published by the Accounting Standards Board (IASB) in order to develop an internationally common accounting language in financial reporting.

Principles of Measurement: It is the defined characteristic of an item that can be measured in accounting.

Value in Use and Fulfilment Value: It is a measurement basis that is based on future cash flows and reflects entity-specific assumptions.

Chapter 4
Investigative Interviews Conducted by Forensic Accounting and Auditing Professionals

Joan Fico
https://orcid.org/0000-0003-4658-0525
University of Delaware, USA

David William Walsh
De Montfort University, UK

ABSTRACT

Interviews conducted by both forensic accountants and auditors are an important task associated with either role in gathering information that progresses inquiries. Auditors interview clients about the collectability of accounts receivable, or the appropriateness of significant accounting estimates such as goodwill impairment. Forensic accountants interview clients when financial fraud is suspected in cases of asset misappropriation, bribery, larceny, and financial statement fraud. However, training in the task and the literature concerning how the task should be undertaken is disjointed, outdated both by the science and developments in practice undertaken elsewhere. Anecdotally, although new auditors spend nearly twenty five percent of their engagement time performing interviews and partners spend nearly forty percent performing interviews, there is virtually no formal training on how to conduct an interview at the undergraduate and graduate level.

DOI: 10.4018/978-1-6684-5483-1.ch004

Copyright © 2023, IGI Global. Copying or distributing in print or electronic forms without written permission of IGI Global is prohibited.

INTRODUCTION

Interviews conducted by forensic accountants and auditors are an important task associated with either role in gathering information that progresses inquiries. For example, auditors interview clients about the collectability of accounts receivable, or the appropriateness of significant accounting estimates such as goodwill impairment. Internal auditors perform interviews to ensure the system of internal controls are present and functioning and evaluate new and old systems periodically for weaknesses. Internal auditors are frequently called upon to investigate fraud within the organization. Forensic accountants interview clients when financial fraud is suspected in cases of asset misappropriation, bribery, larceny, and financial statement fraud. However, training in the task and the literature concerning how the task should be undertaken is disjointed, outdated both by the science and developments in practice undertaken elsewhere. Anecdotally, although new auditors spend nearly twenty five percent of their engagement time performing interviews and partners spend nearly forty percent performing interviews, there is virtually no formal training on how to conduct an interview at the undergraduate and graduate level (Seipp and Lindberg 2012; Wang et al. 2020). Leinicke et al. (2005) report, “interviewing is both a regular and important task undertaken by auditors at all stages in their careers”.

The AICPA’s *Pre-Certification Core Competency Framework* states that communication and critical thinking skills are an important part of students’ competencies. Interviewing is one important aspect of communication and critical thinking (Wang et al. 2020). Furthermore, although interview training textbooks exist aimed at the budding criminologist, there are no resources aimed at preparing the new forensic accountant or internal or external auditors to conduct a skilled interview. Porter and Crumbley (2012) report, “the forensic accounting profession is not at the leading edge of interview training. The most successful interviewers command these skills because they are beneficiaries of comprehensive training.” Turning our attention to preparing students to perform a high-quality interview (that includes the skills required for all aspects of communication with colleagues and clients) is not only essential to students’ development, but to the profession (Leinecke et al., 2005; Seipp and Lindberg 2012). The accounting curriculum should include such training for the profession. There is a brief discussion of the interview as oral evidence in auditing textbooks. Arens et. al. (2020) define oral evidence as, “the obtaining of … oral information from the client in response to specific questions during the audit.” A discussion of investigative interviewing techniques would be appropriate during a discussion of *how* to collect oral evidence and how to design appropriate questions. Second, rapport building, an essential component of interviewing, can be introduced in any first session as a way that students can learn more about each other while practicing structured rapport building techniques.

The nature of the interviewing task in these domains has come to be viewed not so dissimilar as to those conducted by law enforcement agencies, where the goal is to establish from victims, witnesses, and suspects (some of whom for a whole range of reasons may be reluctant to talk) detailed information concerning what has happened to progress cases. Such transfer of understanding from that domain has led to a growing number of publications that illustrate how the developments in law enforcement interviews in certain parts of the world can be equally applicable to other contexts such as forensic accounting and auditing (e.g., Rachlew, Loken and Bergestuen, 2022; Stacey and Page, 2013). Thus far, the techniques have been applied to a wide range of practices and are used by medical professionals, salespeople, and psychologists.

Developments have occurred in the last twenty years or so in several countries (e.g., England and Wales, Norway, and Australia) that have seen the police service in those countries move away from a confession-seeking approach that had so dominated their previous interviews with those suspected of crime. Often it has been found in the countries that the old approaches (where the focus of the interview was not to gain an accurate account, but rather to assign blame) has been argued to have led to false confessions and/or false information (Kassin and Gudjonsson, 2004). Neither outcome represents a satisfactory position. Criminal investigations, need to be based on reliable information.

This premise also applies to the essential inquiries that forensic accountants, and internal and external auditors undertake as part of their responsibilities when they seek information from people. Forensic accountants seek information that can be used in a criminal investigation and the connection between a criminological interview and a forensic interview is similar in its effort to gain an accurate account that is used in a legal proceeding. We can apply similar techniques to auditing (especially internal auditing) to seek information about processes, controls, and fraud. For example, when seeking an understanding of a newly designed budgeting system, the internal auditor builds rapport, carefully plans the interview questions based on a skeletal understanding of the budgeting system, and asks questions about how the new budgeting system works. This allows the internal auditor to assess the adequacy of internal controls. Information collected that lacks both detail and accuracy will undermine these important goals of collecting reliable information.

However, in England and Wales it was regularly found that the police did not achieve these goals regardless as to whether the interviewee is a criminal suspect or a witness. In 1992 such circumstances in England and Wales led to a new interviewing framework. Fundamental to this approach was the need to foster conditions where interviewees were able to provide detailed, accurate and relevant information. In this chapter, we detail this revised approach, termed *investigative interviewing*.

This paradigm is also equally applicable to the forensic accounting interview, as well as to internal and external auditing. For example, rapport building, a critical component of investigative interviewing, is essential to all types of interview settings in accounting. To obtain information, the interviewee must be relaxed and comfortable with sharing information with the interviewer. Planning the interview questions and understanding the appropriate types of questions to ask are useful skills to introduce within the forensic accounting and auditing curriculum.

THE INTRODUCTION OF AN INVESTIGATIVE INTERVIEWING MODEL

In England and Wales, as a result of various high-profile failed cases, the new interviewing philosophy/approach and training courses was introduced. These provided officers with a framework called 'PEACE'. PEACE is an acronym for the five phases of the framework, these being, **P**reparation and **P**lanning undertaken prior to an interview, **E**ngaging with the interviewee at the interview's outset and **E**xplaining what the respective roles were to be expected of all those present during the interview, before gathering an **A**ccount (and if needed, clarifying and challenging that account), and then finally bringing the interview to a **C**lose. Once the interview had ceased there would be expected an **E**valuation both of the case and of the officer's own interview performance.

The PEACE framework has since been adopted in similar forms in other countries (such as Scotland, Australia, New Zealand, Norway, Ireland, and Canada – see Walsh, Oxburgh, Redlich & Myklebust, 2016). What is common about all these forms is that they are underpinned by the goal of gaining a detailed and reliable account from interviewees who are first given the opportunity to provide their side of the story. The framework is also applicable to interviews with victims and witnesses. The PEACE framework has been introduced in the United States and can be found in many police training programs[1] and is already in use in professional auditing programs[2].

In England and Wales, various studies have examined use of the framework in actual interviews conducted by the police (see Clarke & Milne, 2001; Griffiths & Milne, 2006; Griffiths, Milne, & Cherryman, 2011; Leahy-Harland & Bull, 2017; Oxburgh, Williamson, & Ost, 2006; Soukara, Bull, Vrij, Turner, & Cherryman, 2009). These field studies have also included interviews conducted as part of fraud investigations (Walsh & Bull, 2010, 2012a, 2012b, 2015; Walsh & Milne, 2008). Consistent across all these studies has been the finding that interviewing malpractice occurred rarely after the introduction of the PEACE model. As such, the ethos of PEACE as an interview technique that respects interviewees, is non-oppressive, not confession-oriented, and (thus) non-coercive has become an essential part of the investigative interviewing paradigm and practice in England and Wales.

Observational studies have often found a greater emphasis on investigators asking open questions, such as those pre-fixed by the instructions; Tell, Explain, or Describe (Oxburgh, Myklebust, & Grant, 2010). However, many studies (e.g., Clarke & Milne, 2001; Izotovas, Kelly & Walsh, 2021; Walsh & Bull, 2010; 2015) have commonly found limitations regarding its use in practice, such as those relating to investigators

1. Developing good questioning strategies where there is a suitable arrangement of good questions asked (and bad question types avoided) when attempting to gain reliable details from interviewees. This subject will be covered in more depth later in this Chapter, including its use in accounting or auditing interviews.
2. Developing a logical structure to the interview (where the interview is divided into several sub-topics to ensure that all relevant topics are covered and none are missed in the search for detailed information from interviewees (Shepherd & Griffiths 2021). In forensic accounting and auditing contexts such a good order of sub-topics could be established by using a flowchart of procedures, by incorporating checklists, or by reference to FASB standards to determine their correct application.
3. Interviewers not providing either intermittent and final summaries (or ineffectively providing them when they did undertake these tasks). Such summaries are useful in ensuring the interviewer has understood what has been said by interviewees. In turn, such recognition by interviewees that they have been understood correctly prompt them to continue to disclose further information (Shepherd & Griffiths, 2021). It also allows interviewers the opportunity to realise what matters are still yet to be covered in interviews and to identify where clarifications are required concerning those details already provided by interviewees. Internal auditors confirm their understanding when gathering information when evaluating operational efficiency. External auditors gain an understanding of the clients processes and must confirm their understanding with the client in order to reliably document the client's systems and processes.
4. By not seeking clarifications first, before challenging interviewees about any inconsistencies in their accounts, Challenges may well be appropriate when that which is said by the interviewee is compared to that which is either already – and indisputably - known, that which clearly contradicts what those interviewees have already said, or that which at first sight is beyond any credulity). However, interviewers were often inappropriately challenging interviewees. had they first clarified details given by interviewees before challenging them where they may

have found that such inconsistencies and contradictions were a product of, say, unclear and insufficient questions asked earlier that had failed to obtain the required details, memory failings that typically occur, and interviewers falsely assuming what had happened. In contrast, where inconsistencies did require challenges, some interviewers failed to challenge the interviewee (and thus the account given by them contained unresolved matters, and the interviewee was not invited to explain these contradictions). Alternatively, where interviewers did challenge interviewees, they were found too aggressive either in their tone of voice, behaviour or language. That is to say, that interviewers do not need to be hostile and confrontational when challenging interviewees but need to show them in a conversational manner any matters of continuing dispute. Indeed, such aggressive techniques have been found to be counter-productive, being ones that were associated with obtaining impaired accounts from interviewees and increasing (but not overcoming) interviewees' resistance and lack of cooperation. Forensic accountants and auditors find that interviewees, especially in instances of fraud, report their practiced accounts of events leaving out self-incriminating details.

5. Associated with the above point, interviewers failing to effectively build and maintain rapport. Again, later in the Chapter this area will be given further coverage. At this point, it is sufficient to say that the development of rapport between interviewer and interviewee is a crucial element when gathering detailed information in any accounting, auditing, or forensic accounting context.
6. Closing the interview effectively. Field studies have often found this phase of the interview be given inadequate attention by interviewers. Here, interviewers have the opportunity to summarise what has been said in the interview (the importance of summarising has already been noted). They also have the opportunity then to seek if the interviewee wants to add or alter anything that has been said, as well as advising the interviewee what is to happen next. Such activities in this final phase of the interview can leave the interviewee with a positive impression of the interviewer's professionalism, while allowing for rapport to be maintained and continued should there need to be further interviews to be conducted with the interviewee.

In addition to the above issues, research also found that two of the PEACE model's components; **P**lanning and **P**reparation, and **E**valuation were often conducted poorly (Clarke & Milne, 2001; Walsh & Milne, 2007). The importance of planning and preparation was evidenced in a study of fraud investigators that found association between its prior undertaking before interviews and the gathering of a comprehensive account during them (Walsh & Bull, 2010). Walsh and Milne (2007) and Walsh and Bull (2011) both conducted surveys of fraud investigation personnel, finding that insufficient time was an offered explanation for planning/preparation not being thoroughly conducted. Planning of interviews should involve gaining background details, planning the order of topics to be introduced, ensuring awareness of the relevant legislative and procedural requirements, and making references to appropriate GAAP and authoritative guidance or PCAOB guidance. In a forensic audit, planning not only includes gaining an understanding of how the internal controls should work, but also how they could be overridden, or manipulated.

Furthermore, comprehensive effort to plan an audit or fraud examination interview is often not undertaken in auditing and forensic accounting. To a very limited extent, audit inquiries are planned if one considers the use of checklists. Checklists prompt auditors to ask specific question topics. However, without experience, auditors and forensic accountants do not have the skills to react to deviations from the expected checklist responses. Training enhances the skills needed to plan appropriate questions and follow up questions to subject's responses.

Kim, Walsh, Bull, & Bergstrom (2018) found that planning was not, however, strongly associated with perceived time pressures, as those prior surveys conducted by Walsh and his associates have found when asking fraud investigators why they did not undertake planning (Walsh & Bull, 2011; Walsh & Milne, 2007). Kim et al., found that financial investigators' decision whether to plan was more linked to their beliefs in their own abilities to interview without needing to undertake such groundwork beforehand. Rating one's own competence is a matter that is connected to evaluation, the final element of the PEACE model (Evaluation). In cases of those who investigate human trafficking and labour exploitation, their ability to assess accurately their interview skills was examined. Walsh, King, and Griffiths (2017) found human trafficking investigators' ratings of their own skill levels to be consistently exaggerated when compared to independent assessments. Indeed, interviewers have stated that they received little or no training in the evaluation task, admitting to undertaking it only rarely, if at all and they seldom received feedback from their supervisors (Clarke & Milne, 2001; Walsh & Bull, 2010; Walsh & Milne, 2007). Feedback on performance has been long found in training and educational domains as an important feature of sustaining performance and skill learned in the training room (Rouiller & Goldstein, 1993).

Griffiths and Walsh (2018) tended to find that human trafficking investigators, assessed by these researchers as skilled, were also those more honest when providing a reflective account of their own interview skills, being also more thoughtful as to how they should plan to improve their skills. Those human trafficking investigators assessed as less skilled, were less reflective, being ones to seek excuses for their performance on situational factors, also being less inclined to plan to improve future performance, and those who tended to avoid undertaking certain activities in practice (such as developing a logical structure for their interviews, rapport building, and effective evidence disclosure).

Any problem would be less evident in the auditing environment because review and feedback are already fundamental aspects of the structure of the supervision of the audit. However, this rather depends on whether supervisors have an agreed set of interview standards, that they commonly apply. Cherryman and Bull (2001) found that this was not the case in their study of criminal investigators. Such inattention to self-evaluation of their own interview skills (or indeed, any supervisory evaluation) may be related to the shortfalls of investigative interviewing in practice.

One of the interviewing skills that the PEACE framework innovatively emphasised over 30 years ago, rapport building, is nowadays commonly understood to be a key feature of investigative interviewing (Abbe & Brandon, 2014; Gabbert et al., 2021). Rapport has been defined as that which involves a 'working alliance' (Vanderhallen, Vervaeke, & Holmberg, 2011), that is characterised by mutual trust and respect between interviewer and interviewee (Russano, Narchet, Kleinman, & Meissner, 2014). Walsh and Bull (2012a) found that rapport was built where fraud investigators were more conversational when (at the start of the interview) explaining the purpose of the interview to interviewees and that their information was important, ensuring that interviewees were comfortable and understood what was expected of them in the ensuing interview. Certain tasks to be employed in that later information-gathering part of the interview (such as encouraging interviewees to provide more information, summarizing, active listening and resolving any contradictions in their account). When these techniques were found to be conducted less skilfully, or not at all, the interviews were associated with a breakdown in rapport. Furthermore, the quality of interviewer rapport was found to be positively associated with the amounts (relevant) information provided by the those suspects of fraud.

Another task deemed crucial to rapport development concerns evidence disclosure. Briefly, evidence already held can be presented either initially in an interview, at the end of the interview or gradually throughout the interview. Walsh, Milne and Bull (2016) found from their survey of investigators, almost all of whom were those who interviewed white collar crime suspects, tended to favour the gradual disclosure approach. However, there was found much less consensus as to what order this ongoing disclosure should take (e.g., strongest piece of evidence introduced either first or last, or whether evidence, regardless of its strength, be disclosed chronologically etc.). Walsh and Bull (2015) found that fraud investigators, trained in the PEACE framework, who revealed evidence they held at or towards the start of the interview were those assessed as less skilled and very often were those who failed to gain detailed accounts. Those interviewers who opted for gradual disclosure of evidence (and those who disclosed evidence only towards the end of the interview once they had obtained a full account) were those seen as more skilful interviewers and were those more likely to obtain more information from interviewees.

Bull and Soukara (2010) examined the techniques undertaken by PEACE-trained interviewers where suspects had initially denied any involvement in criminal activity (though acknowledging their guilt later in the interview). Bull and Soukara noted either at the time of such admissions, or shortly before, interviewers were disclosing gradually the information/evidence held (rather than, say, in a single phase at the start of the interview). Similar findings were also found in subsequent studies following the implementation of PEACE (Leahy-Harland & Bull, 2017; Walsh & Bull, 2012b; Walsh & Bull, 2015). An interesting point is that these findings contrast with those of studies conducted before officers were trained in the PEACE framework (e.g., Baldwin, 1993; Moston et al., 1992). In those studies, all the available evidence/information was often fully disclosed at the beginning, and it was rare that suspects changed their story from denying involvement in the offence to that of admitting such participation or association. However, PEACE trained officers, undertaking an information-gathering approach (involving gradual disclosure), were found to overcome such denials at levels of occurrence far outstripping those found in pre-PEACE studies. Such a finding suggests that the PEACE framework (when employed skilfully) is not only associated with the gaining of more information from suspects, but also overcoming resistance (without using unethical techniques).

These findings followed the work conducted around the world that have examined the perspective of interviewees (e.g., Cleary & Bull, 2019; Holmberg and Christianson, 2002; Kebbell, Hurren and Mazerolle, 2006). These studies involved the researchers talking to convicted offenders of most serious crimes. Common to the findings in these studies is that while half of suspects approach interviews with the firm intent to either provide full admissions or denials, the other half also waited to see how they were treated before deciding which of these two strategies to undertake. Co-operation was found positively associated the interviewers' willingness to (i) allow them to talk and provide explanation and their version of events; (ii) listen to them; (iii) be open minded and non-judgmental and (iv) be compassionate and empathetic. Those who said that they did not co-operate attributed such denials to their treatment by those interviewers whom they viewed as dominant and aggressive.

A further key skill that has been found to problematise officers conducting interviews after the introduction of PEACE, is that of questioning strategies. Here, Griffiths and Milne (2006) offer a model known as the Griffiths' Question map (GQM). Griffiths and Milne (2006) identify eight question types and find that utilizing three, specific "good" question types, "open" "probing" "appropriate-closed", asked in a specific order, yield the most productive account of information. That is, they recommend, that when entering the account gathering phase of the interview, that interviewees should be asked to freely recall their knowledge of the matter in hand (whether it be details of a procedure or a specific incident or a series of incidents). An example of an open-ended question is "you said that you recorded journal entries for the collection of accounts receivable. Can you tell me about that?". From that first account, a series of sub-topics can be developed each commencing with a request for information (that is, tell me, explain to me, or describe to me). Thereafter, it is likely, that such accounts may need probing for finer details (these questions are typically prefaced with terms as "what", "where", "when", "which", "who" and "how"). Let's assume the client reports that the accounts receivable is aged and an aging report is generated. The interviewer might ask, "when is the report reviewed?", and "who reviews the report?". Sometimes they can also begin with "why", though care should be taken that interviewees are asked only to explain what they can be reasonably assumed to know, rather than attempt to provide answer based on speculation. For example, asking the reasons why a particular procedure (like a review of aged receivables) is conducted is acceptable, whereas asking why a third party thought that they had followed the procedure is less so. Those questions defined as "appropriate closed" (which ask for either affirmation or refutation) are intended as those only to be used for confirming or clarifying information already supplied by interviewees. They are known as "inappropriate ones" if used at any other time because while they may give correct information that information is limited. For example, the question "are you responsible for the receipt of cash payments for accounts receivable" requires a simple dichotomous response, whereas (a better question) would be to ask, "explain to me what happens when a customer pays their account in cash".

Thus, in recapitulation, a good question strategy begins with an open question, likely followed by probing questions to get the fine details and also appropriate closed one(s) where necessary, before moving on to the next topic (where the strategy repeats). Other question types such as leading ones are not intended to gather detailed information but to more direct interviewees toward answers presumed by the interviewer. For example, "you review the aging reports and call the late payers regularly, correct?" These should be then avoided. That is, the objective of any interview should be to gather detailed reliable information, rather than to give (assumed) information. Good interview techniques (such as good questioning strategies, rapport, and evidence disclosure) can influence the outcomes of fraud interviews (Walsh & Bull, 2015).

However, while studies examining aspects of the PEACE model are important to our understanding of the effectiveness of information gathering in ascertaining reliable accounts from interviewees, such techniques do not operate in isolation of each other. Recently, studies have begun to examine a coalition of techniques. For example, Walsh and Bull (2015) examined three forms of evidence disclosure by interviewers (i.e., early, gradual, and late presentation) alongside questioning strategies (following Griffiths & Milne, 2006). They found that gradual disclosure, when accompanied by open and probing questions yielded more information from suspects than did the other two methods of evidence presentation, regardless of how questions were put to suspects in those other sets of interviews. Izotovas, Kelly, and Walsh (2021) took this type of interview analysis yet one stage further by using a taxonomy first utilised by Kelly, Miller, Redlich, and Kleinman (2013). These latter authors identified a maximum of six domains in any one interview (that is, *rapport and relationship building*, *context manipulation*, *emotion provocation*, *confrontation/competition*, *collaboration*, and *presentation of evidence)*. Kelly et al. postulated that these domains would be helpful to the gaining of better oversight when studying interview practices, due to the more holistic view undertaken when conducting this type of research of police interviews (see Kelly et al., 2013 for a fuller description of these domains).

Izotovas, Kelly and Walsh (2021) found that interviews tended to commence with rapport being built, good questions being asked, and evidence being gradually disclosed. As the interview progressed in the face of either denials or an absence of co-operation, the interviewers became increasingly confrontational, and asked more 'bad' questions (such as leading ones). The result was that rapport between interviewer and interviewee was found to decrease (or disappear), they became more hostile and they failed to gain either co-operation, or as much information they should have aimed to obtain. In short, they became less skilful. The level of skill matters when conducting audit and forensic accounting procedures. As found in several studies (e.g., Walsh & Bull, 2010, 2012a. 2012b, 2015), it is not merely the performing of certain tactics (such as rapport building, questioning strategies, and evidence disclosure) that matters, but the levels of skills too.

That said, research examining interviewers who are trained in the PEACE framework has found them not adopting a coercive confessions-centred approach found so prevalent before its introduction. Likewise, tactics, such as bluff, trickery and telling lies about what evidence is held are barely seen now in interviews in England and Wales. Likewise, maximisation techniques (that is, those where interviewees are, for example, told things will get worse if they do not give information/tell the truth) or minimisation ones, where the interviewee is induced into giving information (e.g., tell me now, as it will be better for you) are also virtually non-existent. Confession rates remained constant after the introduction of PEACE training compared to the rate before its implementation into everyday practice. However, as Walsh and Bull (2010) found, more reliable information is forthcoming- and that should be the real goal of interviews. The investigative interviewing approach underlines the importance of better investigations, information and intelligence gathering, rather than determining case resolution by the presence or absence of a confession made by a suspect during their interview. As such, transference to other domains is argued as quite appropriate, where the need for detailed information is vital.

However, as has been noted, studies examining PEACE-trained interviewers' practice have found them to be of an inconsistent quality in terms of their skill levels. Leahy-Harland and Bull (2017) have, however, found that officers who were highly skilled and engaged wholly with the PEACE model conducted interviews that gather detailed accounts from suspects.

The accounting curriculum has minimal to no coverage of interviewing techniques. Question types are listed and briefly described in some audit textbooks. For example, Arens et.al (2020) states only, "when the auditor wants to obtain information about the client's method of recording and controlling accounting transactions, the auditor usually begins by asking the client how the internal controls operate. Later, the auditor performs audit tests using inspection and observation to determine whether the transactions are recorded (completeness objective) and authorized (occurrence objective) in the manner stated".

There is no formal training on how to develop rapport, or how to plan an interview with a client, suspect, or witness. The inclusion of investigative interviewing techniques in audit and forensic accounting courses will enhance students' knowledge of essential skills required of them in the profession. Furthermore, the inclusion of interviewing techniques satisfies the AICPA's *Pre-certification Core Competency Framework* requiring students to develop communication and critical thinking skills.

REFERENCES

Abbe, A., & Brandon, S. E. (2014). Building and maintaining rapport in investigative interviews. *Police Practice and Research, 15*, 207–220. doi:10.1080/15614263.2013.827835

Arens, A. A., Beasley, M. S., Elder, R. J., & Hogan, C. E. (2020). *Auditing and assurance services: an integrated approach* (17th ed.).

Baldwin, J. (1993). Police interview techniques: Establishing truth or proof? *British Journal of Criminology, 33*, 325–351.

Bull, R., & Soukara, S. (2010). A set of studies of what really happens in police interviews with suspects. In G. D. Lassiter & C. Meissner (Eds.), *Interrogations and confessions* (pp. 81–96). American Psychological Association.

Cherryman, J., & Bull, R. (2001). Police officers' perceptions of specialist investigative interviewing skills. *International Journal of Police Science and Management, 3*, 199– 212. https://doi.org/. 1177%2F146135570100300302 doi:10

Clarke, C., & Milne, R. (2001). National Evaluation of the PEACE Investigative Interviewing Course. *Police Research Award Scheme Report No. PRAS/149*. London: Home Office.

Cleary, H. M. D., & Bull, R. (2019). Jail inmates' perspectives on police interrogation. *Psychology, Crime & Law*, *25*, 157–170. doi:10.1080/1068316X.2018.1503667

Fico, J., & Walsh, D. (n.d.). *A review of the accounting and forensic auditing literature as it applies to interviewing people as part of the job role.*

Gabbert, F., Hope, L., Luther, K., Wright, G., Ng, M., & Oxburgh, G. E. (2021). Exploring the use of rapport in professional information-gathering contexts by systematically mapping the evidence base. *Applied Cognitive Psychology*, *35*, 329–341. doi:10.1002/acp.3762

Griffiths, A., Milne, B., & Cherryman, J. (2011). A question of control? the formulation of suspect and witness interview question strategies by advanced interviewers. *International Journal of Police Science & Management*, *13*(3), 255–267. doi:10.1350/ijps.2011.13.3.219

Griffiths, A., & Milne, R. (2006). Will it all end in tiers? Police interviews with suspects in Britain. In T. Williamson (Ed.), *Investigative interviewing: Rights, research and regulation* (pp. 167–189). Willan.

Griffiths, A., & Walsh, D. (2018). Qualitative analysis of qualitative evaluation: An exploratory examination of investigative interviewers' reflections on their performance. *Psychology, Crime & Law*, *24*(4), 433–450. doi:10.1080/1068316X.2017.1390115

Holmberg, U., & Christianson, S.-A. (2002). Murderers and sexual offenders' experiences of police interviews and inclination to admit or deny crimes. *Behavioral Sciences & the Law*, *20*, 31–45. PMID:11979490

Izotovas, A., Kelly, C. E., & Walsh, D. (2021). The Domains of PEACE: Examining interviews with suspected sex offenders. *Journal of Police and Criminal Psychology*.

Kassin, S. M., & Gudjonsson, G. H. (2004). The Psychology of Confessions: A Review of the Literature and Issues. *Psychological Science in the Public Interest*, *5*(2), 33–67. doi:10.1111/j.1529-1006.2004.00016.x PMID:26158993

Kebbell, M. R., Hurren, E. J., & Mazerolle, P. (2006). Sex offenders' perceptions of police interviewing: Implications for improving the interviewing effectiveness. *The Canadian Journal of Police & Security Services*, *4*, 67–75.

Kelly, C. E., Miller, J. C., Redlich, A. D., & Kleinman, S. M. (2013). A taxonomy of interrogation methods. *Psychology, Public Policy, and Law, 19*(2), 165–178. doi:10.1037/a0030310

Kim, J., Walsh, D., Bull, R., & Bergstrom, H. (2018). Planning ahead? Factors influencing investigators' attitudes towards planning for interviews with suspects. *Journal of Police and Criminal Psychology*, *33*, 158–174. doi:10.100711896-017-9243-z.104

Leahy-Harland, S., & Bull, R. (2017). Police strategies and suspect responses in real-life serious crime interviews. *Journal of Police and Criminal Psychology*, *32*(2), 138–151.

Leinicke, L. M., Ostrosky, J. A., Rexroad, W. M., Baker, J. R., & Beckman, S. (2005). Interviewing as an Auditing Tool. *The CPA Journal*, *75*(2), 34.

Milne, R., & Bull, R. (1999). *Investigative interviewing: Psychology and practice*. Wiley.

Moston, S., Stephenson, G. M., & Williamson, T. (1992). The effects of case characteristics on suspect behaviour during police questioning. *British Journal of Criminology*, *32*, 23–40.

Oxburgh, G. E., Myklebust, T., & Grant, T. (2010). The question of question of question types in police interviews: A review of the literature from a psychological and linguistic perspective. *International Journal of Speech Language and the Law*, *17*, 45–66.

Oxburgh, G. E., Williamson, T., & Ost, J. (2006). Police officers' use of emotional language during child sexual abuse investigations. *Journal of Investigative Psychology and Offender Profiling*, *3*, 35–45.

Porter, S. F., & Crumbley, D. L. (2012). Teaching interviewing techniques to forensic accountants is critical. *Journal of Forensic & Investigative Accounting*, *4*(1), 122–146.

Rachlew, A., Loken, G.-E., & Bergestuen, S. T. (2022). *A Guide to the Professional Interview*. Anthem Press.

Rouiller, J. Z., & Goldstein, I. L. (1993). The relationship between organizational transfer climate and positive transfer of training. *Human Resource Development Quarterly*, *4*, 377–399.

Russano, M., Narchet, F., Kleinman, S., & Meissner, C. (2014). Structured interviews of experienced HUMINT interrogators. *Applied Cognitive Psychology, 28*. 847–859. doi:10.1002/acp.3069.

Seipp, E., & Lindberg, D. L. (2012). A Guide to Effective Audit Interviews. *The CPA Journal*, *82*, 26.

Shepherd, E., & Griffiths, A. (2012). *Investigative interviewing*. Oxford University Press.

Soukara, S., Bull, R., Vrij, A., Turner, M., & Cherryman, J. (2009). What really happens in police interviews with suspects? Tactics and confessions. *Psychology, Crime & Law*, *15*, 493–506.

Stacey, H., & Page, A. (2013). *Investigative interview: a guide for the workplace*. Publicious Publishing.

Vanderhallen, M., Vervaeke, G., & Holmberg, U. (2011). Witness and suspect perceptions of working alliance and interviewing style. *Journal of Investigative Psychology and Offender Profiling*, *8*(2), 110–130. doi:10.1002/jip.138

Walsh, D., & Bull, R. (2010). The interviewing of suspects by non-police agencies: What's effective? What is effective! *Legal and Criminological Psychology*, *15*, 305–321.

Walsh, D., & Bull, R. (2011). Benefit fraud investigative interviewing: A self-report study of investigation professionals' beliefs concerning practice. *Journal of Investigative Psychology and Offender Profiling*, *8*, 131–148.

Walsh, D., & Bull, R. (2012a). How do interviewers attempt to overcome suspects' denials? *Psychiatry, Psychology and Law*, *19*, 151–168.

Walsh, D., & Bull, R. (2012b). Examining rapport in investigative interviews with suspects: Does its building and maintenance work? *Journal of Police and Criminal Psychology*, *27*, 73–84.

Walsh, D., & Bull, R. (2015). The association between evidence disclosure, questioning strategies, interview skills, and interview outcomes. *Psychology, Crime & Law*, *21*, 661–680. doi:10.1080/1068316X.2015.1028544

Walsh, D., King, M., & Griffiths, A. (2017). Evaluating interviews which search for the truth with suspects: But are investigators' self-assessments of their own skills truthful ones? *Psychology, Crime & Law*, *23*, 647–665. doi:10.1080/10683 16X.2017.1296149

Walsh, D., & Milne, R. (2007). Giving PEACE a Chance. *Public Administration*, *8*, 525–540.

Walsh, D., & Milne, R. (2008). Keeping the PEACE? A study of investigative interviewing practices in the public sector. *Legal and Criminological Psychology*, *13*, 39–57.

Walsh, D., Milne, R., & Bull, H. (2016). One way or another? Criminal investigators' beliefs regarding the disclosure of evidence in interviews with suspects in England and Wales. *Journal of Police and Criminal Psychology*, *31*, 127–140.

Walsh, D., Oxburgh, G., Redlich, A., & Myklebust, T. (2016). *International developments and practices in investigative interviewing and interrogation*. Routledge.

Wang, Y., Chiu, T., Wang, T., & Debreceny, R. S. (2020). A Classroom Exercise on Building Auditors' Interview Skills. *Journal of Emerging Technologies in Accounting*, *17*(2), 93–101. doi:10.2308/JETA-19-07-07-31

KEY TERMS AND DEFINITIONS

Accounting Curriculum: The subjects studied during a course of study by accounting students

Forensic Accounting: An investigative field of study within accounting utilizing accounting skills for the purpose of uncovering fraud, embezzlement, or to analyze financial information.

Investigative Interview: An interview conducted to obtain a detailed factual account of events or information.

Oral Evidence: Oral information provided by an interviewee in response to specific questions by the interviewer/auditor/forensic accountant.

PEACE Model: A non-accusatory interview model used to gather information during an inquiry or investigation.

Question Types: There are seven question types that include open, probing, appropriate-closed, inappropriate-closed, leading, multiple questions, statement questions are used during the interview to gather information.

Rapport: Mutuality or harmony developed in an interpersonal interaction

ENDNOTES

1 https://www.fis-international.com/services?filter=Police%20Courses

2 https://www.fis-international.com/services?filter=Financial%20Courses

Chapter 5
Changes, Challenges, and Choices:
An Approach to the Future of Accounting Education in a Turbulent World

Helena Martins
https://orcid.org/0000-0002-0749-917X
ESCE, Instituto Politécnico de Setúbal, Portugal & CEOS, ISCAP, Polytechnic of Porto, Portugal & Nova School of Business and Economics, Portugal

Tiago Cunha
https://orcid.org/0000-0002-6842-9968
CIICESI, ESTG, Polytechnic of Porto, Portugal

Amélia Oliveira Carvalho
https://orcid.org/0000-0002-3204-5188
CIICESI, ESTG, Polytechnic of Porto, Portugal

Cecília Carmo
https://orcid.org/0000-0002-1883-5490
GOVCOPP, ISCA, University of Aveiro, Portugal

Gianluigi Baldacci
Nova School of Business and Economics, Portugal & LUISS Guido Carli, Rome, Italy

ABSTRACT

Crises deriving from pandemics, extreme weather events, wars, and shifts in technological paradigms are becoming the new normal, adding to the paradigm shifts already underway in the accounting profession due to profound changes in the way people work and information is managed. In this context, there is an agreement from both academics and professionals that, in addition to technical skills, there are other "soft" skills that are critical for value creation by accountants. This chapter proposes a reflection on key soft skills for the future of the accounting profession, especially considering the turbulent times ahead, with a special focus on the role of higher education institutions.

DOI: 10.4018/978-1-6684-5483-1.ch005

Copyright © 2023, IGI Global. Copying or distributing in print or electronic forms without written permission of IGI Global is prohibited.

INTRODUCTION

Accountants perform an important role in the organizational value chain, and it is fairly consensual that the accounting profession is undergoing a paradigm shift due to revolutions in technology and in the labor markets, moving towards a more leadership-oriented role. Further, crises have arguably become the new normal with a constellation of factors eliciting small to paradigm shifting changes and challenges: from pandemics, extreme weather events, and wars to shifts in technological paradigms, the impact on the operations of a multitude of organizations is undeniable and brings forth the need to focus on accountants' competencies in dealing with this type of evermore recurring events.

In this context there is an agreement from both academics and professionals that, in addition to technical skills, there are other "soft" skills that are critical for value creation by accountants.

Higher Education Institutions (HEIs) have a crucial role in developing future accountancy professionals' competencies especially through bachelor's and master's degrees, but they also play a role in lifelong learning, offering continuous training to accountants already employed in the labor market.

In this chapter, we focus on three main dimensions about the future of accounting education: what the literature says that will be a priority, what dealing with constant crisis will mean for professionals in the future, and what strategies should HEIs undertake to help their graduates cope with the challenges ahead. To this purpose, we perform a three-dimensional approach, which allows us to identify: the "changes" occurred in the accounting profession's competency profile; the "challenges" that derive from a turbulent, crisis prone environment and the "choices" which may allow HEIs to better prepare their graduates to the labor market as well as to gain a competitive advantage in accounting education, distinguishing themselves from the others.

BACKGROUND

In the 21st century, accounting and the accounting profession have undergone some of the greatest transformation processes of which there is historical record. According to Kuhn (1970, cit in Shortridge & Smith 2009), the reasons that lead to revolutionary processes are the existence of anomalies or significant crises that force deep and structural changes instead of small adjustments and evolutions. This is an accurate depiction of the contemporary challenges facing the accounting profession, given the amount and speed of emerging changes, the transformation of the industrial economy into an information economy, the increase in globalization

Figure 1. Chapter perspective

and the surge in available information and its processing capacity (Shortridge & Smith, 2009). Additionally, accounting services have become increasingly broader and more diversified, which has triggered the need for accountants to specialize in specific areas that make up the profession (Bui & Porter, 2010).

Institutions that regulate the accounting profession have long been highlighting the need for accountants to develop behavioral, communicative and interdisciplinary skills, in order to bring their curriculum closer to the needs of the market, seeking, among other objectives, to maximize the satisfaction of accountants in relation to their profession (Strawser, Flagg, & Holmes, 2000), but also allowing them to deal with the uncertainty and constant change of the work context, as well as with the ever-present social responsibility (Kavanagh & Drennan, 2008).

Thus, it is essential to align the needs between the education of accountants and the job market so that there is an adjustment between the supply and demand of skills' profiles. This effort aims at meeting the needs of the labor market currently marked by constant evolution and improvement of information systems and globalization (Mohamed & Lashine, 2003), but also crises that due to contemporary circumstances (exploding technological developments, dramatic demographic growth, immigration, ecological disasters, and geopolitical trends) disrupt our lives at an ever-increasing pace and breadth (Linor, Ergas, Alpert, & Ariav, 2020).

Accounting and the accounting profession is thus facing 1) changes that are paradigm shifting and that stem from the way relevant information is stored, shared and treated, as well as the changes in the way people work and what is expected from them, 2) challenges that are transversal to society but have very specific impacts in the accounting profession and role deriving from an environment that is and will keep being prone to crises that may alter dramatically circumstances in a short period of time (e.g. pandemics, war, etc.) and 3) choices regarding the way students and professionals may prepare and cope with the previously mentioned changes and challenges, in a lifelong learning perspective but also in terms of HEIs.

MAIN FOCUS OF THE CHAPTER

Changes

It is unequivocal that the accounting profession has undergone significant changes both in terms of the functions within the competence of accountants and in the way in which these same functions are performed. In this section we will discuss five major changes: the need for the accounting profession to widen its functions and responsibilities as it becomes more of an interdisciplinary field (Carnegie & Napier, 2012); the enduring need for strong and solid ethical standards and practices; the need for good IT competences; the impact from the generalization of use of AI, and the urgent need for improvement in soft skills.

Leading the charge in the prompts for changes in the accounting profession is arguably the beginning of the 4th Industrial Revolution (4th IR) marked by the introduction of artificial intelligence can be highlighted, which allowed the expansion of the scope of automated tasks in the accounting profession.

The tools that the accountant has to carry out his activity currently offer the ability to automate more structured, predictable and repetitive tasks, which exist in abundance in the accounting area (Kokina & Davenport, 2017): the mere recording of accounting documents is nowadays a very narrow definition of the accounting profession (Jackling & De Lange, 2009).

As the driving forces of the market arguably shift from politics to economics, there is an accelerated evolution of the market and thus also a greater need to produce reliable and real-time information to assist in decision-making in companies both internally and externally (Haller, 2002), there is a sophistication and evolution of the financial treatment and disclosure and a replacement of merely financial accounting by business reporting which includes variables such as human resources, production control, sustainability (Lai & Stacchezzini, 2021), and even the relationship with the companies' stakeholders, making accounting a more interdisciplinary field (Carnegie & Napier, 2012) and a more comprehensive and complex science (Carnegie, 2014).

According to the World Bank Group, the information produced by accounting is one of the main guarantees of global economic growth and sustainability given that at the level of the private sector, accounting legitimizes and makes the financial information produced, increasing investment, whereas at the level of the public sector, it guarantees greater transparency and allows for a more efficient management of resources (Venter, Gordon, & Street, 2018). As both financial and non-financial stakeholders require more holistic, integrated representations of sustainability from organizations, this too should become one of the areas accountants must focus on (Lai & Stacchezzini, 2021). The awareness of accountants for the impact of their actions on the public and the development of sensitivity to social responsibilities thus becomes fundamental for the continuity of the profession (IAESB, 2014b) .

Although contemporary, the idea that accountants can assume a wide array of tasks and responsibilities is not new (Bui & Porter, 2010), and a hallmark example of this is the key role accountants play in small and medium companies, where they often ensure the majority of management support, namely functions associated with the financial analysis and reporting. It is thus up to accountants to generate all the information and gather all the resources that can support decision-making and choices regarding the strategy and direction of small and medium-sized companies (Bahador & Haider, 2012) .

However, being competent as an accountant from the viewpoint of information users does not always translate into ethical behavior and attitudes. Sometimes accountants end up transgressing the ethical and deontological principles inherent to their profession for the benefit of the personal interests of company managers, jeopardizing the well-being of society and information users in general. It is the role of the accountant to alert the companies in which they work for, of errors, irregularities and frauds that may be committed and not to agree with them, thus guaranteeing the independence of their work (Duska, 2005).

Although the ethical issues inherent to the accounting profession further develop with increasing professional experience, it is essential that accountants continue to expand their learning throughout their careers and their lives.

The introduction of information technologies in accounting has brought about two types of changes in the work of accountants. It has given rise to a set of new methods and working models using information technologies, which in turn also lead to the emergence of new skills that accountants must have in order to be able to process and produce information through these new resources (Ku Bahador & Haider, 2012).

Accounting Information Systems (AIS,) are one of the main tools that allowed accountants to obtain good performances in processing large amounts of information in a timely manner. AIS are becoming increasingly complex; this methodology comprises the collection, processing and dissemination of the aforementioned information (Guragai, Hunt, Neri, & Taylor, 2017), requiring specifically skilled workers .

The most recent evolution of the AIS in accounting has also been marked by the introduction of new concepts such as the balanced scorecard and business intelligence, existing business models (Trigo, Belfo, & Estebanez, 2014), which allow the interconnection of accounting with other areas of the business, such as human resources or production management. AICs already play a leading role in the activity of large companies, and in small and medium-sized companies this weighting has increased over the years (Grabski, Leech, & Schmidt, 2011). Further, information technologies, make it possible to respond to customer needs more effectively and efficiently, complementing and aiding to the work of accountants (Bahador & Haider, 2012).

The Standard Audit File for Tax (SAF-T) was created and developed by the Organization for Economic Cooperation and Development (OECD) with four main purposes: the reduction of burden by automation, moving from collecting aggregates to individual records, tax compliance process redesign, increasing the taxpayer's responsibility for evaders' misconduct. SAF-T is an example of a procedure that accountants initially considered to be just an additional cost-generating work due to the obligation of adapting the company to the requirements of SAF-T reporting, SAF-T proved to be more complex and caused changes in terms of financial control procedures, standardization of financial reporting, and knowledge of new IT concepts such as the eXtensible Markup Language (XML) (Auksztol & Chomuszko, 2020). In the same sense, blockchain technology, initially developed as a method for documenting cryptocurrency transactions, is seen with the potential to be applied at the accounting and auditing level (Stanciu et al, 2019).

It is thus essential that accountants are associated with this evolutionary process from its genesis, at the risk of not being able to follow its evolution in more advanced stages, running the risk of their curricula being considered obsolete by the marketplace. However, this process alone does not allow anyone to be able to play the role of accountant, because it becomes necessary to put into practice technical skills, interpreting, filtering and reporting information, actions that are only within the reach of accounting professionals (Wessels, 2005). At a more advanced stage, we are witnessing the introduction of artificial intelligence (AI) in accounting, which, like other information technologies, has allowed the development of a set of tools with a view to meeting the needs of the market, increasing the efficiency of the work of resources humans in this professional area (Trigo et al., 2014) .

Marshall & Lambert (2018) argue that the inclusion of AI in accounting does not aim to extinguish human jobs, but rather to value human capital by improving its performance. The tasks with less preponderance in the work of the accountant are now performed using AI, and, therefore, human resources will be able to spend their time only on unplanned tasks that do not present the characteristics conducive to a correct adaptation to an intelligent system. This effect on human capital is called augmented intelligence (Marshall & Lambert, 2018) .

The refutation of the idea of extinction of the accounting profession is further reinforced by the existence of tasks that require business knowledge and interpersonal relationships with company representatives. Because these are tasks with an emotional component and that involve human relationships by nature, the role of human resources becomes preponderant in the treatment of information. If there is a widespread adoption of artificial intelligence by accounting either in the form of specialized systems or in the form of neural networks, some implications will arise from this adoption. On the one hand, we must consider the biases arising from the raw information, the biases arising from the human resources that developed the aforementioned tools and the divergences between the tools and human resources in the interpretation of conclusions, as they limit the quality of the results produced. On the other hand, the complexity and depth with which the tools solve the problems that are proposed must be taken into account, as they often go beyond the capacity of human understanding, which limits the analysis of results and the achievement of conclusions. (Kokina & Davenport, 2017). From an optimistic perspective, artificial intelligence will make it possible to overcome human limitations, thus increasing the spectrum of human intelligence; from a pessimistic perspective, artificial intelligence will superimpose its autonomous decision-making capacity on the human capacity to do so, thus placing humans in a position of inferiority and total dependence (Makridakis, 2017) .

Makridakis (2017) predicts that in about two decades artificial intelligence will be the focus of human lives, both in their daily lives and in their professions. It is believed that its impact will be greater than that of the industrial revolution and the digital revolution at the same time, so its effects on human life will be many.

The size of the company is an influencing factor regarding the profile of employees that companies seek to perform accounting functions. While small and medium-sized companies look for and value the technical skills of candidates and professionals, large companies essentially look for job candidates with behavioral skills, thus valuing critical thinking, proactivity, and communication skills in their various forms and visionary spirit. (Bui & Porter, 2010). The possession of technical skills is unanimously considered crucial to improve the performance and legitimacy of the information produced (Vafeas, 2009); however, over the years, non-accounting and vocational skills have taken on greater weight in terms of market needs (Hassall, Joyce, Arquero Montaño, et al., 2005) .

An increase in market competitiveness forced accountants to hold and develop a wider range of skills, namely in terms of behavioral skills and skills in the field of information systems (Bui & Porter, 2010) .

A wider range of skills assists in the performance of the daily tasks of an accountant, but also adapts to unstructured problems that may arise, In the specific case of information technologies, a wider range of skills leads to efficiency (Ku Bahador & Haider, 2012). However, behavioral skills and information technologies are, at the same time, the two components in greatest deficit in the curriculum of accountants, and those that are understood to be the most critical for the future of the profession (Wessels, 2005; Bahador & Haider, 2012) .

Challenges

Exploding technological developments, dramatic demographic growth, immigration, ecological disasters, and geopolitical trends disrupt our lives at an ever-increasing pace and breadth (Linor, Ergas, Alpert, & Ariav, 2020). This summation of critical events can be referred to as VUCA, a terminology, coined by the U.S. Army War College, describing the Volatile, Uncertain, Complex, and Ambiguous multilateral world that has resulted since the end of the Cold War (Kingsinger & Waich, 2012). Recent events illustrate and support these claims: the COVID19 pandemic, emerging armed conflicts in Europe, technological revolutions, etc.

Looking to the future, numerous factors suggest that other pandemics will be inevitable, and that the world must prepare for them (Dodds, 2019). In particular, phenomena such as deforestation and the decrease in biodiversity significantly increased risk, in the sense that they carry with them the higher probability of natural disaster and bio events (Tollefson, 2020). Other sources of crisis are climate change and associated extreme weather events, but also geopolitical tensions, therefore the risk of wars (including trade wars) and the threat of terrorism could rise. Of note in this regard are the tensions between West and East, the crisis between Ukraine and Russia (Bebier, 2015) and the strains over China's claims over Taiwan (Albert, 2016). In addition to these factors, it is necessary to consider technological advancement, the rise and implementation of profoundly disruptive technologies such as artificial intelligence, blockchain and the internet of things (Bublitz, et al., 2019) that constitute innovations capable of radically changing the approach to work, education, and even society itself.

The moments of crisis are unique situations and, to overcome them, it is usually necessary to put into practice paradigms of behavior and operations different from the usual ones (Jankelová & Mišún, 2021).Overcoming moments of crisis arguably falls under the field of crisis management, a specific area of management, using approaches and methods to deal with certain functions of the subject under conditions of negative effects caused by extraordinary events (Tomastik, Strohmadl, & Cech, 2015).

The crisis manager function requires a great deal of knowledge, skills, and experience, to manage the demanding process of an extraordinary event both mentally and physically. Thus, beyond technical skills, professionals are required to possess additional skills, generally in the field of soft skills, including intuition, ability to deal with people, decision making, stress management, creativity and innovativeness (Tomastik, Strohmadl, & Cech, 2015), but also strategic planning, problem solving, message production, information management, communication management, and problem management. Therefore, skills and competencies beyond those related to academic training or technical expertise are necessary (Coombs, 2014).

The study conducted by Kim (2021) particularly emphasizes how leadership in crisis situations is one of the crucial elements in successfully resolving such events. In analyzing the field of nursing, the author identified six key attributes of crisis leadership namely: clear, quick, and frank communication and a high degree of collaboration; information sharing; decision making and fair prioritization; trust building; and competence. Because leadership is fundamental to crisis resolution (Kim, 2021), it is possible to highlight how the listed skills of the leader that constitute necessary competencies for dealing with crisis.

Analyzing the need for changes in the educational system in a VUCA world, the importance of social-emotional skills in the management of critical situations is emphasized (Linor, Ergas, Alpert, & Ariav, 2020). In this sense, skills like self-management, communication, empathy, and self-awareness derive their relevance from the fact that they influence how well people adjust to their environment and allow to act and adapt to rapid changes as they happen (Linor, Ergas, Alpert, & Ariav, 2020).

In addition, the work of Jankelová and Mišún (2021) analyzed the skills that proved to be the most useful for managers in the agricultural sector in facing the acute crisis phase of COVID-19. The research conducted highlights the importance of "hard thinking" that is the ability to work with estimates, assumptions and in a condition of lack of information. The managers who managed the crisis best possessed: communication skills, empathy and teamwork, leadership, and decision-making skills.

A summary of these competencies is presented in Table 1.

Table 1. Key competences in a crisis

Author	Role or Sector	Competencies
Coombs, 2014	Crisis Manager	Strategic planning, problem solving, message production, information management, communication management, and problem management
Tomastik, Strohmadl, & Cech, 2015	Crisis Manager	Intuition, broad experience, ability to deal with people, decision making ability, stress management ability, creativity, and innovativeness, should be able to make priorities and have action ability
Linor, Ergas, Alpert, & Ariav, 2020	Education	Socio-emotional skills, self-management, communication, empathy, and self-awareness
Sun-Ju, 2021	Nursing (leader)	Clear, quick, and frank communication and a high degree of collaboration; information sharing; decision making and fair prioritization; trust building; and competence.
Jankelová & Mišún, 2021	Agricultural Managers	Hard thinking, communication skills, empathy, teamwork, leadership, decision making skills.

A crisis can involve, in general, three types of risk for an organization, namely public safety risks, financial loss and reputation loss and it can broad the scope of an organization, its stakeholders or, more generally, to an entire sector (Coombs, 2014). In extreme cases, the loss of human life may also be at risk (e.g. toxic material spill or an injury caused by negative work conditions, bombing near a nuclear site, etc.).

All these aspects are closely interrelated. For instance, a risk to public health and safety could lead to a loss of reputation and, consequently, to a financial loss. Moreover, such damage to an organization's reputation and finances would inevitably involve its stakeholders, fueling a climate of distrust that would only worsen the damage created by the crisis.

In this sense, Özdemir et al. (2010) highlight how the impact of a crisis can negatively affect several components of an organization, leading to failures in internal communication, a decrease in the quality of decision-making, inadequate coordination, a deterioration in organizational culture, confusion in the allocation of responsibility and a growing mistrust and demoralization among staff. Considering an entrepreneurial dimension, to assess the produced effects, it can be also useful to identify the elements that, by varying, can clearly show the impact of the crisis. In the work of Ritter and Carsten (2020) six different types of impact of a crisis are identified based on the characteristics that define a given business model (Table 2).

Table 2. Classification of business models according to the impact of a crisis

Business Model Type	Crisis Impact
Antifragile Business Model	The organization performs well during the crisis. As stated by Taleb (2012), some systems improve under stress, and in this case, the crisis becomes an element of growth and development.
Robust Business Model	Many areas of the business are not affected by the crisis as well as some areas changed only in secondary aspects not influencing the business model itself.
Adaptive Business Model	Business models that need to change considering a crisis. Adapting the business model, the organization can reemerge in sustainable way. The management has the responsibility of developing and implementing new business alternatives.
Suspended Business Model	The business model is temporary suspended and restarted after the crisis ends. The organization changes its paradigm of operation.
Aided Business Model	Business model unable to support itself in a crisis starting to depend on outside support. For example, the organization may need to be helped by the government through different types of support.
Retired Business Model	This business model ceases to exist during the crisis as the cost of getting the business through the crisis exceed the potential profits after the crisis.

(Ritter & Carsten, 2020)

Although crises are generally identified as a negative factor, it should be noted that the definition adopted intend them as an uncertain situation possessing latent risks and opportunities. A crisis is, therefore, "an unstable time or state of affairs in which a decisive change is impending either one with a distinct possibility of a highly undesirable outcome or one with a distinct possibility of a highly desirable and extremely positive outcome" (Özdemir, et al., 2010).

When managed in the correct way, crisis offer change, learning and growth opportunities (Özdemir, et al., 2010). In fact, crisis may open a window in which question the assumptions that were unquestionable, testing targets, experiences, and habits. In addition, responding to the contingency the organization can learn, through the analysis of the adopted measures and through a proper feedback structure. It should not be forgotten that the sum of change and learning can bring new operating patterns inside the organization, deeply influencing various components of the organization environment like stakeholders' trust or organizational culture.

In summary, the vast majority of competences identified in crisis management are soft skills that either have to do with the ability to regulate one's thoughts and emotions in a scenario of turmoil, but also the ability to communicate, collaborate and coordinate group efforts. These are elements that are consistent with the scope of (soft) skills identified in the literature for the future of accounting and the accounting profession. This means that a clear effort in educating accounting professionals in this area is not only an option, but also a must.

Choices

The changes and challenges previously presented are thus conducive of shifts in the accounting professional's competency profile (cf. Figure 2). These changes – which have already begun taking place - are bound to change deeply not only accounting processes and working methods, but also the accounting professional's duties and responsibilities. Considering this fact, it is essential that accountants are equipped with a set of skills that allow them to continue to offer value to the market and to make the existence of the profession relevant (Bui & Porter, 2010), which leads us to the choices regarding the way institutions may deal with these elements.

In the context of any professional activity, learning, especially at the university level, serves to reduce asymmetries between the skills of students in the area in question and what the labor market expects of them. According to Yorke (1992), to develop a training model it is necessary to understand who will be positively and negatively affected by it. According to the author, there are two target audiences in any training area. On the one hand, the students, as they are the ones who will attend the courses and therefore the latter must be shaped according to their interests and to represent an added value for them. On the other hand, the employers who will

Figure 2. Discussed changes and challenges and their consequences regarding the profile of competencies of the accounting professional

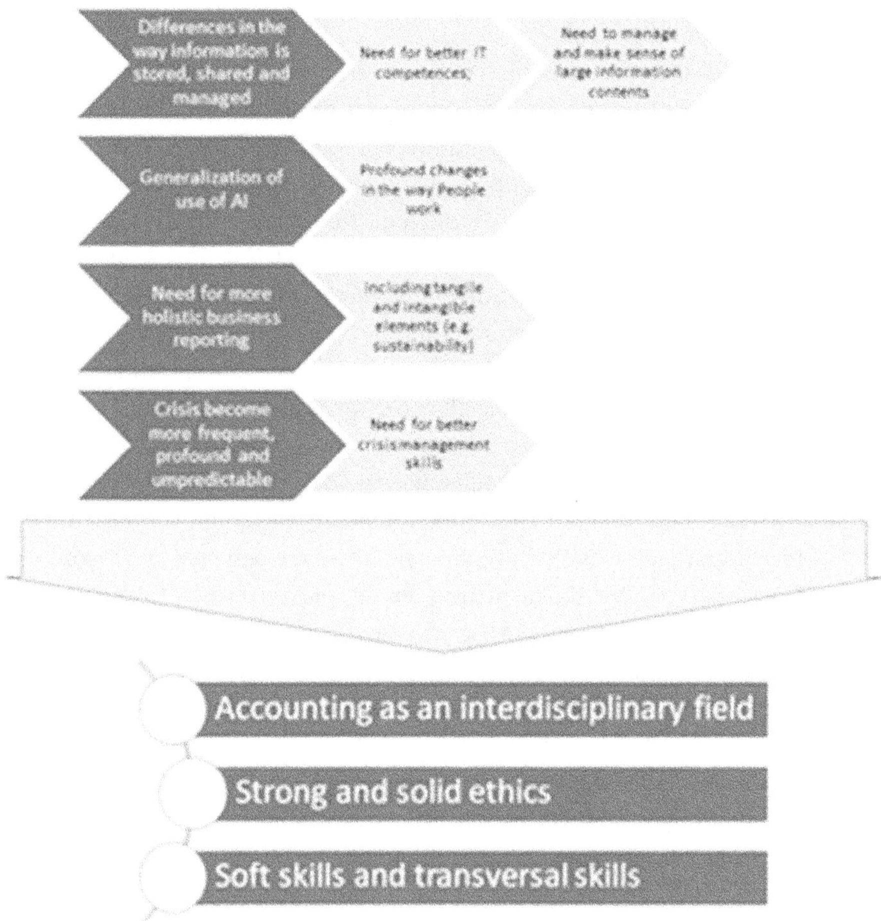

recruit the students and, as such, the courses must comply with the needs of the market. The objective for any educational institution is to ensure a balance between what are the aspirations and goals of students and what are the needs and demands of the job market (Hassall, Joyce, Arquero Montaño, et al., 2005).

In a study developed by Cunha et al. (2022), the authors looked into the curricular structures of an entire European country's Accounting Education programs to find that despite the clear and consensual statements in the literature regarding the need to broaden the horizons of the accounting profession and education, the vast majority of credits (80% to 90%) were attributed to hard skills and learning rules and regulations that could be upended by the time students reach the end of their formal education. This study is in line with the majority of the literature, where it seems clear that there is a distinct gap between academics and professionals as to how the education of an accountant should be and what competences to be developed (Pratama, 2015) .

Since the 1980s, it has been recognized by both students, faculty, and employers that study plans in accounting are inadequate and unsuitable for the labor market that has proved to be increasingly modern, technologically evolved and constantly changing. Clearly, the skills developed in the study plans do not coincide with the needs of employers, which makes it difficult for recent graduates to adapt and integrate into the labor market (Cunha et al, 2022). While employers tend to focus on skills to be part of a work group, universities seek to develop in their students a better intellectual capacity and greater autonomy.

Another factor to consider is the misperception that accounting students have of the accounting profession, the functions they perform and the content of accounting courses. In short, there are three reasons that justify the existing divergences between the expected competences and the competences held by accounting students. First, there are differences between the expectations of faculty and employers regarding the skills that recent graduates should have. Second, there are personal and institutional limitations on the part of students and institutions that prevent faculty from developing the competences of these students in the way they would like to. Finally, there are also limitations on the part of faculty reflected in their teaching methods that make it difficult for students to learn (Bui & Porter, 2010) .

Aside from the limitations of individuals, from the perspective of accounting students, the idea remains that these skills are not worked on and there is a strong tendency to train students to suit large companies (Hassall, Joyce, Arquero Montaño, et al., 2005) instead of adjusting to different contexts. It is expected and desirable by the job market that the development of non-technical skills allows accountants to have disruptive thoughts and attitudes towards the basic concepts of accounting. However, the labor market also plays an active role in the development of behavioral skills, insofar as it must value and demonstrate in practice the importance of this type of skills, so that educational institutions are sensitized to address them in their study plans. If carried out, this approach would occur even before the approach to technical skills so that students are "first educated and then trained" (Jackling & De Lange, 2009) .

An increase in market competitiveness forced accountants to hold and develop a wider range of skills, namely in terms of behavioral skills and skills in the field of information systems (Bui & Porter, 2010).

These skills allow, on the one hand, to assist in the performance of the daily tasks of an accountant, but also to adapt to unstructured problems that may arise, as well as, in the specific case of information technologies, to help in the introduction and efficient use of these (Ku Bahador & Haider, 2012) .

The HEI 4 developed by the IAESB, on the other hand, corroborate the idea described above, adding that behavioral skills should first be taught in isolation from other subjects, ending up being interconnected with them throughout the study plan, similarly to what happens in the labor market (IAESB, 2014b).

Thus, HEIs, as well as other institutions (e.g., local and international regulatory bodies in both the accounting profession) should reinforce their investment and resources geared towards the development of transversal competencies (such as user-level IT competencies and languages), strong and solid ethical principles and soft skills, including socio-emotional skills, self-management, communication, empathy and self-awareness, which may be conducive of better adaptability to circumstances, stress and change management and teamwork, vital elements for the future of accounting.

SOLUTIONS AND RECOMMENDATIONS

Considering the changes, challenges, and choices we presented above, it is clear that the accounting community and higher education institutions need to reconsider the way they conceptualize the accounting profession and role, and the way students and professionals are educated. It is necessary that resources and conditions be made available to accounting professionals and students so that they can invest in their education: lifelong learning is a fundamental factor both for accountants who are already part of the market, in order to correspond to the new needs of the profession, or for students who attend accounting courses who seek to develop the necessary skills before their first contact with the profession. HEIs especially have a responsibility to their students and the community to be at the forefront of this trend, namely regarding themes to be addressed throughout the study plan and the methods and techniques that must be used to transmit this knowledge. The objective is to once again ensure transversality and uniformity throughout the world without affecting the quality of education (David McPeak, Pincus, & Sundem, 2012).

Thus, in the coming years HEIs and the accounting community (professional institutions, chambers, orders, syndicates, and accountant organizations professionals alike) will need to reconsider the weight and contact hours dedicated to soft skills and transversal competencies (especially ones more related with IT competences, ethics and soft skills. Beyond specific courses, due to their transversal nature these elements can be practiced and included in nearly all subject matters through active pedagogical models and strategies. Thus, developing teamwork and communication skills can be the result of working in a team for group presentation or project;

problem solving can be stimulated with problem and project-based learning; self-management can be stimulated with the need to put one's emotions in check in a challenging assignment.

The development of these transversal skills as well as greater sense of ethics and value from the beginning of the accountancy professional education and through lifelong learning is fundamental in order to prevent the profession from becoming obsolete (Daff, 2021). Considering that higher education plays a major role in improving and broadening the skills of accountants (Jackling & De Lange, 2009), the development of new skills and the improvement of the accountant's curricula are an emerging need.

FUTURE RESEARCH DIRECTIONS

Future research should further these topics conceptually as well as empirically. Conceptually, and as the accounting profession keeps shifting, research should strive to make sense of the shifts and trends, reconceptualizing perceptions and attributions of accounting and the accounting profession; it is also important to keep reflecting on the future of accounting education and strategies to adapt to the 4.0 world and to comply both with professional guilds and accreditation. Empirically, data should be collected and analyzed from different stakeholders' points of view, including accounting professionals, students, organizations and HEIs. Longitudinal studies aiming at understanding graduates' adaptation to the job market and success throughout their careers, namely regarding the time until they are employed, the type of functions they occupy, and the remuneration received.

It is also considered relevant to explore, within the behavioral skills and transversal skills, which in the future will be more critical for the profile of accountants, given that there is at the same time the need for accountants to be more interdisciplinary and more endowed with interpersonal skills. Finally, a study is suggested in which the evolution of study plans over time is analyzed, comparing their structure before the last change occurred in each of them respectively with their current structure, in order to understand if the changes that have occurred have resulted in a convergence with market needs or, on the other hand, in a departure.

CONCLUSION

Following the traditional concept of accountant described by Carnegie & Napier (2010), the accountant or "bean counter", only needed technical skills insofar as the functions performed were merely processing financial information and reporting it without requiring any type of contact with customers and other parties involved in the business and mostly consisted of repetitive, predictable tasks. Although in the past the success or failure of an accountant was mostly dependent on the greater or lesser number of technical skills, nowadays transversal skills also assume a significant weight in the range of skills of an accountant.

These changes stem from the growing participation of accountants in decision-making within companies, as advisers of not only financial but also non-financial departments, thus demanding greater relational and communication skills from accountants.

Given that the field of action of accountants has been expanded, they should seek to be as interdisciplinary as possible, thus allowing them to be able to intervene in both financial and non-financial areas. Accountants nowadays must develop and hold skills regarding oral and written communication, teamwork, analysis, and management of unstructured problems, IT and interpersonal relationships.

The development of generic skills such as those described above should allow accountants to develop their emotional intelligence, which according to Richins, Stapleton, Stratopoulos & Wong (2017) and Fernandez & Aman (2018) are the most difficult human skills to be replicated by artificial intelligence.

Higher education in accounting thus assumes a leading role both in the preparation of accounting students who aspire to practice the profession, and in offering continuous education to accountants already employed in the job market, to guarantee the updating of their knowledge. Hence there is a need to review the study plans in accounting is imminent; Robley, Whittle & Murdoch-Eaton (2005) suggest an annual review of study plans, so that all market changes are replicated in academic terms.

This rather consensual reality among the literature is engrossed by the fact that we live in increasingly turbulent times, where crisis will become more regular and more intense in the disturbances they cause as well as in the changes they will prompt. Thus, accountants will benefit from not only being able to make sense of information and communicate it clearly with their coworkers and stakeholders in regular times, but these competencies are heightened in importance and need in times of crises.

The accounting profession, due to the highly structured and repetitive nature of many core tasks has become one of the areas in which technological advances have had the most impact (Makridakis, 2017; Uwizeyemungu, et al., 2020). It seems clear that the way forward in the future of accounting will be to add new competencies to the core of the profession, especially in terms of soft skills for collaborating and leading, but also sense making and dealing with crisis situations in stride.

ACKNOWLEDGEMENTS

This research was supported by FCT- Fundação para a Ciência e Tecnologia (Portugal), national funding, under the projects UIDB/05422/2020, UIDB/04728/2020, UIDB/00124/2020, UIDB/04058/2020, UIDP/04058/2020 and UIDP/00124/2020 and the Social Sciences DataLab - PINFRA/22209/2016), POR Lisboa and POR Norte (Social Sciences DataLab, PINFRA/22209/2016).

REFERENCES

Albert, E. (2016). China-Taiwan Relations. *Council on Foreign Relations, 7.*

Auksztol, J., & Chomuszko, M. (2020). A data control framework for SAF-T reporting: A process-based approach. *Journal of Entrepreneurship Management and Innovation, 16*(1), 13–40. doi:10.7341/20201611

Bahador, K. M. K., & Haider, A. (2012). Information technology skills and competencies—A case for professional accountants. In Abramowicz, W., Domingue, J., Węcel, K., (eds.) Business Information Systems Workshops, pp. 81–87. Springer: Berlin/Heidelberg.

Bebier, A. (2015). Crimea and the Russina-Ukranian Conflict. *Romanian Journal of European Affairs, 15*(1), 35–54.

Bublitz, M., Oetomo, F., Sahu, S., Kuang, A. X., Fadrique, L., Velmovitsky, P., & Morita, P. (2019). Disruptive technologies for environment and health research: An overview of artificial intelligence, blockchain, and internet of things. *International Journal of Environmental Research and Public Health, 16*(20), 3847. doi:10.3390/ijerph16203847 PMID:31614632

Bui, B., & Porter, B. (2010). The expectation-performance gap in accounting education: An exploratory study. *Accounting Education, 19*(1-2), 23–50. doi:10.1080/09639280902875556

Cambridge dictionary. (2022, May 2). Business Model. *Cambridge Dictionary*. Cambridge. https://dictionary.cambridge.org/it/dizionario/inglese/business-model

Carnegie, G. D. (2014). The present and future of accounting history. *Accounting, Auditing & Accountability Journal, 27*(8), 1241–1249. doi:10.1108/AAAJ-05-2014-1715

Carnegie, G. D., & Napier, C. J. (2012). Accounting's past, present and future: The unifying power of history. *Accounting, Auditing & Accountability Journal*, *25*(2), 328–369. doi:10.1108/09513571211198782

Coombs, T. W. (2014). *State of Crisis Communication: Evidence and the Bleeding Edge*. Research Journal of the Institute for Public Relations.

Cunha, T., Martins, H., Carvalho, A., & Carmo, C. (2022). Not Practicing What You Preach: How Is Accounting Higher Education Preparing the Future of Accounting. *Education Sciences*, *12*(7), 432. doi:10.3390/educsci12070432

Dodds, W. (2019). Disease Now and Potential Future Pandemics. The World's Worst Problems, (pp. 31-44). Springer. doi:10.1007/978-3-030-30410-2_4

Duncan, J., & Schmutte, J. (2006). Change in Accounting Programs: The Impact of Influences and Constraints, 16.

Duska, R. F. (2015). The responsibilities of accountants. *The Geneva Papers on Risk and Insurance. Issues and Practice*, *30*(3), 410–424. doi:10.1057/palgrave.gpp.2510042

Fernandez, D., & Aman, A. (2018). Impacts of robotic process automation on global accounting services. *Asian J. Account. Gov.*, *9*, 123–132. doi:10.17576/AJAG-2018-09-11

Grabski, S. V., Leech, S. A., & Schmidt, P. J. (2011). A Review of ERP Research: A Future Agenda for Accounting Information Systems. *Journal of Information Systems*, *25*(1), 37–78. doi:10.2308/jis.2011.25.1.37

Guragai, B., Hunt, N. C., Neri, M. P., & Taylor, E. Z. (2017). Accounting information systems and ethics research: Review, synthesis, and the future. *Journal of Information Systems*, *31*(2), 65–81. doi:10.2308/isys-51265

Hadar, L. L., Ergas, O., Alpert, B., & Ariav, T. (2020). Rethinking teacher education in a VUCA world: Student teachers' social-emotional competencies during the Covid-19 crisis. *European Journal of Teacher Education*, *43*(4), 573–586. doi:10.1080/02619768.2020.1807513

Haller, A. (2002). Financial accounting developments in the European Union: past events and future prospects. *European Accounting Review, 11*(1), 153-153-190.

Hassall, T., Joyce, J., Montaño, J. L. A., & Donoso Anes, J. A. (2005). Priorities for the development of vocational skills in management accountants: A European perspective. *Accounting Forum*, *29*(4), 379–394. doi:10.1016/j.accfor.2005.03.002

IAESB International Education Standards Board. (2014). *IES 4, Initial Professional Development—Professional Values, Ethics, and Attitudes*. IFAC.

Jackling, B., & De Lange, P. (2009). Do accounting graduates' skills meet the expectations of employers? A matter of convergence or divergence. *Accounting Education, 18*(4-5), 369–385. doi:10.1080/09639280902719341

Jankelová, N., & Mišún, J. (2021). Key Competencies of Agricultural Managers in the Acute Stage of COVID-19 Crisis. *Agriculture, 11*(1), 59. doi:10.3390/agriculture11010059

Kim, S. J. (2021). Crisis leadership: An evolutionary concept analysis. Applied nursing research. *ANR, 60*(1), 151454. PMID:34215477

Kingsinger, P., & Waich, K. (2012, July 9). *Living and leading in a VUCA world.* Thunderbird University. http://knowledgenetwork.thunderbird.edu/research/2012/07/09/kinsinger-walch-vuca/

Kokina, J., & Davenport, T. H. (2017). The Emergence of Artificial Intelligence: How Automation is Changing Auditing. *Journal of Emerging Technologies in Accounting, 14*(1), 115–122. doi:10.2308/jeta-51730

Lai, A., & Stacchezzini, R. (2021). Organisational and professional challenges amid the evolution of sustainability reporting: A theoretical framework and an agenda for future research. *Meditari Accountancy Research, 29*(3), 405–429. doi:10.1108/MEDAR-02-2021-1199

Makridakis, S. (2017). The forthcoming Artificial Intelligence (AI) revolution: Its impact on society and firms. *Futures, 90*(1), 46–60. doi:10.1016/j.futures.2017.03.006

Marshall, T. E., & Lambert, S. L. (2018). Cloud-based intelligent accounting applications: Accounting task automation using IBM Watson Cognitive Computing. *Journal of Emerging Technologies in Accounting, 15*(1), 199–215. doi:10.2308/jeta-52095

Mcpeak, D. W., Pincus, K. V., & Sundem, G. L. (2012). The International Accounting Education Standards Board: Influencing Global Accounting Education. *Issues in Accounting Education, 27*(1), 743–750. doi:10.2308/iace-50121

Mohamed, E. K. A., & Lashine, S. H. (2003). Accounting knowledge and skills and the challenges of a global business environment. *Managerial Finance, 29*(7), 3–16. doi:10.1108/03074350310768319

Özdemir, L & Balkan, M. (2010). *The Positive and Negative Effects of Crisis on Organizations: An Application*. Research Gate.

Pratama, A. (2015). Bridging the gap between academicians and practitioners on accountant competencies: An analysis of International Education Standards (IES) implementation on Indonesia's accounting education. *Procedia: Social and Behavioral Sciences, 211*(1), 19–26. doi:10.1016/j.sbspro.2015.11.004

Richins, G., Stapleton, A., Stratopoulos, T., & Wong, C. (2017). Big data analytics: Opportunity or threat for the accounting profession? *Journal of Information Systems, 31*(3), 63–79. doi:10.2308/isys-51805

Ritter, T., & Carsten, P. L. (2020). Analyzing the impact of the coronavirus crisis on business models. *Industrial Marketing Management, 88*(1), 214–224. doi:10.1016/j.indmarman.2020.05.014

Robley, W., Whittle, S., & Murdoch-Eaton, D. (2005). Mapping generic skills curricula: A recommended methodology. *Journal of Further and Higher Education, 29*(3), 221–231. doi:10.1080/03098770500166801

Shortridge, R. T., & Smith, P. A. (2009). Understanding the changes in accounting thought. *Research in Accounting Regulation, 21*(1), 11–18. doi:10.1016/j.racreg.2008.11.010

Stanciu, V., Pugna, I. B., & Gheorghe, M. (2019). New coordinates of accounting academic education. A Romanian insight. Paper presented at *the 14th International Conference on Accounting and Management Information Systems (AMIS IAAER)*. Bucharest Univ.

Strawser, J. A., Flagg, J. C., & Holmes, S. A. (2000). Job perceptions and turnover behavior of tenure-track accounting educators. *Journal of Accounting Education, 18*(4), 315–340. doi:10.1016/S0748-5751(01)00004-5

Taleb, N. N. (2012). *Antifragile: Things that gain from disorder*. Random House.

Tollefson, J. (2020). Why deforestation and extinctions make pandemics more likely. *Nature, 584*(7820), 175–176. doi:10.1038/d41586-020-02341-1 PMID:32770149

Tomastik, M., Strohmadl, J., & Cech, P. (2015). Managerial competency of crisis managers. *Procedia: Social and Behavioral Sciences, 174*, 3964–3969. doi:10.1016/j.sbspro.2015.01.1141

Trigo, A., Belfo, F. P., & Estébanez, R. P. (2014). Accounting Information Systems: The Challenge of the Real-time Reporting. *Procedia Technology, 16*(1), 118–127. doi:10.1016/j.protcy.2014.10.075

Vafeas, N. (2009). Is accounting education valued by the stock market? Evidence from corporate controller appointments. *Contemporary Accounting Research, 26*(4), 1143–1174. doi:10.1506/car.26.4.6

Venter, E. R., Gordon, E. A., & Street, D. L. (2018). The role of accounting and the accountancy profession in economic development: A research agenda. *Journal of International Financial Management & Accounting*, *29*(2), 195–218. doi:10.1111/jifm.12080

Wessels, P. L. (2005). Critical information and communication technology (ICT) skills for professional accountants. *Meditari Account. Res.*, *13*(1), 87–103. doi:10.1108/10222529200500006

Yorke, M. (1992). Quality in higher education: A conceptualization and some observations on the implementation of a sectorial quality system. *Journal of Further and Higher Education*, *16*(1), 90–103. doi:10.1080/0309877920160210

KEY TERMS AND DEFINITIONS

4th Industrial Revolution (4th IR): This refers to the abrupt changes in the way people work and produce after the introduction of artificial intelligence in the workplace and production systems.

Accounting Information Systems: These are IT tools that allow for the processing of large amounts of information in a timely manner.

Artificial Intelligence: An umbrella term that refers to different IT systems that are able to make decisions on their own and evolve/learn from their experience.

Crisis Management: The field of management that specifically addresses the coping with and leveraging of adverse and potentially damaging situations to the organization and individuals.

Soft Skills: A set of skills associated with the social and emotional components of work and life, that are generally geared towards coping with a person's own emotions as well as others' and translates in being able to cooperate well with others and function well on their own.

Transversal Skills: An umbrella term that refers to all skills that can be used in multiple settings of work and life. They include soft skills, as well as some technical skills like speaking different languages and using IT with proficiency.

VUCA: VUCA is an acronym for Volatile, Uncertain, Complex, and Ambiguous, originally coined by the U.S. Army War College that has become more mainstream in light of the increase in quantity, intensity, and duration of crisis in the contemporary context, especially after the COVID19 pandemic.

Chapter 6
The Uniform Accountancy Act and CPA Evolution:
What the New Regime Means for Accountancy

Nina T. Dorata
St. John's University, USA

Adrian T. Fitzsimons
St. John's University, USA

Vincent J. Shea
St. John's University, USA

Mark M. Ulrich
CUNY Queensborough Community College, USA

ABSTRACT

This chapter explores evolution implications, evaluates their impact, and sets the stage for future research. Academic programs, CPA candidates, and potential employers are contemplating the significant implications of evolution. Those implications are wide and impactful for the academy, recruiters, and ultimately, CPA candidates and the future CPA pipeline. The evolution exam requires a common core in audit, regulation, financial accounting, and reporting with technology and business concepts embedded and one required discipline of business analysis and reporting or information systems and controls or tax compliance and planning. For the first time in history, the CPA candidate will bring a different knowledge set to the exam. The reason for this is that a candidate will choose a discipline compared the identical candidate knowledge requirement that currently exists since the CPA exam was offered. That change, in addition to the knowledge requirement for technology application, has broad implications for the academy and the profession. These issues are explored in this chapter.

DOI: 10.4018/978-1-6684-5483-1.ch006

Copyright © 2023, IGI Global. Copying or distributing in print or electronic forms without written permission of IGI Global is prohibited.

INTRODUCTION

On October 13, 2020, the Board of Directors of the National Association of State Boards of Accountancy (NASBA) approved amendments to the Uniform Accountancy Act (UAA) Model Rules that pertain to the education requirements for those wishing to obtain licensure in the accounting profession as a certified public accountant (CPA) (NASBA, 2020). The Model Rules provide guidance for students, educators, and regulators on the education needed to enter the evolving CPA profession in the years ahead. The amendments to the Model Rules were developed jointly by the CPA Evolution (Evolution) initiative sponsored by the American Institute of Certified Public Accountants (AICPA) and the NASBA Uniform Accountancy Act Committee (the Committee).

In June 2021, AICPA and NASBA released the Model Curriculum (MC), which was a six-month endeavor providing education content guidance to academics as programs recalibrate curriculum to align with Evolution. The MC was later updated in November 2021 and the AICPA released the proposed blueprints for the Evolution CPA exam in June 2022.[1] The UAA provides guiding principles for the MC and licensing jurisdictions that also regulate education requirements to sit for the CPA exam and for licensure. Beginning in January 2024, Evolution reformats the CPA exam to a core knowledge representing three exam parts covering accounting, audit, and tax, which includes digital acumen. Candidates select a fourth part in one of three disciplines: Business analysis and reporting (BAR), Information systems and controls (ISC), and Tax compliance and planning (TCP).

Unless jurisdictions prohibit otherwise, the discipline-based exam may be taken before the core exams. The MC guidance for discipline-based content assumes the core knowledge as a prerequisite, which implies that graduate courses in a 150-hour licensure program would most likely deliver discipline content. If jurisdictions maintain 120-hour sit requirements, candidates will need to exercise caution when considering sitting for discipline exam in advance of the core exams.

This article explores Evolution implications, evaluates its impact, and sets the stage for future research. Academic programs, CPA candidates, and potential employers are contemplating the significant implications of Evolution. Those implications are wide and impactful for the academy, recruiters, and ultimately, CPA candidates and the future CPA pipeline.

HIGHLIGHTS OF UAA MODEL RULES

Degree Requirements

Several jurisdictions do not require applicants desiring to sit for the Uniform CPA examination to have obtained a bachelor's degree – 120 credit hours is sufficient, and most do not require a Bachelor's degree in accountancy. Some jurisdictions include coursework that must be completed before an applicant can sit for the examination. However, international candidates may choose to sit for the examination from jurisdictions with the lowest sit requirements, which may result in some applicants have taken the examination before completing their first accounting course. The UAA Model Rules require a CPA applicant to earn a graduate degree and/or a baccalaureate degree at an accredited college or university and have earned a minimum of six semester credit hours at the undergraduate level or three semester credit hours at the graduate level of principles or introductory accounting content.

Accounting Content

The UAA Model Rules require a CPA applicant to earn a minimum of 24 semester credit hours of accounting courses content at the undergraduate or graduate level, requiring a minimum of three semester credit hours in each of the following accounting content areas: (a) financial accounting and reporting for business organizations, (b) financial statement auditing, (c) taxation, (d) accounting information systems. In addition, applicants must earn a minimum of twelve semester credit hours in some or all of the following accounting content areas: (a) financial accounting and reporting for government and not-for-profit entities; (b) attestation engagements; (c) managerial or cost accounting; (d) mergers and acquisitions; (e) tax and financial planning; (f) fraud examination; (g) internal controls and risk assessment; (h) financial statement analysis; (i) accounting research and analysis; (j) tax research and analysis; (k) data analytics, data interrogation techniques, and/or digital acumen in an accounting context, whether taken in the business school or in another college or university program, such as the engineering, computer science, or math programs; (l) ethics (accounting course); or (m) other accounting-related content areas included in the Uniform CPA Examination Blueprints or as may be approved by the Board.

Business Content

The UAA Model Rules require a CPA applicant to earn a minimum of 24 semester credit hours (or the equivalent) of business content, other than accounting, at the undergraduate and/or graduate level, covering some or all of the following subject-matter content: (a) business law, (b) economics, (c) management, (d) marketing, (e) finance, (f) business communications, (g) statistics, (h) quantitative methods, (i) information systems or technology, (j) data analytics, data interrogation techniques, and/or digital acumen (whether taken in the business school or in another college or university program, such as the engineering, computer science, or math programs), (k) ethics (business course), and (m) other business-related content areas included in the Uniform CPA Examination Blueprints or as may be approved by the Board. Unlike the current and past exams, the MC does not provide business law the same prominence as it once did in the CPA exam; rather, Sarbanes-Oxley Act of 2002, Securities and Exchange Commission regulations, and laws related to taxation are examples of the limits of law tested in the MC.

Program Accreditation

NASBA recognizes that accredited accounting and business programs are viewed as quality programs because of requirements to adhere to accreditation standards. Nevertheless, despite accreditation, NASBA requires transcript review for candidates seeking to sit for the Uniform CPA exam. Even though the Model Rules remove the Council for Higher Education Accreditation (CHEA) requirement, the Board may recognize CHEA as an acceptable accrediting organization.

The Model Rules established three levels of accreditation. Level 1 accreditation represents the most comprehensive review at the accounting program level; whereby, separate accreditation exists for the institution through regional accreditation agencies such as Higher Learning Commission, Middle States Commission on Higher Education, New England Commission on Higher Education, Northwest Commission on Colleges and Universities, Southern Association of Colleges and Schools Commission on Colleges, and WASC Senior College and University Commission), the business school through AACSB and Association of Collegiate Business Schools and Programs (ACBSP), and the accounting program through AACSB, as examples. In a Level 2 accreditation, the institution and the business school are both accredited by a NASBA recognized organization that includes not only the AACSB but also the ACBSP. Level 3 accreditation represents the least comprehensive review as accreditation is only completed by a regional accreditation organization at the institution level. Institutions without Level 3 accreditation generally are not recognized by NASBA.

The UAA is silent with respect to accreditation status for accounting programs of foreign institutions of higher education and institutions that have specialty accreditation from an approved Department of Education specialty accreditation organization but are not accredited by a regional accreditation organization. That silence demands a meticulous transcript review if the education is obtained outside the U.S. and the program is not AACSB accredited. It is evident that candidates who list their home address outside of the U.S. most likely have some of their education taken outside the U.S. NASBA (2020a) reports that these candidates represent 11.4% of all exam section taken in 2019. NASBA reports "A total of 9,122 candidates from 98 countries other than the U.S., sat for 22,663 sections." The data show for

2019, Japan ranked first with 2,248 candidates, which represented an increase of 21.4% from 2018.

According to the AACSB, of the 937 accredited institutions, 190 are Level 1, of which 11 reside outside of the U.S. Of the 747 Level 2 programs, 386 reside outside the U.S.[2] ACBSP accreditation represents 700 programs with approximately 15% holding a separate ACBSP accounting accreditation (ACBSP, 2021). Approximately 43 of the ACBSP programs reside outside the U.S.; none hold the separate accounting accreditation. The UAA is silent on classifying ACBSP accounting accreditation as a Level 1 status.

NASBA (2020a) reports overall passing rates of approximately 60% and 66%, for overall and first time test takers, respectively, for programs that have Level 1 AACSB accounting accreditation. For AACSB Level 2 accreditation, the comparable pass rates are lower at approximately 52% and 57%, respectively. Comparable pass rates are further lower for Level 2 ACBSP accreditation at approximately 43% and 46%, respectively.

SKILLS AND COMPETENCIES: ASSURANCE OF LEARNING

The UAA prescribes not only technical based knowledge, but also professional skills for a newly licensed CPA. Most of these skills center on critical thinking, with significant emphasis on ethics and professional skepticism. Acquiring content knowledge and professional skills are equally important, but not easily equally learned. The classroom may provide challenges to deliver that knowledge; however, the UAA allows for multiple internship experiences that may meet the challenge in limiting the skills' gap. Lastly, the UAA guidance implies that 150-hour should be obtained before a candidate "sits" for the exam. Since the 150-hours program was implemented for licensure, most jurisdictions do permit candidates to sit with 120 credits. There is no indication that the 120-hour sit requirement will change for most jurisdictions. The result being candidates sitting for the exam absent certain requisite skills that education and/or experience could provide.

The following table summarizes the skills and competencies prescribed by the UAA:

Below is a discussion of certain professional skills prescribed by the UAA and challenges to attain them.

Critical Thinking

In 1987, the National Council for Excellence in Critical Thinking (Council) defined critical thinking as the intellectually disciplined process of actively and skillfully

Table 1. UAA summary of skills and competencies

Skills	Description	Application
Critical Thinking	Conceptualizing Applying Analyzing Synthesizing Evaluating	Risk assessment Management Measurement Interpretation Reporting Research Systems and Process Technology and Tools
Professional Skepticism	Attitude State of mind Built over time Requires refinement	Critical assessment Auditor requires knowledge, skills, competencies, integrity Persuasive evidence Robust risk assessment

conceptualizing, applying, analyzing, synthesizing, and/or evaluating information gathered from, or generated by, observation, experience, reflection, reasoning, or communication, as a guide to belief and action The Council states that in its exemplary form, critical thinking is based on universal intellectual values that transcend subject matter divisions: clarity, accuracy, precision, consistency, relevance, sound evidence, good reasons, depth, breadth, and fairness are elements of critical thinking (ITEN, 2015). The Council also states that critical thinking entails the examination of those structures or elements of thought implicit in all reasoning: purpose, problem, or question-at-issue; assumptions; concepts; empirical grounding; reasoning leading to conclusions; implications and consequences; objections from alternative viewpoints; and frame of reference are examples.

When the AICPA issued its functional competencies or those technical competencies most closely aligned with the value contributed by accounting professionals, it advised that those competencies add value to business and contribute to a prosperous society (AICPA, 2021a). Several of the functional competencies listed below, clearly require the auditor to exercise critical thinking. They are:

- Risk Assessment, Analysis and Management – to assess, analyze and manage risk using appropriate frameworks, professional judgment, and skepticism for effective business management.
- Measurement Analysis and Interpretation – to identify and apply appropriate, reliable, and verifiable measurements to analyze data for a given purpose and intended use.
- Reporting – to identify the appropriate content and communicate clearly and objectively to the intended audience, the work performed, and the results

as governed by professional standards, required by law, or dictated by the business environment.

- Research – to identify, access and apply relevant professional frameworks, standards, and guidance, as well as other information for analysis and to make informed decisions.
- Systems and Process Management – to identify the appropriate business processes and system(s), related frameworks, and controls to assist in the design and use of systems for efficient and effective operations.
- Technology and Tools – to identify and utilize relevant technology and tools to analyze data, efficiently and effectively perform assigned tasks as well as support other competencies.

The AICPA contends that employers on average believe that only approximately 57% of college graduates are proficient in using critical thinking skills (AICPA, 2020). Critical thinking requires not only skills that include identify, analyze, conclude, and then communicate, but also requires faculty understanding of cognitive development, which may be different among students. The challenges to develop stronger critical thinking skills may be overwhelming; however, starting with smaller cases or tasks, assessment that is neither wrong nor right but focus on the next higher order critical thinking skills are examples of making progress to improving critical thinking skills.

Professional Skepticism

Professional skepticism is defined in the Public Company Accounting Oversight Board (PCAOB) standards as an attitude that includes a questioning mind and a critical assessment of audit evidence. Professional skepticism should be exercised in all aspects of the audit process, it is particularly important in those areas of the audit that involve: (a) significant management judgments, (b) transactions outside the normal course of business, (c) possible misstatement due to fraud or error in an audit, or (d) critical assessment of audit evidence. The PCAOB states in Staff Audit Practice Alert No. 10*: Maintaining and Applying Professional Skepticism in Audits,* that when auditors do not appropriately apply professional skepticism, they may not obtain sufficient appropriate evidence to support their opinions or may not identify or address situations in which the financial statements are materially misstated (PCAOB, 2012).

Professional skepticism is not easily measured, nor is it cultivated overnight, but rather it is a skill developed over time and one that all auditors should constantly build and refine. The PCAOB noted that it continues to observe instances in which circumstances suggest that auditors did not appropriately apply professional skepticism in their audits. Staff Audit Practice Alert No. 10: *Maintaining and Applying Professional Skepticism in Audits* focuses on the importance of professional skepticism, the appropriate application of professional skepticism in audits, and certain important considerations for audit firms' quality control systems.

Professional skepticism includes the following elements:

- Attributes for the knowledge, skill, competencies, and overall ability of the auditor needed to perform their responsibilities.
- Mindset or the integrity and good faith of the auditor who recognizes the possibility of fraud, misstatement, or misrepresentation of essential facts by management and employees and who is not satisfied with less than persuasive evidence.
- Action or the importance of performing a robust risk assessment, planning the engagement based on the risks involved, ensuring vigorous engagement supervision, and the diligent gathering and evaluation of audit evidence.

The PCAOB has cited numerous cases that have linked audit deficiencies with a lack of professional skepticism described below (PCAOB, 2012). The cases not only describe the neglect to exercise skepticism, but also, the accounting context demonstrates complex judgements where skepticism may prevail.

Examples and situations noted by the PCAOB that point to insufficient skepticism include testing of assumptions and modeling for level two financial instruments, inventory reserve calculations, and asset impairments for both intangibles and fixed assets. The PCAOB also cited insufficient sensitivity testing for subsequent events with respect to debt covenants and entity going concern as examples of inadequate application of skepticism.

The professional literature describes various call for emphasizing ethics education in accounting programs and in particular, professional skepticism (Fei Gong, Kim, & Harding, 2014; Mintz, 2017, 2018). The challenges in ethics education are succinctly stated by Mintz (2018): "the problem is that students often parrot back what they believe the professor wants to hear rather than what they truly feel." Gong Kim and Harding studied professional skepticism in an experimental setting where expectations are known and not known in advance. Like Mintz (2018), Gong et al. (2014) finds that when preferences are not known, professional skepticism is elevated. Otherwise, when preferences are known in advance, participants will respond to ethical situations with greater ease and with minimal fear of retribution from in-line responses.

Educating students to apply critical thinking skills that require application of professional skepticism could be a tall order. Students need to exercise professional skepticism in the context without known expectations (Gong et al. (2014) and any professional experience as a point of reference is cognitively challenging because to be a skeptic requires evaluation from broader and deeper perspectives. As an example adult cognitive development consists of five stages until it reaches expert critical thinking; most undergraduate students only achieve stages one through three (AICPA 2020 pgs. 7-8).

Academics have tested professionals' skepticism in experimental settings and results show difficulties exist in exercising independence, recognizing conflicts of interest, and maintaining a skeptical mindset (Braun & Stallworth, 2009; Mintz, 2017). To mitigate deficiencies in applying professional skepticism, licensing jurisdictions could again require professional experience prior to sitting for the discipline-based exam. However, an experience requirement may be considered a barrier to the profession. Although the AICPA views knowledge derived from experience necessary for the exam, there is no indication that licensing jurisdictions are reconsidering an experience requirement to sit for the exam.[3]

Research and Communication

The UAA Model Rules, require all CPA candidates to earn a minimum of two semester credit hours in research and analysis and two semester credit hours in oral and written communications relevant to the course content through a discrete undergraduate and/or graduate accounting course, or integrated throughout the undergraduate and/or graduate accounting curriculum. All colleges or universities would be required to provide evidence of coverage under integration. The semester credit hours earned through discrete courses in research and analysis in accounting and in oral and written communications may fulfill two of the semester credit hours of the accounting subject matter requirements.

Required Ethics

An ethics program would be required to provide, at a minimum, a foundation for ethical reasoning that includes core values of integrity, objectivity, and independence. The UAA Model Rules require all CPA applicants to earn a minimum of three semester credit hours in an undergraduate and/or a graduate course listed or cross listed as an accounting or business course in ethics. The UAA Model Rules require the program of learning to provide students with a framework of ethical reasoning, professional values, and attitudes for exercising professional skepticism and other behavior that is in the best interest of the public and profession.

As an alternative, the UAA Model Rules allow colleges or universities to choose to integrate the ethics course throughout the undergraduate and/or graduate accounting or business curriculum. Universities must provide evidence of coverage under integration. Proof of coverage may be provided through specific evaluation by a specialized or professional accrediting organization recognized by the Board. Evidence provides the Board with assurance that the program of learning has been adequately covered and has the equivalent of three semester credit hours minimum. Alternate methods for proof of ethics coverage may be determined and approved by the Board following scrutiny. As an example, approximately half of the jurisdictions specify either the credits or type (accounting or business) ethics within the education requirements for licensure.[4] Ethics studies continues following licensure with required ethics continuing professional education.

Digital Acumen

Digital acumen is a combination of digital ambition and digital ability that can be used to help business professionals understand the transformative power of digital technologies, as well as, to help them develop the vision and ability to execute that knowledge. Digital acumen entails professionals staying abreast of digital trends, understanding the implication of digital trends on their business, and knowing how to leverage new technologies and to take effective action, quickly.

Internship Programs and Independent Study

A significant change in the Model Rules centers on pre-approved internship programs and independent study to help ensure students receive valuable educational experiences. Internships, according to the Model Rules, are defined as a faculty pre-approved and appropriately supervised short-term work experience, usually related to a student's major field of study, for which the student earns academic credit and/or receive compensation. Internships and independent study options will lend value to candidates' decisions in choosing Evolution's discipline exams in either BAR, ISC, or TCP. Depending on which semester the internship is taken, the internship could make finishing the CPA exam dependent on completing the internship. Additional value may be obtained from the experience knowledge, which may improve passing outcomes for the Evolution discipline-based exams. Internship experiences could further expose students to applying critical thinking skills, especially professional skepticism. Still, if licensing jurisdictions permit candidates to sit for the discipline-based exam before any internship experience, that may dispel any knowledge derived from professional experiences.

Independent Study

The Model Rules define independent study as academic work selected or designed by the student with the pre-approval of the appropriate department of a college or university under faculty supervision. This work typically occurs outside of the regular classroom structure. Independent study programs: (a) provide knowledge and skills not easily communicated in class, (b) enable learners to identify a problem, gather data, and take responsibility for conclusions, (c) provide useful practice in the process of learning, (d) meet the convenience needs of the learner, (e) develop self-motivation, concentration, and discipline, and (f) require the learner to individually complete all work (Rafoth, 2020).

Additionally, the Model Rules would set the maximum of nine (9) semester credit hours for internships and independent study that may count towards the education subject matter requirements and would describe the content of those courses. The Model Rules limit the nine semester credit hours to a maximum of three semester credit hours that may apply to accounting course content requirements, and three semester credit hours that may apply to business course content requirements and the remainder applied to elective credit. That application assumes overall program requirements permit flexibility in choosing internships for course credit.

CANDIDATES SITTING FOR THE EXAM BEFORE EARNING 150-HOURS: WHO DECIDES?

Missing from the UAA Model Rules is the "Sit 120" rule that most licensing jurisdictions currently have in place, which allows candidates to starting taking the exam following completion of 120-hours or completion of a baccalaureate degree. Section 5 of the January 2018 AICPA/NASBA Uniform Accountancy Act Standards for Regulation state that "The education requirements for a certificate, which must be met before an applicant is eligible to apply for the examination prescribed in subsection (d), shall be at least 150-hours of college education including a baccalaureate or higher degree conferred by a college or university acceptable to the Board, the total educational program to include an accounting concentration as determined by the Board rule to be appropriate (AICPA/NASBA, 2018)." Unlike the 2020 Model rules published solely by NASBA, there is no requirement to attain 150-hours before an applicate is eligible to apply for the exam (NASBA, 2020).

The AICPA/NASBA UAA Committee indicates that candidates should complete 150-hours of education before sitting for the exam; therefore, it is reasonable to expect that candidates would gain practical experience through internships while preparing for the uniform CPA exam. The exam tests the content knowledge to reflect the minimum skills and knowledge required of a CPA.[5] That implies professional experience lends valuable content knowledge for the exam; therefore, it could be inferred that the exam is designed to be taken after some professional experience.

Understandably, as a document prescribing educational policy, the UAA Model Rules do not suggest experience requirements to sit for the exam nor does it set jurisdiction education requirements. Like the MC, the UAA Model Rules is just that, a model. Licensing jurisdictions determine education, sit, and experience requirements to attain the license. The AICPA determines uniform CPA exam content. There is a substantial difference when jurisdictions allow 120-hours sit rules or have other policies to allow sitting for the exam prior to earning 150-hours. Not only do candidates take the exam prior to obtaining experience, but candidates can sit for the exam before earning the UAA Model Rules-prescribed education requirements.

Having simultaneous discussions over the exam's educational and experience requirements is a solution to resolve the discrepancy among the AICPA's intended candidate profile, the UAA's Model Rules to sit for the exam, and jurisdictions' sit and license requirements. The CPA Evolution's initial plan was to adopt the engineering model; however, Evolution narrowly focuses on the engineering model for exam core and disciplines. Evolution does not consider the more extensive path of an engineer, in which licensing jurisdictions may require not only education but also experience prior to sitting for exams. Only taking a true holistic approach could better prepare CPA candidates that the profession demands.

THE ACCOUNTING PIPELINE TRENDS AND CPA EXAM PASS RATES AND BEC

It has been reported that since the implementation of the 150-hour requirement for licensure, the accounting pipeline to licensure has been challenged with significant declines in the candidates and the number (Allen and Woodland 2006). Recent declines have been reported in the 2019 AICPA Trends Report. Yet AICPA student surveys of the Evolution model indicate either more or continued high interest in pursuing the CPA license.[6] Very recent enrollment, pass rate trends, and evolution transition plans may provide glimpses of the CPA pipeline for near future. Programs may face challenges to deliver Evolution disciplines could further downward trends in enrollments.

Pipeline Trends

Overall, master's and baccalaureate degrees conferred in accounting declined 6.2% from 2016 to 2020. Private colleges and universities experienced a greater share of the decline, with baccalaureate degrees conferred falling 8.18% (compared to 4.15% for public institutions) and master's degrees conferred falling 10.50% (compared to 6.77% for public institutions) during the same 2016-2020 period (IPEDS, 2021).

The decline in degrees conferred is consistent with the declines in the CPA exam pipeline that is presented in the 2019 AICPA Trends Report. That report shows a decline of 23.3% for the same period. Fortunately, CPA pass rates started to increase significantly starting in 2017. Specifically, between 2017 and 2020, overall pass rates increased significantly, from approximately 48% to approximately 56%.[7]

Pass Rate Trends

Pass rates increased during the second quarter of 2020, which started about three weeks following COVID-19 shutdown. Section pass rates during the second quarter of 2020 were 69% but then dropped in the third and fourth quarters to 61% and 51%, respectively. The first, second, and third quarters of 2021 show overall pass rates were steady at 53%, 53%, and 54%, respectively.

Recently released quarterly data from NASBA show a 33% and 20% increase in sections taken and number of candidates, respectively, for the third quarter compared to the comparable quarter in 2020. For the third quarter in 2021, 62% of the candidates passed BEC and 63% passed REG, which represented a 4% increase from prior quarters. Significantly lower passage rates for AUD, and FAR were 47% and 48% respectively, for the 2021 third quarter. BEC obtained the highest pass rates of 62% and 63%, for the first and second quarters, respectively. The annual data for the years 2017, 2018 and 2019 show that BEC averages the highest pass rate for first time test takers of 61%, 78%, and 78%, respectively. [8]

CPA Evolution poses many questions about future pass rates for the CPA exam. BEC, the section which typically has the highest pass rates is being replaced by the candidate's choice of one of three discipline-specific exams. The July 2021 AICPA CPA Exam Blueprints[9] map at least 50% of the BEC content to topics that are taught in lower division courses that are typical of an undergraduate business program (AICPA, 2021b). The discipline-specific exams will have more advanced content typically learned at the upper division or at the graduate level part of a 150-hour program. Collectively, discipline content could be more challenging to candidates than is the BEC content. Further, over two-thirds of the U.S. jurisdictions have 120-hour sit requirements.[10] Because the proposed transition model between pre- and post-Evolution allows substitution of BEC for a discipline-based exam and given BEC's typically higher pass rate, it is reasonable to conclude that there will be a surge sitting for BEC before the January 2024 effective date of the Evolution exam.[11]

It is unknown how the passing rates will trend with the disciplines in place; however, expectancies could be hypothesized. Review programs will be nimble and help candidates learn discipline-based content until the academy not only implements the discipline content, but also the course and/or program structure to deliver it. It reasonable to expect that the discipline exam will have a lower pass rate; therefore, the overall pass rate for the CPA exam could decline, assuming the pass rates for three core part pass rates remain constant post-Evolution. In conclusion, the perception of a harder Evolution exam could be the most significant barrier to the profession since licensing jurisdictions implemented the 150-hour licensing requirement. That barrier is exacerbated by the dismal increase in starting salaries for newly licensed CPAs creating a lower return on education investment relative to other professions requiring only a typical 120-hour undergraduate degrees.

POST-EVOLUTION SATISFACTION ISSUES: WHICH DISCIPLINE TO SELECT?

Evolution will mandate candidates to choose a discipline. It is reasonable to expect that the choice of discipline will signal to recruiters how to implement hiring practices, even though jurisdictions are issuing one CPA license with no discipline designation.[12] Choosing a discipline may be limited to program offerings or what is perceived as most desirable by the profession. UAA prescribed internships could aid candidates in making that choice. Practical experience through internships could also mitigate technology gaps that the Evolution exam platform will struggle to assess.

Discipline Descriptions

In 2024, the uniform CPA examination will require candidates to select one discipline exam in BAR, ISC or TCP.

- For BAR, candidates would be interested in assurance or advisory services, financial statement analysis and reporting, technical accounting, and financial and operations management. The content would have a data analytics focus and assess topics such as financial risk management and financial planning techniques and more advanced technical accounting and reporting topics at higher-skill levels.
- For ISC, candidates would be focused on technology and business controls and in assurance or advisory services related to business processes, information systems, information security and governance, and IT audits. The content would focus on IT and data governance, internal control testing, and information system security, as well as the performance of system and organization controls (SOC) engagements.
- For TCP, candidates would be interested in more advanced tax compliance for individuals, business entities with a focus on personal financial planning and entity planning as well as property transactions. The content would focus

on individual tax planning topics, advanced entity tax compliance coverage, entity planning, including the tax treatments of the formation and liquidation of business entities, and coverage of property transactions, including like-kind and involuntary exchanges and related party transactions.

Digital Acumen

Even though the new examination format broadens the scope of the uniform CPA examinations, it does little to minimize the technology gap between what professionals expect from new CPAs and what the exam continues to be unable to test. As is true with the current exam, candidate's digital acumen and proficiency in using and applying relevant technology tools may not be adequately tested on the new uniform CPA examination. At best, dashboards from which candidates must interpret and draw relevant conclusions could be tested. It is then reasonable to conclude that professionals will continue to be dissatisfied with the technological skills of new CPAs, as examinations alone cannot substitute for appropriate professional experiences or apprenticeships.

CONCLUSION

A tall order is in place for academic programs, jurisdictions, and CPA exam candidates to embrace the Evolution exam prescribed in the UAA Model Rules and the AICPA proposal for the Evolution exam both core and disciplines. Educators, current and future exam candidates must hasten preparation because Evolution is effective January 2024. Academic programs require significant retooling to address core and disciplines' knowledge content, which may entail difficult decisions to limit program delivery. Jurisdictions are charged with the daunting task of evaluating and reregistering academic programs for compliance with the Evolution model and ultimately the AICPA Evolution blueprints. That circumstance arises potentially for at least two reasons: greater emphasis on emerging technologies and the Evolution disciplines. Because the content knowledge differs for each discipline, candidates will no longer bring the same knowledge to the Evolution exam for their chosen discipline as they do for the pre-Evolution exam. Jurisdictions may choose to specify courses for the three unique pathways Evolution provides to licensure or, the most likely scenario is that programs will be responsible for mapping discipline content to specific elective courses.

Candidates will strategize in the remaining time prior to Evolution whether to accelerate, postpone or forgo examination plans. Candidates caught between Evolution and pre-Evolution exams will need to adhere to a transition model, which will preclude taking a discipline with credit given to BEC as being the swing part.[13] Candidates with pre-Evolution education will face deadlines to sit before their education is deemed invalid. Concurrently, career recruiters may implicitly establish preferences for disciplines tied to hiring goals. Nevertheless, Evolution may be a revolution in the education, testing, and ultimately the employing CPA candidates.

REFERENCES

AACSB. (2021). *About Us.* AACSB. https://aacsb.edu/about-us

ACBSP. (2021). *About.* ACBSP. https://acbsp.org/page/about-who-we-are

AICPA. (2020). *How to Help Your Students Become Better Critical Thinkers.* AICPA. https://thiswaytocpa.com/program/CriticalThinking

AICPA. (2021a). *Accounting Competencies.* AICPA. https://www.aicpa.org/interestareas/accountingeducation/resources/accounting-core-competencies-functional.html

AICPA. (2021b). *Uniform CPA Examination Blueprints.* AICPA. https://us.aicpa.org/content/dam/aicpa/becomeacpa/cpaexam/examinationcontent/downloadabledocuments/cpa-exam-blueprints-effective-july-2021.pdf

AICPA. (2022). *Exposure Draft: Proposed 2024 CPA Exam changes.* AICPA. https://www.aicpa.org/resources/download/exposure-draft-proposed-2024-cpa-exam-changes AICPA/NASBA.

Allen, A., & Woodland, A. M. (2006). The 150- Hour Requirement and the Number of CPA Exam Candidates, Pass Rates, and the the Number Passing. *Issues in Accounting Education, 21*(3), 173–193. doi:10.2308/iace.2006.21.3.173

Braun, R. L., & Stallworth, H. L. (2009). If You Need Love, Get a Puppy: A Case Study on Professional Skepticism and Auditor Independence. *Issues in Accounting Education, 24*(2), 237–252. doi:10.2308/iace.2009.24.2.237

Fei Gong, Y., Kim, S., & Harding, N. (2014). Elevating professional scepticism. *Managerial Auditing Journal, 29*(8), 674–694. doi:10.1108/MAJ-08-2013-0914

IPEDS. (2021). *National Center for Education Statistics.* NCES. https://nces.ed.gov/ipeds/use-the-data

ITEN. (2015). Critical Thinking Toolkit. *Learning, A: A Guide to Professional Skepticism.* ITEN. https://www.acilearning.com/blog/professional-skepticism-for-auditors

Mintz, S. (2017). Reimagining Ethics Education. *The CPA Journal, 87*(9), 8–9. https://jerome.stjohns.edu/login?url=https://search.ebscohost.com/login.aspx?direct=true&db=buh&AN=124942823&site=ehost-live

Mintz, S. (2018). Accounting in the Public Interest. (cover story). *The CPA Journal, 88*(3), 22–29. https://jerome.stjohns.edu/login?url=https://search.ebscohost.com/login.aspx?direct=true&db=buh&AN=128446872&site=ehost-live

NASBA. (2020). *UAA Model Rule Requirements - Education*. NASBA. https://nasba.org/app/uploads/2020/10/Oct-20-UAA-Model-Rule-5-1-Education.pdf

NASBA. (2020a). *Candidate Perfomance On The Uniform CPA Examination 2019 Edition*. NASBA.

PCAOB. (2012). *Maintaining and Applying Professional Skepticim in Audits*. PCAOB. https://pcaobus.org/Standards/QandA/12-04-2012_SAPA_10.pdf

Rafoth, M. A. (2020). *Independent Study*. State University. https://education.stateuniversity.com/pages/2080/Independent-Study.html

ENDNOTES

1 See https://thiswaytocpa.com/collectedmedia/files/cpa-evolution-model-curriculum-update.pdf and https://www.aicpa.org/resources/download/exposure-draft-proposed-2024-cpa-exam-changes

2 See https://aacsb.edu/accredited?accreditations=business

3 See https://www.aicpa.org/resources/article/find-answers-to-frequently-asked-questions-about-cpa-exam

4 See https://nasba.org/stateboards/ for access to jurisdiction education requirements for licensure.

5 See https://www.aicpa.org/resources/article/find-answers-to-frequently-asked-questions-about-cpa-exam

6 https://www.journalofaccountancy.com/news/2020/jul/new-cpa-licensure-model-embraces-core-specialization.html

7 2017 through 2019 overall pass rate is reported in the Candidate Performance on the Uniform CPA Examination published by NASBA. Starting with 2020, NASBA paused publication of the annual editions (see https://nasba.org/blog/2021/12/13/candidate-performance-book-publication-paused/). Quarterly performance data are still published by NASBA. The annual 2020 pass rate is calculated by aggregating quarterly pass rates weighted by quarterly sections relative to annual sections taken.

8 Source of data are the Candidate Performance on the Uniform CPA Examination published by NASBA for the respective years.

9 Content is mapped as follows: 1. ERM, Internal Controls and Business Processes (20%-30%), 2. Economics (15%-25%), 3. Financial Management (10%-20%), 4. Information Technology (15%-25%), and 5. Operations Management (15%-25%).

10 Jurisdiction requirements found at https://nasba.org/stateboards/.

11 The current BEC will be eliminated in the Evolution exam with its content expected to be embedded in the Evolution exam content. NYS has approved a transition model that awards credit for an Evolution discipline if BEC is passed by December 2023 until December 2025. See January 26, 2022 Meeting Agenda found at https://www.op.nysed.gov/boards/01262022CPABdMtg.htm. Also see https://nasba.org/blog/2022/02/25/transition-policy/

12 See https://www.aicpa.org/news/article/the-new-cpa-evolution-cpa-exam

13 https://nasba.org/blog/2022/02/25/transition-policy/

Chapter 7
The Effect of COVID-19 on Professional Accountants:
The Evidence of Turkey

Ahmet Kaya
https://orcid.org/0000-0002-0822-4549
Akdeniz University, Turkey

ABSTRACT

Covid-19 has affected the business methods and procedures of almost all professions as well as the economies of the countries. Many professions in Turkey have felt the adverse effects of the pandemic. One of these professions is Certified Public Accountant (CPA). The pandemic has significantly affected accounting practices and the roles of professionals. Therefore, the need to learn in detail from the experts has emerged. So, this study aimed to investigate the effect of the pandemic on the professional activities of CPAs. In this direction, using the interview technique, eight questions were asked to eight professionals, mainly problems, expectations, income status, workload, and work stress. The results of the research revealed that the members of the profession had problems with both government institutions and taxpayers. As a result of the research, the CPAs stated that they had difficulty finding an interlocutor during the pandemic and had severe communication problems. Emphasizing their income has decreased significantly, the CPAs also said that their workload has increased.

DOI: 10.4018/978-1-6684-5483-1.ch007

Copyright © 2023, IGI Global. Copying or distributing in print or electronic forms without written permission of IGI Global is prohibited.

INTRODUCTION

The Covid-19 pandemic, which emerged as a health crisis in Wuhan, China, at the end of 2019, greatly affected the economic and social life in the later process (Topcu & Demirkol, 2021). Covid-19 has started to affect all countries negatively in a short time. As a result of this rapid spread, a series of measures have been taken in countries. Restrictions have begun to be implemented in many areas, from health to economy, education to social life. The Covid-19 epidemic, which emerged as a significant threat, has limited the life activities of individuals and has become a global problem (Güngör Karyağdı, 2021). The measures taken by the states caused a decrease in production and commercial activities, a decrease in the income of individuals, and an increase in unemployment rates. These developments have led to the deterioration of supply chains, the consumption of various products, and decreased demand for some services. Therefore, the balance of supply and demand has deteriorated significantly (Papadopoulou & Papadopoulou, 2020). Covid-19 has been a process in which the normals of life are affected, the known solutions lose their validity, and the importance of psychological immunity is realized. The ways of doing business of the future, whose scenarios have been discussed so far, had to be implemented as new normals with this sudden change. This change process has led to an increased understanding of individuals, questioning their talents and supporting their weak points (Beder, 2021). One of the biggest problems experienced in this process has been the problems encountered in the economic field. At this point, accounting professionals, who ensure healthy communication between businesses and the state, which has great importance in the economy, emerge again. Professional accountants contribute to the beneficial execution of economic activities by providing consultancy to the enterprises in the struggle given in the economic sense and by providing communication between the state and the taxpayer (Güngör Karyağdı, 2021). In such a situation, it becomes challenging to carry out professional activities, especially in occupational groups with intense human relations. The accounting profession is also stressful, where physical and emotional collapse is low and tiring. Dissatisfaction is high due to the heavy workload, constant communication with people and the necessity of completing work at certain times (Buyruk Akbaba & Bulut, 2021).

Our social habits, which we had to change due to the Covid-19 epidemic, have affected business life closely (Tuğay & Dokur, 2020). Many organizations have changed their work environments and have had to offer their employees the opportunity to work remotely. A survey conducted in 2020 reveals that remote workers account for 51 to 75% of the total workforce in firms (Lin & Hwang, 2021). The accounting profession has also significantly affected this change in working habits (Tuğay & Dokur, 2020). Professionals who provide the link between the taxpayer and the state, which acts as a bridge in fulfilling tax-related duties, may face the stress of raising a job with an intense workload. Professionals working under pressure are more likely to make mistakes due to distraction. As a result, professional accountants may be penalized (Buyruk Akbaba & Bulut, 2021). Professional accountants are a part of the broad economic ecosystem as per the general system theory because they provide accounting and consultancy services between the state and businesses within the ecosystem (Topcu & Demirkol, 2021). The accounting profession is known as one with a systematic and static structure. Individuals who acquire this profession have difficulty showing flexibility in the face of environmental changes, and the attitudes and practices of professional institutions on this subject can restrict their professional development (Beder, 2021). Since crowded workplaces are now considered a risk, the remote working system has been adopted, and digital working has been started through computers and new technologies (Katkat Özçelik, 2021). This sudden change, especially with the pandemic, the new order and the working conditions brought by digitalization, has caused adaptation problems and resistance to changes in the CPAs (Beder, 2021). This change due to Covid-19 has also affected the accounting profession, from working conditions to office conditions, from customer relations to ways of doing business. For the accountant, the pandemic has created a series of challenges, such as evaluating the economic consequences and the effects of uncertainties arising from the measures taken on financial statement elements, solving complex incentive plans, adapting to new technology, leading staff and customers in this climate of luck, and protecting both themselves and their clients' jobs (Katkat Özçelik, 2021).

Due to the problems experienced, the state has taken some measures (Güngör Karyağdı, 2021). For example, due to catching the coronavirus, the person practising the profession and the customers with whom she/he signed an intermediary responsibility agreement were given additional time equal to the reporting period (Açıkgöz & Mutlu, 2022). Measures have been taken for certified public accountants and accountants, such as postponing the application for the internship entrance exam and the date of the exam, counting the internship dates from the working time in order to facilitate the benefit of the short-time working allowance, and postponing the payment of the contribution fees for the interns (Şahin & Kumaş, 2022). The period for submitting and paying VAT returns for the 2019 income tax return and February 2020 period and the submission period of the Certified Public Accountant certification reports has been extended. SSI premiums have been deferred for six months (Katkat Özçelik, 2021). With the introduction of the Short Working Allowance, some responsibilities have been imposed on employers. However, due to the employers' inability to keep up with this system, these works are given to the responsibility of the CPA (Mazman İtik, 2021). Also, video conferences and training seminars were held online about the regulations that can be applied in working life due to the coronavirus, and e-transformation and e-applications (Açıkgöz & Mutlu, 2022). Finally, within the scope of the postponement-cancellation application, the export periods were extended, and the application date of the accommodation tax was postponed (Mazman İtik, 2021).

At the end of 2019, digitalization started in the private sector, and the scope of e-transformation has found a wider area. Electronic documents such as e-ledger, e-invoice, e-archive, e-producer receipt, and e-self-employment receipts have become more common and adopted by taxpayers. At this point, the professional groups that play a crucial role in guiding taxpayers in the name of consultancy have been the groups that perform the accounting profession (Güngör Karyağdı, 2021). The job of accountancy and financial advisory is based on human interaction. It has gained legal status in Turkey with the law on “Certified Accounting, Certified Public Accountant and Certified Public Accountant”, numbered 3568. With the amendment made with Law No. 5786 in 2008, individuals who fulfil the general and special conditions specified in the law, as well as pass the professional exams and practice the accounting profession professionally, are entitled to be “public accountant financial advisor” and “sworn financial advisor”. The fields of expertise of the job can be listed as bookkeeping, financial advisor, sworn financial advisor, expert witness, consultancy and auditing. In addition, the business and career fields of the profession are divided into the private sector (dependent on working in a corporate environment), international audit firms and independent work (having an accounting office) (Beder, 2021).

This study investigates how the accounting profession in Turkey has been affected by the Covid-19 pandemic. The study focuses on revealing how accounting professionals have adapted to the emergency changes that have started to be implemented with the pandemic and the problems. It was also aimed to determine and evaluate the effects of the pandemic on the methods of doing business, working styles, stress levels, income change, expectations from the state, intentions to quit and communication methods with their customers and public enterprises. In this direction, it has been tried to examine what problems professional accountants face while helping the state and taxpayers during the pandemic process and while doing their work. Besides the opinions of CPAs on the current process, their views about the steps to be taken in the future will also be obtained. Fundamental issues about what kind of measures can be taken to address the problems and how the processes can be arranged to achieve the highest efficiency level for the state will be discussed. In this respect, this study aims to both provide valuable contributions to the existing literature and to guide practitioners in terms of the strategies they will create and the decisions they will take. Finally, the study results will be a road map for the periods when urgent changes will be necessary due to Covid-19-like situations in the coming years.

LITERATURE REVIEW

The accounting profession is one of the business lines that perform accounting transactions, ensures the practice of accounting science, and is a consultant in managing budgets (Ceylan & Hacıhasanoğlu, 2022: 775). It is a profession that has increased in importance with economic, social, financial and technological changes and is very important for society and business life today (Ayboğa, 2003: 332). Also, it is a profession where the workload is high, human relations are intense, and physical fatigue and stress are even higher, especially in specific periods (Köse et al., 2022: 141). Professional accountants act as a bridge between taxpayers and the state due to their activities (Ceylan & Hacıhasanoğlu, 2022: 775). Professionals provide services to legal entities and persons in the field of accounting finance (Köse et al., 2022: 139). Today, accounting professionals have started to offer consultancy services in terms of finding solutions to the problems experienced by taxpayers, as well as keeping business records and reporting the necessary data to the relevant people (Aydemir, 2015: 72).

Covid-19 was declared a pandemic by the World Health Organization on March 11, 2020 (Ceylan & Hacıhasanoğlu, 2022: 775). Covid-19 has turned into a global epidemic and has become a disease that significantly affects daily life and causes changes in individuals' businesses and daily lives. This unpredictable disease has also affected accounting practices and the roles of professionals (Carungu et al., 2021: 1389). During the pandemic, many professionals across Turkey have started working from home (Köse et al., 2022: 141). Increasing uncertainties and mandatory changes due to the pandemic have disrupted organizations' activities, which has brought along difficulties, especially in the field of accounting (Prawitasari, 2022: 332). The pandemic has revealed that a robust digital transformation strategy is necessary to provide quality services to customers. In addition, members of the profession have experienced a severe transformation from how they do business to their working conditions. The pandemic has accelerated the disappearance of the traditional boundaries of office working life (Azaltun et al., 2022: 67). However, due to the pandemic, the measures taken by the states and new practices have caused the priorities of the taxpayers to change, and this has also affected the accounting professionals (Kaka, 2020: 67).

It is seen that research on the effects of Covid-19 in the field of accounting is carried out on two bases. The first is the research conducted on the impact of the pandemic on financial statements. The second is the studies on the effects of the pandemic on the accounting profession and professionals. For example, Erol and Ayboğa (2021) aimed to determine the impact of Covid-19 on the professional activities of accounting professionals. They stated that the professionals' workload increased, their productivity decreased due to the change in working hours, and they encountered difficulties in their relations with official institutions. Papadopoulou and Papadopoulou (2020) examined how Greek accountants were affected by the Covid-19 outbreak. They found that after the Covid-19 epidemic, accounting professionals had difficulties adapting to emerging business demands and had to change their working routines. Güngör Karyağdı (2021) examined the effects of the Covid-19 pandemic on the accounting profession. As a result, it was found that professional accountants could not make collections, the number of taxpayers decreased, and the workload increased due to consulting businesses.

Topçu and Demirkol (2021) examined the changes experienced by professional accountants before and during the Covid-19 period. It has been determined that there is no difference in the working hours and workload level of the professionals compared to pre-Covid-19. There is a significant difference in the income of the accounting professionals, the collection of receivables, the workload, the level of communication and work stress, and the frequency of remote work compared to before Covid-19. Selimoglu et al. (2021) examined the stress caused by Covid-19 in professional accountants. They determined that professional uncertainties due to legislative changes, document contact and the risk of infection are the primary sources of stress. Buyruk Akbaba and Bulut (2021) examined the professional burnout levels of professional accountants during the pandemic process. They determined that the burnout levels of the professionals are high, that the transition to flexible working hours, the time for filing the declarations and the reduction of the penalties can reduce the burnout.

Beder (2021) determined that the Covid-19 pandemic caused individuals to adapt to unfamiliar working conditions. It has been determined that professional accountants cannot adapt to a world that tends to digitalize. Azaltun et al. (2022) discussed the problems experienced by professional accountants during the Covid-19 process, their working methods, the digital transformation of the accounting profession and accounting-related issues. As a result, they determined that Covid-19 impacted the provision of accounting services, affecting accounting professionals' psychological and technological competencies. Ceylan and Hacıhasanoğlu (2022) determined that the biggest problem of accountants before and during the pandemic was the collection and that members of the profession were deeply affected by stress, increased workload and devaluation. Kaka (2020) explores the effective use of technology, how accountants manage the Covid-19 crisis, and the support accountants need. It has been tried to shed light on accountants' risk compliance issues after Covid-19, emphasizing that adopting digital technology is necessary for accounting firms.

Frumusanu et al. (2020) focused on the impact of the new measures on the activities of professional accountants due to Covid-19. They determined that accelerating digitalization in the financial accounting department is imperative for the pandemic. Mihai et al. (2020) examined the socioeconomic consequences of

Covid-19 on professionals. As a result, they found that professionals adapt to remote work relatively quickly. Working during the pandemic creates additional stress and fatigue but positively affects work-family relationships and productivity. Tugay and Dokur (2020) examined the pandemic's effects on professional accountants' working habits. They found that the working hours have decreased, and the most critical problem is the fear and anxiety of contracting the disease due to compulsory contact with the documents.

Katkat Özçelik (2021) investigated the changes, the effect of financial and economic measures taken by the state, and the problems that arise. The study concluded that the presence of digital technologies is essential and causes the professionals' pre-existing collection problems to increase. Mazman İtik (2021) aimed to reveal the problems experienced by financial advisors during the pandemic process. As a result, most problems are increased workload, loss of income, and difficulties in information flow with taxpayers and institutions. Kose et al. (2022) aimed to determine how professional accountants were affected during the Covid-19 process, how they adapted to the changes made during the epidemic and the problems they faced. They found that male accounting professionals were more affected by the changes, and those male accountants adapted to the new situation more quickly than female accounting professionals.

METHOD

The study aimed to determine and evaluate the effects of the pandemic on the methods of doing business, working styles, working hours and communication methods with customers of professional accountants. In this direction, the interview method has been adopted to analyze the events and developments in the focus of professional accountants uniquely and to determine the evaluations of these individuals who are experts in their fields more accurately. Qualitative research tries to find answers to three questions regarding the subject: "how", "why", and "what". The primary purpose of this type of research is to reveal the perspectives of individuals regarding the research question. Qualitative data are generally obtained through interviews, focus group meetings and observations (Haven and Van Grootel, 2019: 232). The interview technique focuses on the experiences of individuals and the meanings they derive from these experiences, rather than testing the hypothesis or getting answers (Seidman, 2006: 9). In the present study, data were obtained by the semi-structured interview technique. In this technique, the interviewers do not go beyond the questions they have prepared beforehand. However, to reveal different perspectives in line with the answers given by the participants, they can ask additional questions that they have prepared beforehand (Ceylan & Hacıhasanoğlu, 2022: 778).

While CPAs operating in Turkey constitute the research universe, 8 CPAs operating in seven geographical regions were determined as a sample. The data were obtained from face-to-face and telephone interviews between 20.07.2022 and 30.07.2022. Eight questions were asked under the main headings, such as the problems they experienced, working conditions, job stress, income change and expectations from the state. The questions in the interview form are as follows:

1. Have you encountered problems with your business (state, taxpayer) during the pandemic? If your answer is yes, can you explain what problems you are experiencing?
2. Has there been a change in your income during the pandemic process? If your answer is yes, can you explain the income change with the reasons?
3. Has your workload changed during the pandemic process? If your answer is yes, can you tell us what kind of change happened?
4. Have you thought about quitting/changing your profession during the pandemic process? If your answer is yes, can you explain why?
5. Did you have any expectations from the state during the pandemic process? If your answer is yes, what expectations did you have and were these expectations met?
6. Have you experienced work stress during the pandemic process? If your answer is yes, can you explain from what point of view you are experiencing this stress?
7. Have your working conditions changed during the pandemic process? If your answer is yes, can you give information about what kind of changes (remote working, working in the office) there are?
8. What are your expectations about your profession in case of a resumption of the pandemic (full closure, partial closure)?

FINDINGS AND INTERPRETATION

In the present study, a total of 8 CPAs were interviewed. Descriptive information regarding members of the profession is shown in Table 1. Half of the participants are men, and half are women. The ages of the participants ranged from 35 to 59. While the experience of the most experienced participant is 30 years, the experience of the least experienced one is five years. While the most extended interview with the participants was approximately 40 minutes, the shortest interview lasted 20 minutes.

The questions asked are in line with the primary purpose of the research, and the answers are presented below.

Table 1. Descriptive information

Interviewer	Age	Gender	Experience (year)	Average interview time
CPA 1	43	Female	17	30 min
CPA 2	45	Male	22	20 min
CPA 3	59	Female	30	40 min
CPA 4	35	Male	15	30 min
CPA 5	47	Female	25	40 min
CPA 6	40	Female	20	30 min
CPA 7	37	Male	17	20 min
CPA 8	41	Male	5	30 min

Question 1: Have you encountered problems with your business (state, taxpayer) during the pandemic? If your answer is yes, can you explain what problems you are experiencing?

All of the CPAs stated that they had problems during the pandemic. They indicated difficulty finding an interlocutor during the pandemic, had severe communication problems and were exposed to intense calls and demands from taxpayers because the declarations were not extended. Also, they stated that they constantly experience the risk of epidemics due to non-deferred declarations and that circulars, forms and documents are renewed continuously during the said process. Finally, they stated that they tried to manage the process by trial and error and that official institutions did not know about the measures taken and the practices that came into force. The answers given by professionals reveal that they have faced serious problems related to the operation of their work in almost every stage of the pandemic. Especially, adapting to changes and communication difficulties have been the most challenging factors. This situation placed an excessive burden on them to obtain information. Some of the answers highlighting these points are as follows:

"During the pandemic process, I had great problems with government institutions. I could not reach any institution by phone or e-mail. I had to go to the institution for even the slightest problem or consultation in urgent cases. When I went, I had difficulty finding a contact person." (CPA 1)

"We worked as Financial Advisors while others were not working during the pandemic process. Since all the declarations required to be submitted in the legal process were not extended, declarations were given in the legal process by working hard. We were not given the necessary value during the pandemic. Taxpayers constantly disturbed us to take advantage of the incentives. They held us responsible for these incentives. It has made it necessary for us to work during the pandemic by constantly providing state incentives." (CPA 2)

"We were thrown into the middle of the risk at the expense of our lives. Despite all the attempts, we went through this process by being ignored with statements that were not postponed. The undelayed declaration means being in touch and getting the documents of someone with an epidemic. While recovery moves were being made to all sectors, our staff and we overcame this process by going through many material and moral processes." (CPA 3)

"The government institutions are not informed about the measures and practices. The taxpayers are the most easily accessible to us since the taxpayers cannot get a definite answer from the government institutions or cannot reach the government institutions. So, their constant calls to us have thrown us into the responsibility." (CPA 4)

"There were those who had covid in their taxpayers. Having to exchange paperwork." (CPA 5)

"Changes were made in the declaration and payment periods regarding sectors. In this case, the failure to extend the declaration and payment periods in companies operating in more than one sector caused negative behaviours by the taxpayer. In addition, why was the support provided to some sectors not provided to us by other taxpayers? It led to the search for what we can do to get coverage." (CPA 6)

"The State did not give any support to us, and we did all the chores and practice procedures. Since the taxpayers remained closed, the collection problem was serious." (CPA 8)

Question 2: Has there been a change in your income during the pandemic process? If your answer is yes, can you explain the income change with the reasons?

Two of the CPAs stated that their income was not changed. The other six professionals indicated that their revenues had decreased significantly. In particular, they said that they had collection problems from taxpayers and that some taxpayers had to close their workplaces, which directly affected them. They stated they experienced more serious financial difficulties due to the closure, especially in the first months. It has been understood that professionals have experienced a significant loss of income during this challenging period due to inadequate support. Some of the answers are as follows:

"During the pandemic process, my income decreased. I could not get the agreed wages from the taxpayers on time because the companies were in a difficult situation. Their collection was weak, so this situation affected me as well." (CPA 1)

"In this difficult process, many businesses have become unable to pay rent and pay the salaries of their personnel. Naturally, the consultancy fees, which were first sacrificed, were interrupted for months. There were also disruptions in revenue collections during the pandemic process. Closures in workplaces and downsizing caused collection problems." (CPA 3)

"As taxpayers closed their businesses due to the closure and it was unclear when they would reopen, we had collection problems for the first month. Then, some taxpayers began to pay half of the accounting fees, depending on their strength. Our collections have decreased by almost a quarter." (CPA 4)

"We had a collection problem. We could not collect from the workplaces that could not work due to the prohibitions, or we worked for lower wages." (CPA 5)

"During the pandemic, many employers had to close their workplaces because they could not meet the running expenses. Since many employers who decided to continue could not make a profit, we approached them with empathy. We made various sacrifices in this process." (CPA 6)

"Due to the serious collection problem, the income change inevitably reflected. We had problems due to the closure of workplaces." (CPA 8)

Question 3: Has your workload changed during the pandemic process? If your answer is yes, can you tell us what kind of change happened?

All members of the profession stated that their workload had increased significantly. In particular, they noted that the initiatives to alleviate the economic impact of the pandemic on businesses are carried out directly through them. Due to this situation, their workload has increased significantly. They stated that they are constantly busy without the concept of overtime and bear the burden of the published circulars, especially the short-time working allowance. In addition, they stated that there is information pollution through various channels, especially the media, and the taxpayers who are worried about this situation constantly disturb themselves to get information. It has been observed that the workload of professionals has increased and there have been difficulties in announcing new regulations. As a result, many taxpayers seeking information have further intensified the already busy schedules of these professionals. Important excerpts from the answers are as follows:

"My workload and chores doubled under the name of working from home. Previously, I could rest at least in the evening or on the weekend, but moving the work to our home under the name of working from home limited our social life." (CPA 1)

"During the pandemic process, we have done all the procedures such as short-time working allowance and work permits for companies and employees in the pandemic. The workload due to these transactions has increased." (CPA 2)

"With the enacted laws and new laws, many chores have been left on our shoulders. Such as short-time working allowance and aid practices. If we add these to the postponement that could not be made to the declarations, our risk in our offices never decreased." (CPA 3)

"Due to the circulars and the statements made on TV, our phone was rarely silent. People were calling 24/7. Taxpayers were extremely nervous and extremely scared about how the process would work. There was an excessive amount of information pollution, and hearsay information and interpretations in their way caused extreme confusion." (CPA 4)

"The largest workload in social security institution transactions (such as short-time working allowance, cash wage support)." (CPA 5)

"While the density of documents decreased in some sectors, the density increased in others. There is no document density if your taxpayer portfolio is not focused on a certain sector. It just shifted. The workload did not decrease as the obligation to be declared continued." (CPA 6)

"Works such as entering short-time working allowance information increased the workload." (CPA 7)

"The workload is too much, plus we handled all official transactions and practices. Financial support practices were handled through us. All legislative changes were reflected us." (CPA 8)

Question 4: Have you thought about quitting/changing your profession during the pandemic? If your answer is yes, can you explain why?

Half of the CPAs said they are considering quitting/changing their profession due to this tiring and intense process. The remaining half answered no to this question. One of the most important reasons for those considering quitting their job was that they thought they were left alone in this challenging process. In particular, they stated that they could not see the value and attention they expected and their demands and needs were not considered at the intense pace. However, despite these difficult work and living conditions, half of the professionals said they love their profession and do not intend to quit. In this process, it has been understood that professionals are feeling isolated and as a result, some are considering quitting their profession. It has been particularly noticed that despite the heavy workload, they are not receiving the recognition they deserve. Some of the striking answers given are as follows:

"Yes, the pandemic process has been very tiring and even now, I have taken steps to enter the trade. If these steps are satisfactory, I will leave this job." (CPA 1)

"No. I like my job. However, the required value for my profession is not given by the relevant institutions." (CPA 2)

"I thought. I think it could have been academics or another field related to commerce. The only reason is that while we wait for a burden to be taken from us, the state worries about income and ignores us." (CPA 3)

"Yes. While most of the place was closed during the pandemic, we continued to work day and night, and our earnings were zero when it was extremely risky. We had no earnings on the statement. Most of the merchants' notifications and the burden of informing the merchants fell on us. However, we were not provided with anything in terms of income and support. If I had the slightest income from anywhere else, I would leave this profession immediately." (CPA 4)

"I never thought." (CPA 5)

"Yes, I thought so now. If I had a regular income to replace my life, I would not practice this profession for a minute. We are drowning in legislation. We could not do our work because of the workload." (CPA 8)

Question 5: Did you have any expectations from the state during the pandemic process? If your answer is yes, what expectations did you have and were these expectations met?

It is seen that seven of the members of the profession have expectations in this process. On the other hand, one CPA emphasized that he did not have any expectations. They stated that the CPAs have expectations, such as providing them with financial incentives and facilitating the declaration and VAT. Also, they are being supported by being treated equally as they are given to other sectors. They stated that they fulfilled all the tasks assigned by the state, but their wishes were ignored, and the authorities remained indifferent on a few fundamental issues (VAT, declaration). The members of the profession have been understood to not receive sufficient incentives and their expectations are not met despite having high expectations. Some of the answers highlighting these points are as follows:

"I have no expectations from this government." (CPA 1)

"Incentives were not given to us during the pandemic. On the contrary, benefiting from incentives was prevented." (CPA 2)

"We had expectations for ourselves and our family, but nothing was done. Financial support was denied. Even if it was temporary, they did not reduce the VAT rate from 18% to 8%. While trying to help all industries, we ignored them. Our expectations for improvement in conditions, flexibility in declaration times, and financial support were not met." (CPA 3)

"They could lighten our workload and suspend statements and notifications. They could have combined the declarations for two months instead of monthly. They could provide us with financial support. During the pandemic, many professionals with Covid were sentenced to work sick at home. When it started to increase, the practice brought 15 days extensions to be provided by the practice." (CPA 4)

"The social security organization for artisans and the self-employed did not bring convenience was a problem for employers and us. Our most important expectations were convenience in declarations and VAT and collections." (CPA 5)

"Yes, there were many declarations and payment deadlines in some sectors, but sooner or later, it was impossible to accumulate the work because the declaration obligation continued. Some sectors were excluded, and declarations had to be submitted on time. In terms of business, we did not have any reduced obligations. However, we faced both financial losses as well as going to the office. Making sectoral restrictions was not a realistic approach. An equal benefit should be provided to all taxpayers. Many sectors were given cash aid, and we should have been included in these sectors." (CPA 6)

"I expected that VAT rates would be reduced from the general rate to the discount rate." (CPA 7)

"Yes, it certainly did, but we did not receive any support, but we pulled out all irrelevant workloads. The state should see us as its employee and stop burdening them with whatever work is required." (CPA 8)

Question 6: Have you experienced work stress during the pandemic process? If your answer is yes, can you explain from what point of view you are experiencing this stress?

Seven of the CPAs stated that they experienced work stress in this process. Worrying about catching the virus, being unable to get the job done, legislative changes, insufficient official announcements, conflicting official procedures and practices, and the inadequacy of official institutions' systems have been the primary sources of stress. Professionals have had a very stressful period, primarily due to the frequent changes in legal regulations. Also, the constant effort to keep up with new legislation or circulars and the desire to respond to taxpayers' problems while doing all these. In this process, it has been observed that professionals are quite stressed and experience intense stress due to both illness and work-related pressures caused by the physical circulation of documents. Some of the striking answers given are as follows:

"Yes, it was a very stressful process, the tension caused by the increasing workload negatively affected my way of doing business. When new laws, communiqués and drudgery were added, this negatively affected our health." (CPA 1)

"Yes. We have done all the procedures such as short-time working allowance. We have always experienced the anxiety and stress of not completing such transactions on time. Our sleep is gone." (CPA 2)

"We went through processes that were very difficult in terms of both health and workload." (CPA 3)

"Yes. The main causes of work stress were insufficient explanations, conflicting practices, the inadequacy of the state database, constant system problems, constant circular and practice changes, financial difficulties, statement and notifications, and responsibility stress." (CPA 4)

"I experienced stress due to the illness of the personnel, the quarantine, the worry of not being able to complete a job, the drudgery imposed on us." (CPA 5)

"Yes, as a team, we had to do most of the work at home. Providing continuous access to documents was challenging without being in an office environment. The biggest worry was that when you got sick, things would pile up. Because force majeure was not declared." (CPA 6)

"The stress level has peaked due to the constant calls of all taxpayers and related irrelevant people. Aside from the fear of the pandemic, let alone the fear of life, we are trying to cure people's problems, and many of our colleagues lost their lives for this cause." (CPA 8)

Question 7: Have your working conditions changed during the pandemic process? If your answer is yes, can you give information about what kind of changes (remote working, working in the office) there are?

Seven of the professionals stated that their working conditions have changed. They indicated that they started working from home, especially at the beginning of the pandemic and then they continued to work in the office again. On the other hand, they stated that although they started to work in the office after working from home, they took work from home and worked hard even on the weekends. They noted that the concept of working hours disappeared, and all the conditions were forced to produce a job. In this process, it has been understood that professionals work partially remotely and partially in the office, and therefore they do not have a regular schedule and work overtime. Some answers are as follows:

"Yes, my working conditions have changed. Before the pandemic, I was just doing my job in the office, now I do it everywhere." (CPA 1)

"Our remote working time was concise. Since it is not possible to make a statement without income and expense documents, we moved from the office to work. The concept of working hours is gone." (CPA 3)

"Yes. We worked in the office during the day and continued to work at home in the evenings. Also, we could not go out on the weekend." (CPA 4)

"We had to work from home for a while, but we had to continue from the office. Working with gloves and mask was difficult." (CPA 5)

"Yes, we worked from home for about two months in the first months of the pandemic. We had to switch to this method to avoid putting public transportation personnel at risk. Since we were out of scope during the mandatory closure periods, we could come to the office and work. Some people got sick in our office. We closed our office every time we got sick and continued working from home." (CPA 6)

"In the first stage, the system of working at home was adopted. Then, with the exemption, the office house continued to be mixed. Working in the office has always been more beneficial." (CPA 8)

Question 8: What are your expectations about your profession in case of a resumption of the pandemic (full closure, partial closure)?

Two of the members of the profession have no expectations. The remaining six professionals have different expectations. The main expectations are VAT reduction, the extension of declaration periods, improvement of income management systems, financial support, force majeure due to the disease and giving the necessary value. It is seen that the CPAs, whose expectations were not met in this challenging process, are in great despair. Although they have emphasized that they have some expectations, it is understood that they do not have hope of meeting these expectations. They stated that taxes, an important source of income for the state, are regularly obtained thanks to them. However, they are not given the necessary value despite undertaking such a critical mission. The professionals had quite high expectations, but these expectations were not met. Therefore, it has been observed that they have no hope if a similar process occurs again. Some of the striking answers are as follows:

"I do not have any expectations. I don't think it will be better. Unfortunately, it will be worse. That is why I want to improve the trading part." (CPA 1)

"Let us be given the necessary value. We are the ones who declare the taxes. Relevant institutions collect taxes with the declarations they receive. They have no value in return." (CPA 2)

"After all these attempts, everything that remains unanswered is now psychologically complicated to deal with. On some issues, the burden seems to fall on us again due to the lack of room and unity. Financial support, the extension of declaration periods, currently working revenue management systems, VAT reduction." (CPA 3)

"I have no expectations from this profession. Because so far, none of our expectations has come true. After this time, there is no need to enter an expectation state. We are the free freight carriers of the state." (CPA 4)

"Force majeure should be imposed on all taxpayers, including our profession." (CPA 5)

"In the extension of the declaration periods, determinations covering all taxpayers should be made in place of the sectoral approach. In the pandemic, support payments should be made without data entry for the support paid to employers and their employees. Payment of support for our financial losses will reduce our losses. Our or our employees' catching the disease should be considered as force majeure and added to our declaration periods." (CPA 6)

"Assuming that the collection will decrease, I expect a discounted rate to be applied in VAT rates." (CPA 7)

"Our expectations are high, but none of them will come true. It is necessary to be close to the political power and solve all professional problems. There will be a request for financial support, but it will not be given." (CPA 8)

DISCUSSION

This research aimed to address the problems, working conditions, incomes, expectations, perspectives on their professions and stress levels experienced by the members of the profession during the pandemic period by using the interview technique. As a result of the research, the CPAs stated that they had difficulty finding an interlocutor during the pandemic and had severe communication problems.

Emphasizing that their income has decreased significantly, the CPAs also said that their workload has increased. Half of the professionals have considered quitting their job. The members of the profession who stated that the working conditions had significantly changed and the concept of overtime had disappeared have experienced work stress. However, they stated that their expectations, especially VAT reduction and extension of declaration periods, were not met despite their difficulties. These findings of the study are similar to the results of similar studies. Erol & Ayboğa (2021) found that the professionals' workload increased, they experienced collection problems and were affected negatively. Also, their productivity decreased due to the change in working hours, and they encountered difficulties in their relations with official institutions. Similarly, Papadopoulou & Papadopoulou (2020) found that members of the profession had trouble adapting to legislative changes and new demands and had to make changes in their working routines. Güngör Karyağdı (2021) found that professional accountants could not make collections, the number of taxpayers decreased, and the workload increased due to consulting businesses.

In this process, it has been understood that professionals are feeling isolated and as a result, some are considering quitting their profession. It has been particularly noticed that despite the heavy workload, they are not receiving the recognition they deserve. The members of the profession have been understood to not receive sufficient incentives and their expectations are not met despite having high expectations. In this process, it has been observed that professionals are quite stressed and experience intense stress due to both illness and work-related pressures caused by the physical circulation of documents. In this process, it has been understood that professionals work partially remotely and partially in the office, and therefore they do not have a regular schedule and work overtime. The professionals had quite high expectations, but these expectations were not met. Therefore, it has been observed that they have no hope if a similar process occurs again. Ceylan & Hacıhasanoğlu (2022) found that the biggest problem of accountants before and during the pandemic was the collection and that members of the profession were deeply affected by stress, increased workload and devaluation. Mihai et al. (2020) found that working during the pandemic creates additional stress and fatigue. Mazman İtik (2021) found that most problems are increased workload, loss of income, and difficulties in information flow with taxpayers and institutions. Tugay & Dokur (2020) found that the most important is the compulsory contact with the documents that taxpayers/customers deliver or send by courier and the fear and anxiety of contagion due to this. However, the research results differ from the findings of similar studies. Topçu & Demirkol (2021) found no difference in working hours and workload level of professional accountants compared to pre-Covid-19. Tugay & Dokur (2020) found that the working hours of professional accountants decreased, and Mihai et al. (2020) found that professionals quickly adapt to remote work.

The answers given by professionals reveal that they have faced serious problems related to the operation of their work in almost every stage of the pandemic. Especially, adapting to changes and communication difficulties have been the most challenging factors. It has been understood that professionals have experienced a significant loss of income during this challenging period due to inadequate support. It has been observed that the workload of professionals has increased and there have been difficulties in announcing new regulations. As a result, many taxpayers seeking information have further intensified the already busy schedules of these professionals. In the current research, the primary source of stress was the anxiety of catching the virus, the fear of not being able to complete the job, the changes in the legislation, the inadequacy of the official institution explanations, the conflicting official procedures and practices, the insufficient systems of the official institutions. These results are similar to the findings of other studies. For example, Selimoglu et al. (2021) found that factors such as the deterioration of the functioning of the classical accounting profession and changes in the way of doing business, professional uncertainties due to legislative changes, document contact and the risk of virus transmission are the primary sources of stress.

CONCLUSION AND RECOMMENDATIONS

This research aimed to determine the experiences of CPAs in business life during the pandemic. In this direction, a total of eight questions, mainly problems, expectations, income status, workload, and stress, were asked of eight professionals. The results of the research revealed that the members of the profession had problems with both government institutions and taxpayers. They stated that they had issues due to the lack of protective measures, especially the communication problem with official institutions. Taxpayers indicated that they were worried that the declaration period was not extended, this situation was directly reflected on them, and they experienced collection problems. They stated that taxpayers had to close their workplaces, which affected them, and that they had more serious financial difficulties, especially in the first months. In this process, they stated that their workload increased. Finally, they noted that overtime does not exist due to the legislation and regulations that official institutions frequently change.

Half of the CPAs thought they were alone in this challenging process, did not receive the value and attention they expected, and wanted to leave their profession. Four professionals, on the other hand, stated that they love their job and do not plan to quit, despite this tiring working environment. They noted that they have expectations such as providing them with financial incentives, facilitating the declaration and VAT, and being supported by being treated equally as they are given to other sectors. However, they stated that these expectations were not met in any way. Worrying about catching the virus, inability to get the job done, legislative changes, insufficient official announcements, conflicting official procedures and practices, and the inadequacy of official institutions' systems have been the primary sources of stress experienced by professionals. In addition, members of the profession stated that they started working from home in the first months and then continued working in the office again. On the other hand, they stated that although they began to work in the office after working from home, they took work from home and worked hard even on the weekends. They stated that with the resumption of the pandemic, they had expectations such as VAT reduction, the extension of declaration periods, improvement of revenue management systems, financial support, and force majeure due to the disease and giving them the necessary value.

The data in the research were obtained as a result of interviews with 8 CPAs between 20.07.2022 and 30.07.2022. A total of eight questions were asked to the profession's members under eight main headings. The opinions of the CPAs may differ due to the improvements made on the issues they expect solutions to in the future. Researchers can interview more professionals in future research. In addition to the questions in the current research, they can ask questions in different categories. They can also focus on a specific issue, such as solving problems experienced. In the study, the interview method was preferred. With this method, mixed-patterned research can be carried out using quantitative research methods (surveys).

REFERENCES

Açıkgöz, B. & Mutlu, M. D. (2022). Muhasebe Mesleğinde Dijital Dönüşüm: Covid-19 Pandemi Döneminde Uzaktan Çalışma Uygulamaları. *İnsan ve Toplum Bilimleri Araştırmaları Dergisi, 11*(2), 52-69.

Ayboğa, H. (2003). Globalleşme sürecinde ülkemizde muhasebe mesleği ve meslek mensuplarının eğitimi. *Marmara Üniversitesi İktisadi ve İdari Bilimler Dergisi, 18*(1), 327–359.

Aydemir, O. (2015). Muhasebe meslek mensuplarının karşılaştıkları sorunlar ve beklentiler. *Muhasebe ve Finansman Dergisi*, (67), 71–84. doi:10.25095/mufad.396577

Azaltun, M., Aktaş, A., Yavuzaslan Söylemez, S., Tekbaş, İ., & Atasoy, A. (2022). COVID-19 Pandemisinin Muhasebe Mesleği Ve Muhasebe Meslek Mensuplarına Etkileri Üzerine Bir Araştırma. *Mali Çözüm Dergisi, 32*(171), 65–101.

Beder, N. (2021). Muhasebe Meslek Mensuplarının Yeni Dünya ile İmtihanı. *Anadolu Üniversitesi Sosyal Bilimler Dergisi*, *21*(1), 163–184. doi:10.18037/ausbd.902591

Buyruk Akbaba, A. N., & Bulut, N. (2021). Pandemi Sürecinde Muhasebe Meslek Mensuplarının Mesleki Tükenmişlik Düzeylerinin İncelenmesi. *EUropean Journal of Managerial Research (EUJMR)*, *5*(Özel), 35-48.

Carungu, J., Di Pietra, R., & Molinari, M. (2021). The impact of a humanitarian disaster on the working approach of accountants: A study of contingent effects. *Accounting, Auditing & Accountability Journal*, *34*(6), 1388–1403. doi:10.1108/AAAJ-08-2020-4789

Ceylan, R., & Hacıhasanoğlu, T. (2022). A Qualitative Study on the Problems of Accounting Professionals in Covid-19 Period in Yozgat Province. *Cumhuriyet Üniversitesi İktisadi ve İdari Bilimler Dergisi*, *23*(3), 774–789. doi:10.37880/cumuiibf.1109191

Erol, M., & Ayboğa, H. (2021). Kovid-19'un Muhasebe Meslek Mensuplarının Mesleki Faaliyetlerine Etkisinin Belirlenmesine Yönelik Ampirik Çalışma. *Uluslararası Beşerî ve Sosyal Bilimler İnceleme Dergisi*, *5*(1), 1–12.

Frumuşanu, N. M., Marin, A. M., & Martin, M. (2020). The impact of COVID-19 pandemic on the activity of the professional accountant. *ANNALS ECONOMIC SCIENCES SERIES*, *XX*(2), 922.

Güngör Karyağdı, N. (2021). Muhasebe Meslek Mensuplarının Covid-19 Pandemi Krizini ve Etkilerini Mesleki Açıdan Değerlendirmelerine Üzerine Bir Çalışma: Muş İlinde Bir Araştırma. *Siirt Üniversitesi Sosyal Bilimler Enstitüsü Dergisi*, *9*(17), 20–40.

Haven, L. T., & Van Grootel, D. L. (2019). Preregistering qualitative research. *Accountability in Research*, *26*(3), 229–244. doi:10.1080/08989621.2019.1580147 PMID:30741570

Kaka, E. J. (2020). the Covid-19 Crisis, Risk Compliance and Its Aftermath on Professional Accountants. *Indonesian Journal of Accounting and Governance*, *4*(1), 65–81. doi:10.36766/ijag.v4i1.61

Katkat Özçelik, M. (2021). Covid-19 Salgınının Muhasebe Mesleğine Etkisi Üzerine Bir Olgubilim Çalışması. In T. Öndeş, C. Yerdelen Kaygin (eds.) Covid-19'un Muhasebe ve Finans Yansımaları. Gazi Kitabevi.

Köse, E., Altunay, M. A., & Bekci, İ. (2022). Covid-19 Salgınının Muhasebe Meslek Mensuplarına Etkisi. *Vergi Raporu*, *272*, 138–155.

Lin, H., & Hwang, Y. (2021). The effects of personal information management capabilities and social-psychological factors on accounting professionals' knowledge-sharing intentions: Pre and post COVID-19. *International Journal of Accounting Information Systems*, *42*, 100522. doi:10.1016/j.accinf.2021.100522

Mazman İtik, Ü. (2021). Covid-19 Pandemi Sürecinde Serbest Muhasebeci Mali Müşavirlerin Yaşadığı Sorunlar Üzerine Sivas İlinde Bir Araştırma. *Akademik Sosyal Araştırmalar Dergisi*, *9*(120), 78–91.

Mihai, F., Stan, M., Radu, G., & Dumitru, V. F. (2020). Heavy work investment for the accounting profession in Romania at time of coronavirus pandemic. *Amfiteatru Economic*, *22*(14), 1121–1139.

Papadopoulou, S., & Papadopoulou, M. (2020). The Accounting Profession Amidst the COVID-19 Pandemic. *International Journal of Accounting and Financial Reporting*, *10*(2), 39–59. doi:10.5296/ijafr.v10i2.17001

Prawitasari, P. P. (2022). Will Accountants Still Exist? Challenges of The Accountant Profession In Facing Technological Disruption In The New. In *International Conference on Industrial Revolution 4.0* (pp. 326–350).

Şahin, O. N., & Kumaş, C. (2022). COVID-19 Sürecinde Muhasebe Meslek Mensuplarına Yönelik Alanya Örneğinde Bir Araştırma. *Anadolu İktisat ve İşletme Dergisi*, *6*(2), 142–166.

Seidman, I. (2006). *Interviewing as qualitative research: A guide for researchers in education and the social sciences*. Teachers college press.

Selimoğlu, S. K., Cengiz, A. A., Özdemir, A., & Begüm, Y. A. L. I. (2021). COVID-19 İle Birlikte Muhasebe Mesleğindeki Stresin Yeni Halleri. *Muhasebe ve Denetime Bakış*, *21*(63), 1–18.

Topcu, N., & Demirkol, V. (2021). Covid-19 Pandemi Sürecinin Muhasebe Meslek Elemanları Üzerindeki Etkisi: Yalova Örneği. *Journal of Academic Value Studies*, *7*(3), 344–353. doi:10.29228/javs.52026

Tuğay, O., & Dokur, Ş. (2020). Koronavirüs (Kovid-19) Salgınının Muhasebe Meslek Mensuplarının Çalışma Alışkanlıkları Üzerine Etkileri: Bir Araştırma. *Akademik Sosyal Araştırmalar Dergisi*, *8*(105), 75–86.

Chapter 8
Department of Accountancy: Alternative Offerings

David Y. Chan
St. John's University, USA

Adrian P. Fitzsimons
St. John's University, USA

ABSTRACT

Accountancy departments across higher education have been experiencing enrollment declines and these declines will likely continue going forward. Program directors need to be innovative and diversify their offerings in order to attract students. Traditionally most accountancy programs in higher education have limited their program offerings to two tracks: 1) audit and 2) tax. This chapter provides program directors with strategic direction and guidance on alternative offerings that an accountancy department can implement to expand their offerings and to attract new students. These alternative offerings include higher education programs developed and endorsed by professional associations such as the Institute of Internal Auditors, Association of Certified Fraud Examiners, and ISACA. Program Directors can implement all these programs or in piecemeal. The authors have implemented these programs into their accountancy program at their university or college with success and share with readers how they can get these programs up and running quickly and with ease.

DOI: 10.4018/978-1-6684-5483-1.ch008

Copyright © 2023, IGI Global. Copying or distributing in print or electronic forms without written permission of IGI Global is prohibited.

INTRODUCTION

Traditionally accountancy programs have focused on student career outcomes in financial or managerial accounting, external auditing, and taxation. However, the type of services being offered by the profession has been and is becoming more diverse. For example, the Big Four Accounting Firms and Advisory Firms are offering ever expanding services that include internal auditing, information technology auditing, fraud examination, enterprise risk management, cyber security, robotic process automation, and enterprise resource planning implementation and maintenance. Accountants are well suited for these careers because of their expertise in assurance and advisory. The profession's demand for accounting students with skills and knowledge related to these services have been on the rise (AICPA 2020). Therefore, there is a case for accountancy programs to consider the modernization of their existing programs or to create a new program to service the demand and to expand employment opportunities for their students. Moreover, a diversification of their curriculum may lead to increased enrollment in their program consequently. A variety of accounting careers that a student can pursue upon graduation may help attract those students that may not have had an interest in the traditional careers in accounting (ex. Accounting, Auditing, and Taxation). Capturing a new demographic of students is very desirable considering that accounting program enrollment has been on the decline since 2015 (Burns 2022) and an enrollment cliff is on the horizon in 2025 (Schroeder 2001, Copley and Douthett 2020).

The extension of an existing or the creation of a new program may be arduous from an administrative standpoint. However, there are professional associations that have created higher education academic programs that provide guidance in curriculum development for their respective fields. Universities can seek certification or recognition from those academic programs that meet their requirements. The professional associations include but are not limited to the Institute of Internal Auditors (IIA), ISACA, and the Association of Certified Fraud Examiners (ACFE). The IIA is a professional association that represents the internal audit profession, and their academic program is called the Internal Audit Education Partnership (IAEP) program. Similarly, ISACA is a professional association that represents information system audit professionals and has two model curriculum programs: 1) an Audit and Control Curriculum and 2) an Information Security Management Curriculum. Lastly, the ACFE is a professional association that represents the fraud examination profession and has a Fraud Education Partnership program. A Program Director can explorer these professional associations for synergies or he/she can explore the one with greatest interest from the faculty.

In this chapter, the authors examine the three programs and explore the intricacy of their frameworks to guide Program Directors in quickly adopting these programs.

The authors have assisted their academic institution in implementing these three programs and will provide specific insight in the implementations. Each of these programs have their own unique merits but it is the belief of the authors that the IIA's IAEP program can serves as a foundation for the other complementing academic programs. Accounting programs must be innovative and stand out in today's competitive business school environment and these programs may be a solution in that effort.

INTERNAL AUDIT: INSTITUTE OF INTERNAL AUDITORS

The first academic program that is examined is the Institute of Internal Auditors (IIA) Internal Audit Education Partnership (IAEP) program.

The Institute of Internal Auditing (IIA) defines internal auditing as:

Internal auditing is an independent, objective assurance and consulting activity designed to add value and improve an organization's operations. It helps an organization accomplish its objectives by bringing a systematic, disciplined approach to evaluate and improve the effectiveness of risk management, control, and governance processes.[1]

IAEP program categorized Universities as Centers for Internal Auditing Excellence (Centers), Comprehensive Internal Auditing Programs (Comprehensive), and Internal Auditing Foundation Programs (Foundation). Every school starts the IAEP program as a Foundation program, aspires to become a Comprehensive program, and subsequently aspires to become a Center for Internal Auditing Excellence. This Chapter will provide guidance to an academic institution on becoming a Foundation Program. The IIA developed a IAEP Framework that outlines the requirements to successfully become a IEAP program (IIA 2022)[2]. The successful implementation of such a program will have three pillars: (1) a Faculty IAEP Coordinator (subsequently called the Coordinator), (2) Department support, and (3) Local IIA Chapter support. Each of these pillars will play an integral role in organizing the University to become a part of the IAEP program. However, the success of an IAEP program will significantly depend on the continuous commitment of the Coordinator.

The IIA recommends that the Coordinator to be a full-time educator and a Certified Internal Auditor (CIA) but can be an adjunct or a professional staff member of the University. The faculty member should be very passionate about or see an opportunity in the internal audit profession for students. Furthermore, the IIA encourages the Coordinator be an IIA member[3] and there is a membership discount for educators. The Coordinator should work with their Department to develop an internal audit course (if one has not been created). The Internal Audit course instructor does not need to be the Coordinator but must be a CIA or an appropriately qualified instructor. An appropriately qualified instructor may have years or executive level internal audit professional experience. If the instructor is not an CIA then the IIA's Academic Relations Committee may assess the qualifications of the instructor. The IIA has developed a Global Model Internal Audit Curriculum (subsequently called the Curriculum) that provides guidance on an internal audit curriculum that a University may adopt (IIA 2022)[4]. The Curriculum has recommended courses that can be offered and the related syllabuses.

A Foundation Program is required to have two core course offerings within a university degree program. Therefore, it is important the Coordinator has the support of his/her Department. The program can be housed in an undergraduate or graduate degree program. Table 1 lists the Curriculum recommended core courses and supplemental courses. The Principles of Internal Auditing is required to be one of the two core courses and the other course can be another core course as listed in Table 1. Most accounting degree programs may already offer one or more of the other core courses and can fulfill the two core course requirements by only adding the required Principles of Internal Auditing course to its course offerings (if the Principles of Internal Audit course is not offered). The required Principles of Internal Auditing course must be offered and taught at least annually and the two core courses must have been taught a minimum of one year prior to submitting a Foundation program application into the IAEP Program. Instructor(s) of the Principles

Table 1. Global model internal audit curriculum core and supplemental courses

Course Title	Core/Supplemental Course
Principles of Internal Auditing	Core
Ethics and Organizational Governance	Core
Fraud and Forensics	Core
Information Technology (IT) Auditing	Core
Business Communication Skills for Internal Auditors	Core
Internship and/or Case Studies/Internal Audit Projects	Core
Advanced Internal Auditing	Supplemental
Developing and Managing an Internal Audit Function	Supplemental
Risk Management	Supplemental
Advanced Organizational Governance	Supplemental
Advanced IT Systems and Auditing	Supplemental
Internal Auditing Topics	Supplemental

of Internal Auditing course may encourage their students to pursue the Certified Internal Auditor (CIA) credential offered by the Institute of Internal Auditors.

Once the University has the required course offerings and has determined that the course interest by students is sustainable then the Coordinator should contact their Local Chapter[5]. Each Chapter has an academic relations committee (ARC) and the Coordinator should reach out to the Chair of that committee to set up a meeting to discuss how the local chapter can assist the Coordinator in advancing their program. The Local chapter can also be helpful in helping locate an instructor, provide guest speakers, mentorship for students, offer scholarships, and help students with internships and full-time employment. Moreover, local Chapters typically organize events for their members and students may be invited to those events. The Chapter can play an important role in engaging students and helping with strategizing on making the internal audit program successful. Furthermore, the Chapter can help the Coordinator form an Internal Audit Advisory Board or recommend members to supplement any existing school/department advisory board. An Advisory Board is important to ensure the program remains relevant to the profession.

If the program meets the IAEP Framework requirements, the Principles of Internal Audit course and another core courses have been taught, and the local chapter supports the efforts of the program then the University may submit an IAEP application. The IIA accepts applications twice each year on April 1 and October 1. The IIA will evaluate the program candidate on factors related to curriculum quality, continuity, and sustainability based on the IAEP Program Guidelines and Operating Framework. It is important to note that the IIA will evaluate a program based on a principle versus rule-based approach.

FRAUD EXAMINATION: ASSOCIATION OF CERTIFIED FRAUD EXAMINERS (ACFE)

A Program Director may want to consider adding the ACFE's Fraud Education Partnership program to supplement the IIA's IAEP program or as an individual standalone program.

Joseph T. Wells (Founder of the Association of Certified Fraud Examiners) defines fraud examination as *Resolving allegations of fraud-whether from tips, complaints, or accounting clues-is the discipline of fraud examination. It involves obtaining documentary evidence, interviewing witnesses and potential suspects, writing investigative reports, testifying to findings, and assisting in the general direction and prevention of fraud.* (Wells 2013)

The ACFE has developed an Anti-Fraud Education Partnership that is straightforward for a university to participate[6]. A University only requires committing to implementing a 3-credit hour undergraduate or graduate level course in fraud examination or a related subject. Furthermore, course instructors may encourage students to pursue the Certified Fraud Examiner (CFE) credentials offered by the ACFE. The Anti-Fraud Education Partnership is available to 4-year colleges and universities. The instructor of the course must be a member of the ACFE. The Education Partnership provides Universities with a sample syllabus and related fraud examination course materials such as case studies and videos. By simply offering the Fraud Examination course, the University will satisfy the ACFE's Education Partnership requirement and can also satisfy the second core course requirement in the IIA's IAEP program. Therefore, both programs have synergy and can complement each other well.

INFORMATION TECHNOLOGY AUDITING: ISACA

The inclusion of information technology in a higher education accounting programs is likely prudent given the importance and wide use of technology in organizations today and going forward. Therefore, the demand for professionals with technology and assurance skillsets are likely to increase.

ISACA defines Information Technology (IT) Auditing as *identifying IT risks and the appropriate controls to mitigate those risks to an acceptable level* (Singleton 2014).

ISACA developed two model curricula to provide guidance on 1) information systems audit and control (ISACA 2012)[7] knowledge and 2) information systems security (ISACA 2012)[8] content for universities. The recognition of universities by ISACA that aligned with their curriculums was sunset in 2018 and there are no plans to restart the recognition of universities. However, the curriculums can still be an invaluable resource for universities to help them develop either an information technology audit and control curriculum and/or information security management curriculum that are aligned with the knowledge content that the profession deems as relevant and important.

The information technology audit and control curriculum topics and subtopics are organized according to the major domains for the Certified Information Systems Auditor (CISA) examination. The CISA certification is the most popular certification for information technology or systems auditors and has exam content that the profession determines as essential for their professionals to succeed. As a starting point, an accounting program is likely to be already offering an IT Audit course that may satisfy some of Curriculum requirements. The Program Director can map the course content of their IT Audit Course (if exists) and/or develop new courses to encompass the topics and subtopics described by the Model Curriculum. ISACA provided a useful alignment grid that could be used to streamline the mapping of course(s) content with the Model Curriculum (Appendix 3 - (ISACA 2012)). The topics covered by the ISACA Model Curriculum for information technology audit and control are grouped into five content domains totaling 250 hours:

Domain 1: The Process of Auditing Information Systems (40 Hours)
Domain 2: Governance and Management of IT (60 Hours)
Domain 3: Information Systems Acquisition, Development and Implementation (50 Hours)
Domain 4: Information Systems Operations, Maintenance and Support (50 Hours)
Domain 5: Protection of Information Assets (50 Hours)

Similarly, the information security management curriculum topics and subtopics are organized according to the major domains for the Certified Information Security Manager (CISM) examination. The four CISM domains and their subtopics were used to provide a structure to ISACA Model Curriculum for information security management and are grouped into four content domains totaling 250 hours:

Domain 1: Information Security Governance (50 Hours)
Domain 2: Information Risk Management and Compliance (50 Hours)
Domain 3: Information Security Program Development and Management (105 Hours)
Domain 4: Information Security Incident Management (45 Hours)

The content of each domain in the information technology audit and control curriculum takes between 40 to 60 hours of course delivery time depending on the topics, subtopics, or combination of subtopics. Likewise, the information security management curriculum takes between 45 to 105 hours of course delivery time depending on the topics, subtopics, or combination of subtopics. The Program Director should map the subtopics to the relevant courses and the amount of time spent on each subtopic (Appendix 2 - (ISACA 2012)). A recommended way is to obtain the syllabi and course outlines to inventory what is taught (and time spent) and then to either modify or add content in those courses to meet the content requirements. If the topics/subtopics are not covered in pre-existing course(s) then the Program Director can create new course(s) that will deliver the prescribed content of that Model Curriculum.

Approximately six information technology courses related to the domains is needed to fulfill the 250 hours requirement for each model curriculum assuming a course has fifteen weeks at three hours per week (45 hours per course). Having six IT related courses to meet each Model Curriculum requirements may not be feasible to most accounting programs as these programs typically only have two or three electives available. Furthermore, many accounting departments may not have the faculty expertise to teach these IT-related courses. Therefore, a more comparable approach was to offer two courses in each area: (a) Information Technology Audit I and II or (b) Cybersecurity I and II. These two courses would provide students with a high-level review of the topics and subtopics in each Model Curriculum. The recognition by ISACA of its Model Curriculums ended in 2018 but a university can still use either or both of the Model Curriculums to develop courses to benefit students and be within the means of an accounting department. After a student completes the Information Technology Audit course(s) then they may pursue the Certified Information Systems Auditor (CISA) credential offered by ISACA. Likewise, students may pursue the Certified Information Security Manager (CISM) credential after completing the Cybersecurity course(s).

SYNERGY AND PROGRAM SUCCESS AND OTHER CONSIDERATIONS

The Program Director may approach the three programs in piecemeals or collectively. As mentioned, the IIA's IAEP program can serve as the foundation program. The authors recommend as a starting point to offer the following three courses: 1) Principles of Internal Auditing, 2) Fraud and Forensics (Fraud Examination), and 3) Information Technology (IT) Auditing. The Accounting Department may already be offering the IT Auditing course or some form of the course for meeting the CPA licensing requirements. These three courses will satisfy the requirements for the IIA's IAEP program, the ACFE Education Partnership program, and partially satisfy the ISACA Model Curriculum. As a program becomes successful, the Program Director may wish to add an additional Information Technology Audit course to satisfy the complete ISACA Model Curriculum.

Student enrollment (accounting and non-accounting majors) in the internal audit, fraud examination, and IT audit courses can serve as a metric of success. Moreover, placement of students in employment opportunities related to internal audit, fraud examination, and IT auditing can serve as an additional metric of success. The authors recommend that the Program Director may consider forming a student organization that is focused on alternative careers for accounting students. A student organization is helpful in spreading interests amongst students. Another recommendation is the Program Director may want to partner with the Career Services Center and having them be keener to sourcing internships and full-time employment opportunities in these areas. The local chapters of the professional associations can help support that effort with introductions to employers.

ADVISORY BOARD

An Advisory Board can be an invaluable resource as a Program Director navigates the implementation of all or some of the programs mentioned in this chapter. The authors believe of any higher education program is to place all their students in full time employment upon graduation. Members of the advisory board can provide insight on the demand for entry level talent and whether the local market has the capacity for these employment opportunities. Furthermore, an advisory board can help keep the programs relevant with insight from the profession and can assist with placing students in internships and full-time positions within their own organizations. The Program Director can initially solicit existing advisory board members of the Department or solicit alumni that are interested in giving back to their alma mater. Furthermore, the local chapters of the professional associations may be able to help with selecting members for the advisory board. The board should meet at least annually and the Program Director can provide an update and receive strategic ideas.

FUTURE CONSIDERATIONS

After a Program Director implements all or some of the programs above and had success with the then the he/she may consider advancing the IIA's IAEP program from a Foundation Level to Comprehensive Level and ultimately a Center Level. Currently, there are twenty-two (22) Foundation Level programs, twenty three (23) Comprehensive Level programs, and twelve (12) Center Level programs. The advancement of a Foundation Level program into a Comprehensive Level program generally involves adding another course offering from Table 1, having an active Advisory Board, and having ten (10) students consistently completing the program. Similarly, a Program Director that would like to advance their program to the Center Level will need at least four (4) courses listed in Table 1 and have twenty five (25) students consistently completing the program. As the program continues to grow and becomes successful, the Department of Accountancy may consider implementing an internal Audit track/concentration/diploma or develop a separate Internal audit major/degree undergraduate/graduate program.

CONCLUSION

The purpose of this chapter is to provide Program Directors of accounting programs with a strategic direction on expanding the program offerings from their department beyond the traditional accounting, auditing, and taxation options. The accountancy profession is broader than only these career opportunities. Professional associations related to assurance such as the IIA, ACFE, ISACA have created higher education programs and materials that can guide and support a department in diversifying its offerings and attract students. Nationally enrollment in accounting programs have been trending downwards due to a mix of factors such as demographic changes, uncompetitive wages, and the current lack of student interests in traditional careers in accounting such as accounting, external auditing, and taxation. However, Program Directors can help mitigate this trend and the effects from the looming enrollment cliff in 2025 by considering expanding their program offerings within the Department.

The new programs proposed helps diversify offerings and can attract students perhaps not interested in traditional accounting careers. This will allow the Department's offerings to stay competitive with the other majors in the business school. Furthermore, the new offerings create employment opportunities for students in internal audit, fraud examination, and information technology. These employment opportunities are typically housed in the Advisory practice of an accounting firm and the new program offerings create a talent pipeline for these firms. The assurance background of accountants makes these career paths as natural and compatible extensions. Accounting education is changing, and the future is unknown but those accountancy departments that strategize and plan accordingly can better weather the new climate or lead the next evolution.

REFERENCES

AICPA (2020) *Where Opportunity Meets Value: Business Model Trends for Accounting Advisory Services*. CPA.com

Burns, H. (2022). *The enrollment cliff is coming for higher education, making affordability even more important*. The Business Journals.

Copley, P., & E. Douthett (2020). The Enrollment Cliff, Mega-Universities, COVID-19, and the Changing Landscape of U.S. Colleges. *The CPA Journal*.

IIA. (2022). The IIA's Global Model Internal Audit Curriculum. IIA.

IIA. (2022). *Internal Auditing Education Partnership (IAEP)*. Program Program Guidelines and Operating Framework.

ISACA. (2012). *ISACA Model Curriculum for Information Security Management*. ISACA.

ISACA. (2012). *ISACA Model Curriculum for IS Audit and Control*. ISACA.

Schroeder, R. (2001). A Second Demographic Cliff Adds to Urgency for Change. *Inside Higher Ed.*

Singleton, T. (2014). *IS Audit Basics: The Core of IT Auditing*. ISACA Journal.

Wells, J. T. (2013). *Principles of Fraud Examination*. John Wiley & Sons, Inc.

ENDNOTES

1 https://www.theiia.org/en/about-us/about-internal-audit/

2 https://www.theiia.org/globalassets/documents/about-us/initiatives--awards/academic-relations/iaep-program-requirements-and-operating-framework.pdf

3 https://www.theiia.org/en/membership/

4 https://www.theiia.org/globalassets/documents/about-us/initiatives--awards/academic-relations/global-model-internal-audit-curriculum.pdf

5 https://www.theiia.org/en/about-us/chapters-and-affiliates/

6 https://www.acfe.com/membership/group-membership-and-partnership/anti-fraud-education-partnership

7 https://www.isaca.org/-/media/files/isacadp/project/isaca/membership/academic-advocates/model_curriculum_is_audit-control_3rded-30jan2012.pdf?la=en&hash=0A378D42DE33357B8C087623FEC6D24EC0CF7F51

8 https://www.isaca.org/-/media/files/isacadp/project/isaca/membership/academic-advocates/model-curriculum-infosecmgmt-2nded.pdf?la=en&hash=E5F9E1C7B828836F1E6643CF5D62C0C64F549796

Chapter 9
Professional Competencies for Student Success in an Increasingly Global, Digital, and Virtual World

Ellen D. Bartley
https://orcid.org/0000-0001-8859-4859
Farmingdale State College, USA

ABSTRACT

The pace of technological change is staggering. Together with the effects of the covid-19 pandemic and the entrance of Gen Z into the workplace, the content and nature of accounting is changing significantly. While much attention has focused on technology, several other competencies contribute to a successful accounting career. The more exposure that accounting students have to these competencies, and the more opportunities that they have to develop these competencies as part of their academic preparation, the more likely they are to successfully navigate the transition from university to the workplace. In this chapter, the author examines four competencies for professional success, how academic preparation currently meets those needs, how it might include more, and the influence of Gen Z on the profession.

INTRODUCTION

Accounting education has long provided its students with the body of knowledge required to begin their careers in the accounting profession, which was most often in the public accounting arena. As the knowledge base for the profession has grown,

DOI: 10.4018/978-1-6684-5483-1.ch009

Copyright © 2023, IGI Global. Copying or distributing in print or electronic forms without written permission of IGI Global is prohibited.

so too has its demands that entry-level employees demonstrate at least some of the professional skills that accountants of the past likely developed on-the-job. Each year, top accounting students vie for coveted positions at "Big 4" accounting firms, and the competition for those positions is highly selective. It is presumed that the students interviewing for those positions have the requisite body of accounting knowledge that their degree suggests. It is often some of the other competencies that will distinguish one student from another. In this chapter, the author examines four competencies that accounting graduates need to be successful in an increasingly global, digital, and virtual environment. These are: (1) digital acumen, technological skills, and information literacy; (2) accounting knowledge, as outlined in the revised CPA Evolution Model Curriculum (American Institute of Certified Public Accountants [AICPA] & National Association of State Boards of Accountancy [NASBA], 2021); (3) organizational and communication skills, and (4) intellectual curiosity leading to life-long, self-directed learning.

Accounting Educators

There is a long history of the cooperative working relationship between the accounting profession and accounting educators. Professional associations such as the American Accounting Association, the Institute for Management Accountants (IMA), the AICPA, NASBA, as well as state and local professional organizations provide a wealth of resources for accounting educators. These organizations not only provide accounting educators with the opportunity to stay up to date with the changes in accounting content, but also provide support in teaching effectively. Accounting educators, in turn, work to help students meet the needs of a changing profession. Accounting educators provide necessary technical knowledge, as well as serve as mentors, either formally or informally, to prepare students to enter the accounting profession.

Accounting educators and employers must also embrace change. Educators have the opportunity to help students set realistic career expectations, but need to understand how the workplace is changing. Employers need to understand the implications of the Gen Z mindset on the workforce. Gen Z employees have brought about a paradigm shift, particularly with regard to the expectations of value-based work and work-life balance.

Academic Preparation for the Accounting Profession

Most university accounting programs prepare students for careers in accounting and achieving the qualification of Certified Public Accountant (CPA). These programs provide the framework for students to (1) meet the educational requirement of 150 semester hours, (2) pass the Uniform CPA Examination, and (3) eventually meet the experience requirement by preparing students to enter the profession. Internship experiences, as part of the curriculum, often provide students with the opportunity to observe, participate in, and reflect on their experiences of the profession before formally beginning their careers.

While many states allow students to sit for the exam earlier, all 50 states in the United States currently require the completion of 150 semester hours of education for licensure as a CPA. The 150 semester hours provide students with a solid knowledge base, not just in accounting, but in business management, law, economics, finance, statistics, quantitative methods, data visualization, ethics, and professional communication. These areas provide the opportunity for students to learn more about areas of business that affect how they will carry out their professional work.

While credentialing requirements may vary among jurisdictions, one of the requirements for licensure is the passage of the Uniform CPA Examination. Significant changes to the exam are in progress, with an expected implementation date of January 1, 2024 (Brown 2022, Dorata, 2021). These changes move the exam to a "Core + Discipline" model. All candidates will take, and must pass, three core sections in accounting, audit, and taxation. Candidates must also pass an examination in one of three "Disciplines": analytics, information systems, or tax compliance and planning. Additionally, technology concepts will be infused throughout the examination.

Concurrently with reviewing curricula to adapt to meet the needs of the changing CPA examination, perhaps departments and programs could also assess their ability to meet the needs of accounting majors who do not want to pursue a career in public accounting. The number of CPA candidates has been declining in recent years. Todd Shapiro, Illinois CPA Society president and Chief Executive Officer, said, "It used to be that, if you earned an accounting degree, earning the CPA credential was the given next step regardless of career paths or time commitments—that's no longer the case" (CPA Practice Advisor, para. 3). There are many accounting careers in management accounting, government, in the not-for-profit arena, and in law enforcement that may be drawing students away from a traditional public accounting career path.

Beyond developing technical competency, regardless of career goals, it is important that students engage in active and reflective experiences during their education to prepare them to enter the workplace with realistic expectations. Faculty often play a more or less formal mentoring role in preparing students to enter the profession. They do this by way of classroom discussions, guest speakers, field trips (although limited during the pandemic, hopefully these will return), and engagement with professionals in local chapters of State Societies of CPAs and the IMA chapters. Guest speakers, especially alumni, may also help students understand what their working experiences are going to look like.

FOUR COMPETENCIES

Today's employers seek graduates with more than just minimal educational credentials. They seek graduates with a broad skill set, of which their formal technical knowledge is but one component. "A skill set is a complex combination of work experience and formal learning outcomes used by an employee in the current workplace" (Schislyaeva & Saychenko, 2022, p. 3). Acquisition of technical knowledge is just one component of comprehensive post-secondary education. A review of the literature highlights a wide and growing number of skills that are sought in entry-level accounting staff. If well-developed during their undergraduate and graduate programs, this repertoire of skills will help students be successful as they enter a profession that is rapidly changing. These skills may be broadly categorized into four competencies: (1) digital acumen and information literacy; (2) accounting knowledge, both broad and focused, as the new CPA examination format will reflect; (3) organizational and professional communications skills, commonly referred to as "soft skills," and (4) intellectual curiosity, including a willingness to embrace failure for what can be learned from it, as well as becoming a life-long, self-directed learner. Further, in an increasingly global environment, intellectual curiosity also encompasses an awareness and embrace of diversity, equity, and inclusion. The author examines each of these competencies in the following sections. The need for graduates to develop and demonstrate such a broad set of skills is occurring concurrently with generational shift in entry-level accounting staff. Further confounding the current environment, the students currently entering the workplace completed part of their education during the covid-19 pandemic, which disrupted the way education was delivered for an extended period of time and may influence graduates' expectations for the workplace.

Digital Acumen

While the current generation of accounting students are often touted as being "tech-savvy" or "digital natives" (Parker & Igielnik, 2020), they may not necessarily have the specific technology skills and proficiencies needed for success in the accounting profession. The revised CPA Evolution Model Curriculum (AICPA & NASBA, 2021) uses the term "digital acumen" to more precisely describe the technological skills and knowledge that accounting students will need to know and use in the profession. Excel skills have long been considered the critical technology tool for accountants. However, increasingly, the incorporation of data analytics and the use of artificial intelligence by the accounting profession, necessitates that students be able to use and interpret "big data" and be proficient in the use of such data management, visualization, and analysis tools.

The joint AICPA and NASBA report (2021) on the skills gap addresses critical areas of technology and to what extent they are covered in undergraduate and graduate curricula. This report provides institutions with the opportunity to assess the status of their own programs with regard to changing technology. Vien (2021) notes that, while data analytics has been widely integrated into curricula, other important topics such as Cybersecurity, IT governance, and Systems and Organization Controls, are less widely addressed. It is incumbent upon accounting educators to ensure that their programs continue to evolve as technology does, to address technology in both stand-alone courses that allow for mastery of the technology as well as to infuse technology applications into existing courses to help students develop expertise in the application of this technology.

The term "digital acumen" is used here to also encompass digital literacy skills such as the ability to evaluate sources for authenticity and reliability. Information literacy is an important consideration. Today's students and new entrants to the workplace grew up with a variety of devices literally at their fingertips. This allowed them to find information quickly, but did not always engage them in finding the best or most accurate information, and may "have difficulty vetting information for its legitimacy, use value, and broader implications" (Tulgan, 2016, p. 28). Students report using YouTube videos when they need extra help, forsaking traditional norms such as attending office hours or using institution-based tutoring services. While the use of such tools demonstrates resourcefulness and allows for flexibility, if students are not careful in selecting sources, they may choose material that is, at best, out of context or incomplete, and at worst, inaccurate. Therefore, developing digital acumen necessitates the ability to curate a set of reliable sources upon which to draw.

Finally, digital acumen includes the ability to select among technology alternatives, adapt current technology, and learn new technology to meet the needs of an ever-changing business environment.

From University to the Workplace

While accounting graduates are starting at entry level positions, these positions remain competitive, and employers' expectations are high. Students may need to take advantage of opportunities within and beyond their degree programs to help distinguish themselves. While the CPA Evolution Model Curriculum will help future students, those close to completing their programs may need to find other means of adding to their technical toolbox.

Excel is no longer the only form of technological expertise that accounting firms expect. Rather, they seek students who can analyze a problem and then select and apply the most appropriate tool to solve the problem (Bryant, 2019). Students should take advantage of every opportunity available to develop these skills.

To the extent that they are available at students' institutions, accounting students should give serious consideration to participating in relevant co-curricular activities, such as case study competitions, or completing a minor, microcredential or other digital badge related to data analytics. Case study competitions provide students with an opportunity to develop team work and problem solving skills by applying them to real world problems. EY, one of the "Big Four" accounting firms already embraces microcredentialing as a means for current employees to develop expertise in emerging technologies (McCrae, 2019). This may also be a pathway for those accounting students who are currently preparing to enter the workplace to bridge the gap between their current academic qualifications and the rapidly changing workplace they are entering.

Outside of academia, companies such as Mind Bridge (https://www.mindbridge.ai/) are partnering with colleges and universities and accounting firms to provide technology platforms to help students develop these necessary skills. Accounting firms often provide extensive training as part of the onboarding process and/or as continuing education. For example, in 2011, Deloitte launched Deloitte University, originally in the US and now with international locations (https://www2.deloitte.com/us/en/pages/about-deloitte/articles/deloitteuniversity-leadership-center.html?icid=top) to further promote learning. This is now more important than ever, as the rate of technology change accelerates.

Accounting Knowledge

The revised CPA Evolution Model Curriculum identifies the core and discipline topics relevant to the accounting profession today (AICPA & NASBA, 2021). There is no one-size-fits-all curriculum, as institutions vary in size, resources, and missions. However, there are common goals and objectives regarding curriculum that accounting educators should incorporate into their own programs. Programs should be examined for consistency with both core topics as well as the three discipline areas. The core topics are: (1) Accounting and Data Analytics, (2) Audit and Accounting Information Systems, and (3) Taxation. All three core sections will require the examinee to demonstrate appropriate use of technology (AICPA & NASBA, 2021). Additionally, examinees will be tested on one of three disciplines, and accounting curricula needs to be reviewed for alignment with these disciplines: (1) The Business Analysis and Reporting Discipline option, (2) The Information Systems and Controls Discipline option, or (3) The Tax Compliance and Planning Discipline option (AICPA & NASBA, 2021).

Further, the curriculum has traditionally been set to help students meet the standards for public accounting. Perhaps, there is also an opportunity to offer students tracks within their accounting programs that would help prepare them for careers in management, government, and not-for-profit accounting. Students are eligible to sit for the Certified Management Accounting (CMA) Examination with 120 credits. Perhaps, this credential would allow the opportunity for students planning career paths other than public accounting to demonstrate their expertise.

The Soft Skills: Organizational and Professional Communication Skills

Another set of competencies necessary for academic and professional success is organizational and professional communication skills, often referred to as "soft skills."

This term may unintentionally imply a separate and less important skill set. Soft skills, something perhaps taken for granted by earlier generations and/or was developed over the course of a career, can be taught and need to be developed and adapted for both the face-to-face world as well as the virtual world. In this section, the author examines the demand for, scope of, and challenges in including and measuring soft skills in accounting curricula.

Demand and Scope

"Today, firms admit that flexible skills are as essential to them as, and sometimes even more important than, hard skills" (Schislyaeva & Saychenko, 2022, p. 3). Yet, there is no agreement or single list of what constitutes soft skills. In a review of soft-skills, Martin (2019) distinguishes soft skills from traditional hard (technical) skills as: "non-technical competencies connected to one's personality, attitude, ability, and motivation to interact effectively with others" (p. 42). His review identified the following soft skills, listed here in alphabetical order:

This list is simultaneously exhaustive and incomplete. Some of these skills may develop organically as students mature and gain life and professional experience. In this section, the author focuses on four soft skills that are critical for success in many professions, and, in particular, in accounting. Chabus (2021) identifies these as time management, critical thinking, communication, and collaboration. These skills are already inherently part of accounting education, though accounting educators could make them more explicit, encourage student awareness of these as desirable skills, and be able to provide concrete examples of how students might develop these skills.

Time Management

Organizational skills, particularly time management, are critical components of academic and career success. College students often report that time management is one of their greatest challenges. First year seminars are becoming more common

Table 1.

adaptability	positive attitude
analytical thinking	problem solving
collaboration	professional responsibility
creativity	professionalism
critical thinking skill	relationship building
cultural awareness	self-management
decision making	self-motivation
diversity	sensitivity
emotional intelligence	social intelligence
ethical judgment	social skills
initiative	stress management
innovation	teamwork
interpersonal relationships	time management
moral integrity	trustworthy
negotiation skills	willingness to learn
oral communication	work ethic
persuasion	written communication

place and time management is often one of the challenges addressed. Students who attend school and work and/or participate in sports or other co-curricular activities need to hone these skills early in their academic career, if they are to be successful.

Wolters and Brady (2020) and Thibodeaux et. al. (2017) tie time management to self-regulated learning and ultimately to student academic success. Time management, done well, will include planning and reflection. Students should plan their time, subsequently review their actual performance, revise, and review again in an iterative process until they have mastered the skill.

Critical Thinking

The process of working through the curriculum in an accounting program has long provided students with a myriad of opportunities during which they could develop critical reading, critical thinking and problem solving skills. Despite changes in specific content, these strategies will continue to be important in any accounting program, as well as in the profession.

Critical thinking includes the ability to discern relevant information and to evaluate, select and apply appropriate strategies necessary to solve a problem. Critical thinking further necessitates the ability to assess the initial results to determine if the solution seems appropriate. Some students, particularly those with math anxiety, may be over reliant on calculators and other technology, without assessing the outcome for reasonableness.

Communication

When communication skills are addressed, they tend to focus on oral and written skills. A less-emphasized, though no less important part of communication is listening. In class, students should develop good listening skills, and learn to ask for clarification when necessary. This practice will be important in the workplace; employees need to exercise good listening skills with both supervisors and clients to ensure that they are addressing questions and assignments correctly. Communication for Gen Z, even prior to the pandemic, was increasingly virtual, largely in the forms of text messaging and social media commentary. These forms of communication are much more informal, and generally not appropriate for academic and professional communication.

When students were thrust into a remote learning environment with the onset of the covid-19 pandemic in March 2020, many had never taken an online course before. They quickly learned that a different skill set is required to successfully navigate learning virtually. Because of the suddenness of the pivot to remote learning, and the concurrent demands that the pandemic imposed on students and their families, students may not have initially demonstrated peak performance during that period. As communication continues to have a significant virtual component, it is incumbent upon students to develop professionalism in their communication skills including writing professional e-mails and creating a professional presence on virtual platforms such as Zoom, Google Meets or Microsoft Teams.

Collaboration

Employers look for students who can demonstrate good team working skills. New employees will be expected to both learn from and contribute to the work of their assigned team. As with other soft skills, the more practice students have during their academic career, the better able they will be to contribute in the workplace. Aware of the career demands their students encounter, many instructors satisfy team work skills with group projects or assignments.

While this is a good first step, instructors need to recognize that developing effective team working skills requires two components. One is content-based, the other is process-based. Instructors typically emphasize the content portion of the assignment, but may be less intentional about the group process. King and King

(2021) offer a well-developed resource to help guide instructors in the process portion of the assignment. Awareness of and adherence to roles within the group, as well as honest assessment of themselves and group members, are key skills that students need to learn. Instruction for group assignments needs to be clear and the grading process transparent from the start.

Challenges

While accounting curricula (i.e., hard skills) is typically well defined, a common definition or list of desired "soft skills" is more challenging. Rebele and St. Pierre (2019) argue that there does not exist a clear, agreed upon desirable inventory of soft skills to be included in accounting curricula, no universally agreed upon definitions of such skills, nor a proven way to assess such skills. They further assert that accounting faculty may not be in the best position to teach these skills, as they are often developed outside of the classroom as the student gains professional experience. They maintain "developing soft skills would be an added bonus, but this should never take priority over developing students' technical accounting competence" (p. 77). Though Rebele and St. Pierre are correct in their assertions about the lack of a common list and agreement upon definitions, this author asserts that several of the key soft skills identified in this section align naturally with current technical content and could be, by addressing some of the challenges, surfaced by accounting faculty to help students develop at least some of these skills.

Measurement of the attainment of soft skill outcomes is indeed challenging. Rather than seeking a universally agreed upon measurement, which would delay implementation, and likely be ultimately impossible, it might be better to address measurement in the context of specific assignments, courses, or programs. Rubrics can be a great way to identify the key outcomes on individual assignments. The fact that rubrics would vary from instructor to instructor, or even from assignment to assignment presents students with the reality that in the workplace, not all assignments are the same. It is therefore important as a student, and later as an employee, to understand the parameters, goals, and measurements for each assignment.

Another challenge in including soft skills in the curriculum is to find a place for them. Two possibilities are to integrate them into an existing course(s) or to develop a dedicated course to help students develop these skills. Given the limitations of coursework fitting into a finite semester, if soft skills are taught effectively within an existing course, what current content would have to be omitted? If a dedicated course were developed, what course would have to be dropped from the current curriculum in order to make space for the new course? Are there existing courses that naturally align with one or more of the desired soft skills?

The developmental and experiential nature of soft skill development provides support for integrating soft skill development across the curriculum, rather than as a one-time, stand-alone course. Yet, again, this presents further challenges in identifying which courses would focus on which soft skills and how to measure them. "The main problems with applying soft skills in the workplace are their immeasurability and difficulties with quantifying the skillset" (Schislyaeva & Saychenko, 2022, p. 3). The same challenges of defining, quantifying, and measuring components of soft skills exists in academia. Accounting educators need to define student learning objectives for the skills, develop learning activities to teach the skills, and determine what and how to assess the acquisition of these skills.

Still another challenge is that institutions need to assess the ability of the faculty to teach the desired skills. Many doctoral programs do not emphasize pedagogy, and therefore full-time faculty may not have the pedagogical repertoire necessary to include such soft skill activities in their courses. Adjunct and other part-time faculty may come from practice and may, in fact, be a valuable resource in identifying how soft skills are prioritized and used in practice and assist in the integration of these skills into coursework. Institutions would need to provide professional development support to allow both full-time and part-time faculty to develop these facilitation skills.

Intellectual Curiosity

This author proposes adding Intellectual Curiosity as a distinct competency. There are a number of dimensions of intellectual curiosity that are particularly relevant to academic pursuits and the transfer of learning to the workplace: (1) learning how to learn, (2) an appreciation for diversity, equity, and inclusion, (3) life-long and self-directed learning, (4) learning from failure, (5) metacognition, and (6) experiential learning.

Learning How to Learn

Instructors have a perfect opportunity to model and foster intellectual curiosity and a love of learning in their students. However, "as educators, we sometimes fall prey to the fallacy of equating our covering material with students learning the material" (Pincus, 1997, p. 576). Further, post-secondary instructors may often assume that their students, having been in formal schooling for many years, already know how to learn. That may not be the case. Students may know how to learn about things that interest them; they "just google it" or learn something by watching videos on YouTube. However, do they really know how to learn in the discipline that instructors are teaching? If students "just google" an advanced accounting concept, are they savvy enough to evaluate the source of the information and determine its accuracy before relying on it? While time is very limited each semester, attempting to teach students content without teaching them how to learn in this discipline may be futile. This is particularly true in the accounting principles courses where few students enter with prior formal academic coursework in accounting and may have pre-determined and negative stereotypes about accounting that pose a barrier to learning. Most students are taking a number of courses each term, and those courses may be in different disciplines. Study skills that may work well in one discipline, or at one level, may not work in all disciplines or at all levels. As students advance in their coursework, courses tend to cover higher level learning and require more in depth skills, as Bloom's taxonomy illustrates. Have students progressed in their ability to move from knowledge, comprehension, and application, to analysis, synthesis, and evaluation? (Krathwohl, 2002). Something as seemingly simple as teaching students how to read and use their textbook and course software can go a long way to improving student performance and decreasing frustration for both students and instructors.

Diversity, Equity, and Inclusion

An important aspect of intellectual curiosity in a global environment is to genuinely embrace an openness to learning about people and practices from different cultures. Taking into account multi-cultural perspectives enhances students' personal development as well as their ability to foster interpersonal relationships and make inclusive decisions in the workplace. Employers are increasingly seeking applicants who have demonstrated a commitment and made contributions to diversity (Willis, 2018). Students' backgrounds prior to entering post-secondary education may be rich in or empty of multi-cultural experiences. Students have many opportunities to engage in activities to learn more about other cultures. Study abroad programs at many universities provide students with a way to immerse themselves in other cultures and begin to build or further develop their existing cross cultural competencies.

Life-Long and Self-Directed Learning

One thing that is certain about current students' future careers is that they will change, and the more successful professionals will be those who embrace the opportunities to continue to learn and demonstrate resilience as both the content of work and the way that work is performed continue to evolve. In order to navigate successful careers, much of this life-long learning will need to be self-directed. CPA licensure generally requires a set number of continuing education hours for each period. Although many organizations provide workshops and seminars to facilitate these learning opportunities, it will still be incumbent upon individual professionals to maintain their required level of continuing education. Accounting educators play a natural role in fostering intellectual curiosity, setting an example for and promoting the desire for life-long learning, and scaffolding the skills necessary to help students become self-directed in their learning.

Many programs include a capstone course or project that require students to select a topic to investigate, gather resources, and synthesize and report their findings. While students are generally expected to work independently on these projects, instructors often provide interim deadlines to foster time management and planning skills and to support students as they navigate through the process. This type of project provides students with the opportunity to integrate both technical skills as well as soft skills that they have learned throughout their time in the program. Successful completion of these assignments necessitates exercising time management skills, organizational skills, and communication skills.

Learning From Failure

Intellectual curiosity also encompasses one's ability to accept failure as part of the learning process. Learning often comes as a result of initial "failures." Yet, social anxiety is prevalent among college students worldwide, and may impact the process of learning from failure. For college-aged students, social anxiety may manifest itself in interpersonal interactions, academic performance, and students' personal safety (Lee, et.al, 2022, Brook & Willoughby, 2015). Several of the themes Brook and Willoughby identify have particular relevance to this discussion about soft skills: persistent self-consciousness, expecting and fearing judgement, interpersonal barriers such as mandatory social interaction, and preference for online communication. Post-secondary education seems to provide an excellent opportunity for students to develop these skills in what may be thought of by educators as a safe environment. Yet, the inner turmoil many students experience when called upon for a response in class, when needing to ask for help from an instructor or when being required to make a presentation in class may make the classroom feel like anything but a safe place for some students. The very skills that employers seek in their hiring processes seem to be at odds with students' ability to engage. Although this presents added challenges for instructors trying to teach course content, and now, perhaps, feeling pressure to build in soft skills experiences, it is an important discussion to be had at the university and department level. Particularly in schools of business, students are being prepared to enter the business world, and failure to address the need for soft skill development leaves graduates of business programs less prepared for the job market that they will be facing.

Many Gen Z students enter college having been raised in an environment that, perhaps, pressured achievement over learning (Lahey, 2015), with the unintended consequence that students are inadequately prepared to experience failure, re-evaluate, regroup, and persevere. An examination of the reasons why some people succeed while others fail indicates the role of perseverance, or grit, in creating successful outcomes. In her book, *Grit: The Power of Passion and Perseverance*, Angela Duckworth (2016) retells the story of an interview with Pete Carroll of the Seattle Seahawks, after a 2014 Super Bowl win. In discussing what he looks for in players, he spoke of their grit, their mindset to succeed, of being resilient, of not letting setbacks hold them back, and of not letting challenges deter them. These are the same traits that college instructors would be happy to see in their students. How do students learn when learning is difficult or new? How do they overcome challenges, such as trying to overcome their fear of public speaking by making presentations in class? While grit may not be something that can be taught in accounting classes, instructors can raise an awareness of the need for grit and not giving up when students find coursework challenging. This is especially true in accounting principles courses, where many students, who are not accounting majors, find the work to be challenging and may give up before they really get started. Accounting instructors can help students recognize these challenges as preparation for when they enter the workplace, where they are also likely to face challenges.

Metacognition

Educators are increasingly attentive to the role that metacognition, engaging students in thinking about their own thinking, plays in learning. Instructors are "continually surprised at the number of students who come to college having very little metacognitive knowledge; knowledge about different strategies, different cognitive tasks, and particularly, accurate knowledge about themselves" (Pintrich, 2002, p. 223).

Accounting instructors, as well as instructors in all disciplines, do have an opportunity to help students engage in metacognitive activities. In *Classroom Assessment Techniques: A Handbook for College Teachers,* Angelo and Cross (1993) offer strategies for instructors to use in class to both assess course content as well as helping students to better understand their own learning processes. One such example is an exercise called "The Muddiest Point." At the end of a reading, assignment, exercise or class session, students are asked to identify what point was the "muddiest" (i.e., least clear, most confusing). This simple exercise aids students in thinking about what they learned and articulating what they find confusing. It also provides instructors with timely feedback that allows the instructor to respond, reframe, and clarify concepts before moving on to the next topic.

Experiential Learning

Reviewing the list of competencies employers of today's graduates desire could lead to the conclusion that employers are looking for entry-level employees who already possess the skillsets of more seasoned employees who have had years to hone their skills. Already built into many business and accounting programs is the opportunity for students to participate in internship experiences and/or the Volunteer Income Tax Assistance (VITA) program. These programs provide an opportunity for students to apply the technical skills and are strongly encouraged by the Pathways Commission (2012). Whether explicitly addressed and evaluated, these experiences also provide students with the opportunity to develop their soft skills. In a study of VITA participants at a Midwestern university, researchers observed increases in both technical and soft skill development during the students' participation in the VITA program and provided a helpful rubric for assessing soft skill development (Bootsma et al., 2021).

If the internship program does not already include a metacognitive component, it is never too late to add one. This component requires the student to reflect on, articulate, and then share their experiences in the program. Students should be encouraged to articulate their expectations, goals, and concerns before beginning the program. This provides an opportunity for internship facilitators to help the students set realistic expectations. A mid-semester check-in experience could require the students to reflect on, articulate, and then share their experiences to date. How does the experience, to date, compare with their expectations? What has been particularly interesting and/or challenging? What did they learn about themselves and about the profession? Having prior student interns participate in the reflection may be beneficial for both current and prior student interns. This mid-semester check-in opportunity may provide students with the opportunity to make any necessary adjustments for the remainder of the experience. A similar reflective experience should be conducted as a culminating assignment in the course experience.

GENERATIONAL CHANGES IN THE WORKPLACE

Long before the onset of the covid-19 pandemic, educators were addressing the changes that Generations Y (Millennials) and Z (iGen) brought to the classroom. Employers, in turn, faced generational changes in new employees' approaches to work as these two generations entered the workforce. Employers have been experiencing the shift in the workplace expectations and attitudes of its Generation Y and Z employees.

Gen Y (Millennials) are generally considered to be born between 1980-1992 (Bannon, Ford & Meltzer, 2011). Millennials entering the accounting profession brought with them a level of comfort with technology unlike their predecessors. They were the first generation to be known as digital natives. They were less likely than earlier generations to expect their first job to be their only job. They were the most diverse generation to date, and identified social responsibilities as priorities. This generation seeks more of a balance between their work and personal lives (Clancy, 2012). These trends continued into the next generation.

The current generation of accounting students, those born after 1995, is commonly known as Gen Z (Parker & Igielnik, 2020). Gen Z employees do not generally enter the workplace expecting that their first significant job will be their only one, that they will spend 20-30 years there and then retire. By design and/or by circumstance, members of Generations Y and Z are likely to have career paths that flow smoothly or jump erratically from one position to another. Gen Z enters the post-university workplace with less early work experience than previous cohorts. Schroth (2019) notes that, "in 1979, 60% of teens held a job, while, in 2015, 34% of teens held a job, and it is expected to drop to 25% in 2024" (p. 6). The lack of significant prior work experience may result in a more challenging onboarding process for both new hires as well as the employer and those managing and supervising new employees.

The pandemic further disrupted both education and the workplace. It is important for employers to recognize the implications of the reality, that students now entering the workplace have completed a prolonged portion of their education during the covid-19 pandemic, which, with little warning, disrupted the way by which education was delivered for an extended period of time. It may be too soon to fully grasp the myriad of ways by which the pandemic has influenced work.

IMPLICATIONS FOR EMPLOYERS

Elam and Mendex (2010) find that students expect that their workplace expectations will be met, particularly around these areas: scheduling flexibility, freedom to innovate procedures and processes, frequent positive reinforcement, 40 hours work weeks (as opposed to 60 hours), that their careers will span multiple job changes, some of which may require relocation.

In a joint report about Gen Z and the future of accounting, the Association of Chartered Certified Accountants and the International Federation of Accountants (2021) address both challenges and opportunities for accounting employers. Several significant areas warrant employers' attention. These areas include the values that Gen Z seeks in the workplace, such as the need for authenticity and an alignment of personal goals with those of the organization, being less motivated by compensation and more motivated by work-life balance, the need for, type of, and frequency of feedback desired, and the need for training to be short and visual (Association of Chartered Certified Accountants & International Federation of Accountants, 2021).

Scroth (2019) provides some best practices for onboarding on Gen Z employees. These include:

1. Provide immediate, short-term, and more distant checklists for responsibilities and goals as transition tool from higher education to the workplace.
2. Facilitate communication.
3. Reinforce existing culture and sense of purpose.
4. Provide feedback channels.

While these all provide a good initial strategy, it will be important for the employees' long-term success that they be able to work independently. For example:

1. As new employees move forward, they should be able to both go beyond the checklist, as well as develop future checklists for themselves.
2. While new employees, particularly those who were in school during the early stages of the pandemic, may be familiar with various communication technologies, the swift pivot to the use of the technologies may not have been concurrently undertaken with an eye toward professionalism in those communications. New employees will need to be trained in organizational protocols for such communication.
3. More so than previous generations, Gen Z employees are looking for meaningful work that aligns with their values. Company values need to be clearly articulated and lived out in organizational life, including the ability of the organization and job demands to allow the employee to maintain a work-life balance that aligns with their own values. This is particularly challenging in entry level accounting positions, known for long hours.
4. Feedback provides important communication, particularly to new employees, about how they are performing their work. Employees are more likely to leave companies that fail to distinguish between high and low performers, when it comes to recognition and rewards.

Companies that fail to recognize and reward strong performers have higher rates of attrition, and the same is true for employers that tolerate underperformance. The issue is not compensation below market rates, but rather recognition — both informal and financial — that is not linked to effort and results (Sull et al., 2022, p.3).

Even prior to the covid-19 pandemic, accounting firms were struggling with retaining employees. In a study surveying more than 1,000 employees in five CPA firms, Johnson and Pike (2018) examined employee engagement, employee satisfaction, the employee's intention to stay in the organization. They report that less than 35% of employees at staff, senior, and management levels reported being highly engaged in their work. Further, they identified the top three factors that drive employee engagement: (1) "My job gives me the opportunity to do what I do best," (2) "I believe my personal values are aligned with my firm's values," and (3) "I believe I make a difference at work."

Chamorro-Premuzic and Bersin (2018) note that intellectual curiosity and "learnabiity" are essential to remaining employable. In an effort to retain talent, they provide several solutions for employers and team leaders: (1) Reward continuous learning, (2) give meaningful and constructive feedback, (3) lead by example, and (4) hire curious people.

ITA Group (in Payne, 2022) developed a psychological benefits framework, identifying three areas that employees seek fulfillment, and, when met, lead to greater employee retention. These three areas are: (1) functional benefits, (2) emotional benefits, and (3) identity benefits. The first is what the company helps the employees to accomplish personally or professionally. ITA's Christina Zurek says that this is what gets employees in the door, but rarely what keeps them. It is important to notice the shift in focus: Not "what can you, the prospective employee, do for the company?" Rather, the question that the employer needs to answer for the prospective employee is: "What can we do for you?" The second category, emotional benefits, involves supporting employees in how they feel about the work that they do. The third category, identity benefits, reflect how employees see their work and the company they work for, as reflecting their values. ITA further recommends six initiatives to support this framework: company communication, company-sponsored events, recognition, incentive, professional development, and wellness programs (Payne, 2022).

The challenges employees have faced directly and indirectly by the covid-19 pandemic have further elevated the issue of employee retention. The term "The Great Resignation" has come into common parlance. Accounting firms continue to face challenges retaining top talent. In May 2022, PwC announced a $2.4-billion-dollar investment in its employees. Kaminsky, Vice Chair and Trust Solutions Co-Leader at PwC U.S., said:

'It's clear people's mindsets have changed and so should their employers. We know our people want an experience that matches what they value and what makes them happy. They told us that they want more choice and more flexibility. They want it in a way that is personalized to their needs and interests.' (McCabe, 2022, para 5).

CONCLUSION AND RECOMMENDATIONS FOR FURTHER RESEARCH

Much is expected of today's accounting graduates. The amount and depth of technical accounting knowledge continues to grow at a significant pace. Technology tools continue to change the nature of work in both the classroom and in the workplace. No longer is an excellent grade-point average the biggest factor in determining whether or not a student lands an entry-level position at a top-tier firm. Students are also expected to have accounting knowledge, technical skills, and any number of soft skills mastered by the time they interview for these positions. Prior generations had the luxury of learning many of these additional skills as they progressed in their careers. What is certain for today's graduates is that they will need to continue to learn over the course of their careers. Those students and employees who embrace intellectual curiosity and a love of learning are likely to be the future leaders in the profession.

Accounting educators, likewise, continue to learn not just about changes in accounting knowledge and technology, but about generational changes in students and the implications for learning and preparing students for professional life after graduation. Accounting educators are challenged to not only adapt content, but the pedagogy that they use to deliver the content. There exists a wealth of resources available from numerous professional and educational associations to support educators in their pursuit. Appendix A provides a list of organizations and resources for educators.

Researchers in accounting education and employment experiences should continue to study the integration of soft skills into the accounting curriculum, the onboarding process of Gen Z employees into the accounting workspace, and the reasons for leaving jobs, as well as continued, and likely permanent effects on the workplace and employee retention as a result of the covid-19 pandemic. Changes in technology and employee demands are certain to shape the future of the accounting profession and the way that accounting students are academically prepared to enter that profession.

REFERENCES

American Institute of Certified Public Accountants. (n.d.). *150 hour requirement for obtaining a CPA license*. AICPA. https://us.aicpa.org/becomeacpa/licensure/requirements.html#why

American Institute of Certified Public Accountants & National Association of State Boards of Accountancy. (2021). *CPA Evolution Model Curriculum*. CPA.

Angelo, T. A., & Cross, K. P. (1993). Classroom assessment techniques: A handbook for college professors. Jossey-Bass.

Association of Charted Certified Accountants and the International Federation of Accountants. (2021). *Groundbreakers: Gen Z and the future of accountancy.* ACCAI. file:///C:/Users/user/Downloads/GEN-Z-GROUNDBREAKERS.pdf

Bannon, S., Ford, K., & Meltzer, L. (2011). Understanding millennials in the workplace: Certified public accountant. *The CPA Journal, 81*(11), 61–65.

Bootsma, M., Jeffrey, C., & Perkins, J. D. (2021). Is there learning in service learning? Measuring the extent to which VITA participation improves student technical competence and soft skills. *Issues in Accounting Education, 36*(2), 21–42. doi:10.2308/ISSUES-19-113

Brook, C. A., & Willoughby, T. (2015). The Social Ties That Bind: Social Anxiety and Academic Achievement Across the University Years. *Journal of Youth and Adolescence, 44*(5), 1139–1152. doi:10.100710964-015-0262-8 PMID:25691148

Brown, A. (2022). The CPA exam curriculum is changing. *Accounting Today, 36*(1), 24.

Bryant, S. M. (2019). Bridging the gap between the classroom and career readiness for new accounting graduates. *The CPA Journal.* https://www.cpajournal.com/2019/02/01/bridging-the-gap-between-the-classroom-and-career-readiness-for-new-accounting-graduates/

Chabus, R. (2021). Top soft skills for accounting professionals. *Journal of Accountancy.* https://www.journalofaccountancy.com/newsletters/2021/jun/top-soft-skills-accounting-professionals.html

Chamorro-Premuzic, T., & Bersin, J. (2018). *4 ways to create a learning culture on your team.* Harvard Business Review. https://hbr.org/2018/07/4-ways-to-create-a-learning-culture-on-your-team

Clancy, A. (2012). How to accommodate millennial accountants. *Long Island Business News.* https://www.proquest.com/trade-journals/how-accommodate-millennial-accountants/docview/1017591689/se-2

CPA Practice Advisor. (2021). *Report Examines Decline in Number of CPAs.* CPA. https://www.cpapracticeadvisor.com/2021/06/14/report-examines-decline-in-number-of-cpas/44293/

Deloitte University. (n.d.) *Leadership Center.* Deloitte University. https://www2.deloitte.com/us/en/pages/about-deloitte/articles/deloitteuniversity-leadership-center.html?icid=top_

Dorata, N. (2021). Changes ahead for the big test. *Accounting Today*, *35*(6), 32.

Duckworth. (2016). *Grit: the power of passion and perseverance*. Scribner.

Elam, D., & Mendez, F. (2010). Career Expectations Of Accounting Students. *American Journal of Business Education*, *3*(5), 71–80. doi:10.19030/ajbe.v3i5.430

Johnson, S., & Pike, B. (2018). Employee retention: The state of engagement in public accounting firms and why it matters. *The CPA Journal*, *88*(12), 64–66.

King, A. Z., & King, H. (2021). Developing team skills in accounting students: A complete curriculum. *Journal of Higher Education Theory and Practice*, *21*(7), 116–146.

Krathwohl, D. R. (2002). A revision of Bloom's taxonomy: An overview. *Theory into Practice*, *41*(4), 212–218. doi:10.120715430421tip4104_2

Lahey, J. (2015). *The gift of failure: How parents learn to let go so their children can succeed*. HarperCollins Publishers.

Lee, J., Waldeck, D., Holliman, A. J., Banerjee, M., & Tyndall, I. (2022). Feeling socially anxious at university: An interpretative phenomenological analysis. *Qualitative Report*, *27*(4), 897–919. doi:10.46743/2160-3715/2022.5270

Martin, T. N. (2019). Review of Student Soft Skills Development Using the 5Ws/H Approach Resulting in a Realistic, Experiential, Applied, Active Learning and Teaching Pedagogical Classroom. *Journal of Behavioral and Applied Management*, *19*(1), 41–57.

McCabe, S. (2022, May 6). PwC U.S. announces $2.4B employee investment. *Accounting Today*. https://www.accountingtoday.com/news/pwc-us-announces-2-4b-employee-investment

McCrea, B. M. (2019). Leveling up your accounting and finance credentials. *Insight*. https://www.icpas.org/information/copy-desk/insight/article/spring-2019/leveling-up-your-accounting-and-finance-credentials

Parker, K., & Igielnik, R. (2020). *On the cusp of adulthood and facing an uncertain future: What we know about Gen Z so far*. Pew Research Center. https://www.pewresearch.org/social-trends/2020/05/14/on-the-cusp-of-adulthood-and-facing-an-uncertain-future-what-we-know-about-gen-z-so-far-2/

Pathways Commission. (2012). *Final report.* American Accounting Association.

Payne, E. (2022, April 15). *What it takes to keep top talent: 3 areas of focus*. Benefits Pro. https://www.benefitspro.com/2022/04/15/what-it-takes-to-keep-top-talent-3-areas-of-focus/?slreturn=20220429125753

Pincus, K. V. (1997). Is teaching debits and credits essential in elementary accounting? *Issues in Accounting Education, 12*(2), 575–579.

Pintrich, P. R. (2002). The role of metacognitive knowledge in learning, teaching, and assessing. *Theory into Practice, 41*(4), 219–225. doi:10.120715430421tip4104_3

Rebele, J. E., & St. Pierre, E. K. (2019). A commentary on learning objectives for accounting education programs: The importance of soft skills and technical knowledge. *Journal of Accounting Education, 48*, 71-79. doi:10.1016/j.jaccedu.2019.07.002

Schislyaeva, E. R., & Saychenko, O. A. (2022). Labor market soft skills in the context of digitalization of the economy. *Social Sciences (Basel, Switzerland), 3*(11), 91. doi:10.3390ocsci11030091

Schroth, H. (2019). Are you ready for Gen Z in the workplace? *California Management Review, 61*(3), 5–18. doi:10.1177/0008125619841006

Sull, D., Sull, C., & Zweig, B. (2022). Toxic Culture Is Driving the Great Resignation. *MIT Sloan Management Review, 63*(2), 1–9.

Thibodeaux, J., Deutsch, A., Kitsantas, A., & Winsler, A. (2017). First-year college students' time use: Relations with self-regulation and GPA. *Journal of Advanced Academics, 28*(1), 5–27. doi:10.1177/1932202X16676860

Tulgan, B. (2016). Bridging the soft-skills gap. *Employment Relations Today, 42*(4), 25–33. doi:10.1002/ert.21536

Vien, C. (2021). Wanted: More systems and analytics training for accounting students. *Journal of Accountancy.* https://www.journalofaccountancy.com/news/2021/mar/systems-analytics-training-accounting-students.html

Willis, D. S. (2018). *On the road to champion.* https://www.insidehighered.com/advice/2018/03/26/advice-how-become-diversity-equity-and-inclusion-leader-opinion#.Ys7YnsHPsv8.link

Wolters, & Brady, A. C. (2020). College students' time management: A self-regulated learning perspective. *Educational Psychology Review, 33*(4), 1319–1351. https://doi.org/ doi:10.1007/s10648-020-09519-z

APPENDIX I

Organizational Resources for Accounting Educators

American Accounting Association (AAA) https://aaahq.org

American Accounting Association Teaching, Learning, and Curriculum Section https://aaahq.org/TLC

American Accounting Association Conference on Teaching and Learning in Accounting https://aaahq.org/Meetings/2022/CTLA

American Institute of Certified Public Accountants (AICPA) https://www.aicpa.org

Association of Chartered Certified Accountants (ACCA) https://www.accaglobal.com/

Association to Advance Collegiate Schools of Business (AACSB) https://www.aacsb.edu/

Institute of Management Accountants (IMA) https://www.imanet.org

International Federation of Accountants (IFAC) https://www.ifac.org/

National Association of State Boards of Accountancy (NASBA) https://nasba.org

This Way to CPA https://www.thiswaytocpa.com

Chapter 10
Business Demands of Accounting Students

Frank Manzi
College of Mount Saint Vincent, USA

Mark Martinelli
Synchrony Financial, USA

ABSTRACT

This chapter is an overview of the many gaps accounting students demonstrate as they enter the business world. The gaps to be explored can be separated into two overall categories: technology (these gaps will be referred to in this chapter in a summary fashion as they will be addressed in detail in another chapter) and soft skills, which comprise several gaps that are centered in many ways around communication and management skills. Business demands for accounting graduates go beyond technical skills as they are viewed as future business leaders.

INTRODUCTION

The issue that academia produces graduates that lag in the requirements that business needs to meet the demands of a competitive environment is not new. Three major developments have altered the business environment (as traditionally conveyed by accounting educators to students) and the nature of professional activities of accountants: technology, globalization, and investor power in the capital markets. (Albrecht W.S & Sack 2001) Business moves very quickly which is not only by design but what we as humans expect and demand. Fortunately, business demand for employees still operates under the precepts of free market economics where the

DOI: 10.4018/978-1-6684-5483-1.ch010

Copyright © 2023, IGI Global. Copying or distributing in print or electronic forms without written permission of IGI Global is prohibited.

employee skills and attributes available in the marketplace germinate via the immutable laws of supply and demand. "Basic Excel knowledge is a must, and most students start their jobs with adequate skills. Recruiters are also looking for demonstrated abilities to quickly pick up other software programs." (Ovaska-Few 2017)

Business seeks to obtain a competitive advantage and use that advantage to improve overall profitability. Academia does not necessarily follow the same rules, at least not at the same time related urgency and is more shaped by market forces over a much longer timespan. In the broadest sense Academia follows the same process since the better schools attract more talented students so the immutable forces of supply and demand that drives business also is apparent in the academic world. The main focus of this chapter will be to delve into the educational demands and skills that business require and expect from graduating students.

Our experience tells us that Academia does not react quickly to the changing needs of business. Some of this is philosophical as the purist in Academia will tell you they serve as centers of knowledge and thinking and therefore need to focus on a broad level of education supporting the overall growth of the individual. At least this is what the purveyors of a liberal arts education will tell you. We are not here to denigrate this concept but to instead to analyze Academia's ability of keeping current with the growing demands of their greatest constituents, the business world. The academic world seems to operate under a different timeframe when it comes to educating our youth on the most current precepts of business and society. A lag is to be expected due to the time it can take to develop syllabi, textbooks, and other course material used in a university setting. However, an education topic lag of more than an academic year creates a void that becomes a challenge for businesses hiring college graduates. There is also the education issue that adds to the lag, as some professors are challenged to remain attuned to the ever-changing needs and tools of business. These factors lead to an interesting dichotomy, business changes fast and needs a steady stream of newly graduated employees to help them meet their demands while academia moves at a slower pace thereby not supplying students with the skills they need to be successful.

Business Training Programs

Most companies understand that students coming into the workforce directly from a university will require additional training. This is totally understood when you are training new employees for the specific roles and procedures pertaining to the employing company. This is especially true for the mid-size to large public accounting firms that have tailored systems and processes specific to their firms. Public accounting firms are accountable to the overall public at large in their responsibility for auditing companies to help ensure integrity of their clients' financial reporting.

Figure 1. Bachelor's students: found employment

Year	7 Largest CPA Firms	Other CPA firms	Non-CPA Employers
Bachelor's Students—Found Employment			
2018	43%	34%	23%
2017	68%	21%	11%
2016	62%	19%	19%
2015	40%	32%	28%

Designing audit strategy and audit approach is a little bit of a tightrope because public accounting firms must balance their own profitability while ensuring they are allowing sufficient time to design and perform audit procedures that ensure the financial statements presented by their clients are fairly stated. CPA firms are further constrained by the possibility of lawsuits, whether they be warranted or not, audit failures, company malfeasance, client bankruptcy and several other legal and regulatory issues causing the firms to design their audit processes within an overall business risk framework. In many ways public accounting firms provide intrinsic value to the entire business community as they are the largest employer of accounting graduates and provide graduates with training that will help them be integral to the success of other companies as many of their staff, supervisors and managers venture out of public accounting. As the table below illustrates, in 2018, public accounting firms hired approximately 77% of undergraduate accounting student graduates within their audit, taxation and assurances services practice areas. (Gabbin 2019)

Graduates going directly into private industry are also subject to training programs that are tied directly to the systems and processes at the company. However, such training is much more company software and policies based whereas the public accounting firms are further training students in audit and management skills. Training within private industry is necessary due to the level of complexity and process diversity in the business world. It represents an important aspect of a graduating student's entrance into the workplace. The learning never stops and clearly demonstrates that regardless of how strong a college accounting program may be, it is never as complete to allow a transition from student to professional employee to be seamless.

Business Demands of Accounting Students

To delve deeper into the related soft and hard skills businesses seek from accounting graduates we conducted interviews with professionals serving as senior financial executives amongst a broad spectrum of companies and industries. Our interviewees also included individuals working in the services industry either as external public accountants, internal auditors or consultants. We also included a college professor in our interview process to gain a bit of an academic view of expectations for students entering the workforce.

In total we interviewed twenty-two professionals from a diversity of industries, as described in Table I below, Interview Population Demographics.

Based on the backgrounds of those interviewed the average years' experience of those interviewed was 29.4 years with 60% having started their careers in one

Table 1. Interview population demographics

Interview Population Demographics				
Industry	**Character**	**Size**	**Years' Experience**	**CPA**
Credit Card	Publicly Held	Large	35	Y
Banking	Publicly Held	Large	26	N
Accounting Services	Privately Held	Small	35	Y
Public Accounting	Publicly Held	Large	20	N
Credit Card	Publicly Held	Large	29	Y
Consumer Products	Publicly Held	Large	40	Y
Accounting Services	Privately Held	Medium	40	Y
Public Accounting	Privately Held	Large	20	N
High Technology	Privately Held	Small	25	Y
Public Accounting	Privately Held	Large	35	Y
Human Resource Services	Publicly Held	Medium	32	Y
Advertising	Publicly Held	Large	42	Y
Advertising	Publicly Held	Large	30	Y
Accounting Services	Publicly Held	Medium	20	Y
Public Accounting	Privately Held	Large	33	Y
Education	Not-For-Profit	Medium	11	Y
Banking	Publicly Held	Medium	45	Y
Credit Card	Publicly Held	Medium	20	Y
Credit Card	Publicly Held	Medium	33	Y
High Technology	Privately Held	Small	25	Y
Banking	Publicly Held	Large	20	N
Education	Not-For-Profit	Medium	30	Y

of the top ten nationally recognized external accounting and consulting firms. Moreover, our interviewees were, by the nature of their roles, likely employers and recruiters of individuals that had studied the field of accounting and auditing. Based on their professional level and their involvement in the recruiting process, employers and recruiters are also intimately involved in deriving the specific job descriptions, required skills sets and expectations for successful employment and career expectations.

To help ensure consistency we developed a standard questionnaire that was used for each interview. The questions included both yes and no answers, specific quantifiable answers as well as a section for free form answers to better solicit from the respondents more qualitative thoughts to help us ferret out those skills and issues of most import to business executives exposed to accounting graduates. To give more context and deepen our understanding of the answers, throughout the interview the respondents were asked to provide specific examples they had personally observed or experienced in response to the answers, but more specifically related to any technological needs, expectations, and gaps raised during the interview process.

Questionnaire

1. What is the primary industry your company operates in?
2. What is your title?
3. How many years' experience do you have?
4. What professional certifications do you have?
5. How many employees are in the company?
6. How many people are in your organization?
7. How many accountants and or auditors are in your functional areas?
8. How many accountants and or auditors do you hire per year?
9. Are new hires expected to have professional certifications?
10. Do you hire accountants and or auditors right out of college or after they complete their 150-credit required for CPA licensure?
11. Have you hired college graduates with technology degrees in lieu of hiring college graduates with an accounting degree?
    a. How many?
    b. What percent?
    c. Why?
12. What specific technological skills do you expect from college graduates with an accounting degree?
13. Have you observed a technological skills gap from newly hired college graduates with an accounting degree?
    a. What technological skills gaps have you observed?

  b. Why are these gaps important to mitigate?

14. Do you believe the technological skills gap can be mitigated in the CPA exam or in academia or both?
    a. Please explain.
    b. What changes in the CPA exam would you recommend?
    c. What changes in accounting education would you recommend?
15. Are you fully apprised of the new CPA exam requirements effective January 1, 2024? If yes, do you believe these changes will mitigate the technological skills gap?
16. Do you believe the new CPA exam requirements combined with the current accounting education curriculum will mitigate the technological skills gap?
17. Have you observed other (non-technological) skills gap? If yes, please explain.
18. Please share any final thoughts.

We analyzed the responses on an individual as well as aggregate basis to establish common themes and trends to identify any potential gaps. Whilst our initial focus was to identify the existence of specific technological skill gaps, the responses to our questionnaire also raised other soft skill type gaps which we will further expand upon below. We expect to address the significant gaps identified in the technology skills of new graduates in a subsequent chapter. See Table 2 for a summary chart skill gap identified during our interviews.

Table 2. Interview results summary

	Interview Results Summary									
	Skills Gaps Identified During Interview									
	Communication			Other				Technology		
Industry	Written	Oral	Presenting	Analytical	Critical Thinking	Team Interaction	Professional Skepticism	Excel	Financial Systems	Data Base, Analytics
Accounting Services	X	X	X	X	X				X	
Advertising	X	X	X							
Consumer Products	X	X	X	X	X		X			
Education				X	X			X		X
Financial Services	X	X	X	X	X	X		X	X	X
Technology	X				X		X	X	X	X
Manufacturing				X	X				X	
Not-for-Profit	X	X		X			X	X		X
Public Accounting	X	X		X	X		X	X		X
Staffing	X			X	X			X	X	X
Construction					X		X	X		

Soft Skills Gap

In many ways the term soft skills is in itself a bit of a misnomer. The term soft skills may assume that they are less important than hard or technical skills are which, naturally, is not true at all. Soft skills are much harder to measure, but they are critical for success in the business world and in life in general. The Job Outlook 2008 Survey of 276 employers (Koncz & Collins, 2007) examined the qualities that employers look for in prospective employees. (Beard, Schwieger & Surendran 2008) The chart below is on a 1 to 5 scale with 1 indicating the characteristic was not important and 5 as extremely important supports the importance of soft skills in the workforce.

Figure 2. Results of job outlook survey
(Job Outlook 2008 Survey https://www.naceweb.org/)

Skill	Value
Communication skills (verbal & written)	4.6
Strong work ethic	4.6
Teamwork skills (works well with others)	4.5
Initiative	4.4
Interpersonal skills (relates well to others)	4.4
Problem-solving skills	4.4
Analytical skills	4.3
Flexibility / adaptability	4.2
Computer skills	4.1
Technical skills	4.1
Detail orientation	4.0
Organizational skills	4.0

Technological advancements have caused businesses to expect more of new graduates since they assume these advancements eased much of the detailed burden associated with accountants' skills such as gathering, recording, and properly classifying vast amounts of data. The expectation is that much of the more standardized processes pertaining to financial statement preparation would be done with a few clicks on an ERP report writer or even merely refining a sophisticated Excel spreadsheet. Consequently, prospective employers expect direct hires fresh from college to be more proficient in

- Analyzing information,
- Synthesizing data into actionable activities and
- Communicating information.

To some extent, businesses care much more about the softer skills than they have in the past, and the expectation is that graduates understand this and are proficient in many of the skills that in the past have generally taken experience to hone to perfection. According to a senior consumer products financial executive "it is really more of a combination of having the requisite hard skills and being able to effectively communicate key messages with strong soft skills".

Hard skills are defined as the specific procedural skills and technical expertise that are required to perform a job or more aptly put the 'what' needs to be done. These skills are clearly listed in the job description and are acquired through more highly specific education and training programs. Hard skills are the skills we think of when considering a professional college degree. Examples include accountants must have accounting degrees, lawyers must have law degrees, doctors must have medical degrees and so on. But does that mean that these professionals do not need soft skills? We think not, in fact these soft attributes, or the 'how' something is done, are equally critical and allow professionals to thrive in the interpersonal service orientated economy faced daily. Which is why modern businesses are looking for accounting graduates with a good mix of hard and soft skills as they enter the workforce.

Universities are generally more geared towards educating the hard skills, which are easier to teach and easier to measure success than soft skills are. However, the importance of developing hard skills and using them in conjunction with such soft skills as critical thinking, analysis and data synthesis cannot be underestimated. As a full-service outsourced provider senior financial IT executive told us, "Use and understanding of systems is critical, the staff needs to have an in-depth understanding of end-to-end business operations and the related accounting and financial planning and analysis. Understanding of data manipulation and data interrogation is very important. Including a good understanding of forensic accounting and interaction of different systems and system elements in an ERP system."

For accountants, these hard-technical skills include knowledge-based tasks such as, preparing financial statements, recording financial information, and demonstrating strong data based analytical capabilities. In the past these were the skills that employers sought when hiring college graduates because graduates needed to possess at least a base level of understanding to do the job. Further driving this was the need to have accountants perform manually intensive tasks. However, with the continuing sophistication of business-related technology, the technical aspects of accounting specifically have become less important. Not because the output is not needed but because the ability to generate information and the ready availability of data are so much easier to gather than it was in the past. Therefore, t these types of skills are less critical. Consequently, as certain technical skills become automated, businesses demand more of the higher order skills that include critical thinking and information synthesis. This puts the accounting profession into a conundrum because regardless of the sophistication of accounting reporting software, professionals need to understand the basic building blocks of accounting to understand the interaction of data and its impact on understanding business. The soft skills demanded in the business world can be broken into two broad categories, Communications and Management which we explore below.

THE SO-CALLED SOFT GAPS

Communication

Communication in itself may be too broad of a category as many executives look at it as a combination of verbal and written skills as well as presentation abilities. Communication more specifically defined relates to the ability to effectively inform, influence, persuade and drive decision making. The ability to communicate effectively is extremely important in the business world made more complicated by the growth of social media. The advent of social media communication has only made the ability to get a message across clearly even more critical. Everyone, regardless of their level or position, is representing the company on a continuous basis and is why businesses place a high value on effective, clear, and positive communications skills.

Learning to communicate well should be a top priority for anyone aspiring to lead or advance in a career. Strong technical skills are needed, but technical ability alone will not result in career advancement. Those who develop only technical skills always will work for people who have both technical and leadership abilities, and communication is the key ingredient in leadership as indicated by Hugh B. Jacks, former president, BellSouth Services. (Himstreet, Baty, & Lehman 1993)

The increased focus on representing the business makes effective communication skills apply equally to communication of data analysis in written reports, verbal updates, as well as board presentations. As a financial services financial executive told us, "While the ability to effectively communicate has been a mainstay for accountants and auditors, the use of data has created complex and hard to understand technological terms that need to be better put into clear, concise, understandable terms for non-technical audiences to understand and act upon." Business expects all employees to represent them in a professional and positive manner regardless of level.

Verbal

As the old expression goes, "you only get one chance to make a good first impression." Businesses expect staff to present themselves verbally in a professional and amicable manner. This is probably the easiest positive communication vehicle to master and is first demonstrated during the interview process. It is true that it is extremely personality driven but that does not mean that you are not expected to exhibit positive social norms when having a formal or informal discussion in a business or a social business setting. The idea that you are never off from work when dealing with your peers, friends and even family may sound a bit extreme, but the reality is new hires are expected to represent the company positively in all social interactions. We are all expected to represent ourselves in a professional manner in at all times.

Written

Much has changed with respect to written communication which makes it a more rather than less of a skill to demonstrate in the world of business. This is especially important when communicating via electronic means. It is not a secret that electronic miscommunications can be damaging to a business from all perspectives. It is not just that they can be misconstrued but that they can be easily transmitted to a broad audience internally or externally and damage a company's reputation or even merely misrepresent their position on a specific issue. Today's college graduates, to some extent, are the riskiest from a business reputation perspective as they are more comfortable with living their lives on-line and communicate on social media regularly and in an informal manner. Communications on social media, by their very nature, are less formal and usually not subject to any type of business-like review before they are available in the world for everyone to see. Additionally, much of the formality that traditionally existed in business and societal interactions has significantly changed. Gone are the days of addressing co-workers, let alone partners, as Mister or Miss. We work on a first name basis and have further evolved to where experience and rank confer no privilege. Consequently, newly minted college graduates' adherence to company policies is important to help ensure that new staff are successfully integrated into the company.

Written communication, outside of email, may be much less frequent than in the past, which makes management's focus on strong writing skills even more critical. A senior financial executive in a major financial services company was extremely critical of the academic output and he said, "Communication challenges exist amongst all new staff especially with respect to business and technical writing. The colleges would be better off if they dropped English literature classes and added a business writing class."

The premise is simple, written communications are more formal and need to be constructed in grammatically correct form in proper English and clearly understood. The proliferation of social media, including texting and, to a considerable extent email communication, has caused students to be very lax in using proper grammar, including treat emojis as acceptable business communication. This may work in some industries but, for the most part businesspeople in any industry expect clear, concise, professional, easy to read and informative messages using appropriate formality.

Email, texting and social media communications are also riskier from a legal perspective. Email and other electronic communications can never effectively be permanently deleted. In many ways it is the way these types of communications are viewed and managed that increases the associated risks. Some may view their messages as informal and do not see them as official messages from a company they represent. Unfortunately, in the court of public opinion all of an individual's messaging is automatically attributed as some type of official message from the related company. Letters, memos, reports issued are considered formal and are subject to review and management oversight before they are issued outside a company or even an organization. This level of review is highly effective in ensuring that a company is not misinterpreted or merely just embarrassed by a communication. In our litigious society an errant message communicated broadly can easily turn into a costly lawsuit as well as negatively impact a career or two. Students entering the workforce may need to change their communications behavior to conform to business norms and businesspeople hiring college graduates expect these individuals to have this level of professionalism as they enter the workforce.

Presentations

Business is about making decisions and making those decisions with the appropriate data necessary to weigh all the different competing options available. Many decisions are based on project-based efforts that require a substantial amount of objective and subjective data analysis. Presentations are effective mechanisms for providing management with the ability to make decisions without being forced to pour through the myriad of details necessary to make the decision. Presenting is no longer an optional business management activity especially for accounting professionals.

Presentation style is very personal and a professional's ability to present improves over time. Colleges and universities need to increase their efforts to allow their students to graduate with strong presentation skills with the focus not being on the materials themselves but how well they were presented and what level of informing, persuading, and decisioning they achieved. Much of this comes with practice and critical analysis provided to the students to drive their growth. A prominent CFO told us "Staff is weak in synthesizing various levels of information into a coherent package. Understanding how operational issues can be surfaced with a better understanding of how various bits of data and other information can be pieced together." Young professionals must know their talking points and not rely on reading as a crutch for a presentation.

Presentations are merely stories developed to facilitate decision making and the skill of presenting is the culmination of supporting a position and can also be used to spur discussion driving to a decision. The new staff's presentation ability must include the analysis efforts necessary to drive a position home. The presenter must be an advocate for the position taken, consequently the level of support for a presentation is substantially higher than the information presented. A prominent CFO told us "Staff is weak in synthesizing various levels of information into a coherent package. Understanding how operational issues can be surfaced with a better understanding of how various bits of data and other information can be pieced together. They need to understand how to tell a story with Powerpoint without reading from the slides. Structure and style are important or you can lose the message and the audience."

The presenter should be close to a subject matter expert in the position of the presentation to make their points succinctly in an engaging manner. A key element of all presentations is the ability of the presenter to answer questions of the audience accurately. Research skills that accompany presentations are also important to be highlighted in a university setting.

Management

As noted previously the ability to obtain and summarize data has become much easier with the advent of advanced software functionality. Consequently, this ability is assumed to be present allowing businesses to expect more advanced management skills from new graduates. Management skills such as critical thinking and professional skepticism are expected from graduates right out of the box. In addition, accounting professionals are viewed as potential future managers in financial and operational roles so they are expected to have inherent leadership skills that will become important later in their career as their responsibilities increase.

Critical Thinking

Critical thinking is a higher level of thought expected to help businesspeople dissect business issues into their core components to allow for incisive analysis that address business issues. It is goal orientated, and strong critical thinkers use their skills for problem solving and identifying creative solutions to issues through all aspects of business and business operations. Critical thinking is especially helpful in a business setting where dynamism is the order of the day. There are always many solutions to issues at hand and critical thinking helps a professional surface the best solutions by thinking through problems and being willing to consider many strategies before deciding on the proper course of action. Nothing is taken for granted when presented with a problem. Critical thinking starts with an in-depth assessment of the problem definition to allow the company to identify root causes to increase the possibility of devising a winning solution. The methodology allows all possibilities to be considered in devising viable solutions.

Accounting professionals are accustomed to correlating information attained throughout the company and even the economy to identify threats and opportunities. For example, financial planning and analysis groups found in all public corporations must synthesize varying bits of information to help a company chart a course for success in their normal course of business. Critical thinking business practices live in the three highest levels of Blooms Taxonomy where the application of higher-level thinking can help a company address its problems and meet its goals; namely: analysis, synthesis, and evaluation (see figure below).

Figure 3. Levels of Blooms taxonomy[1]

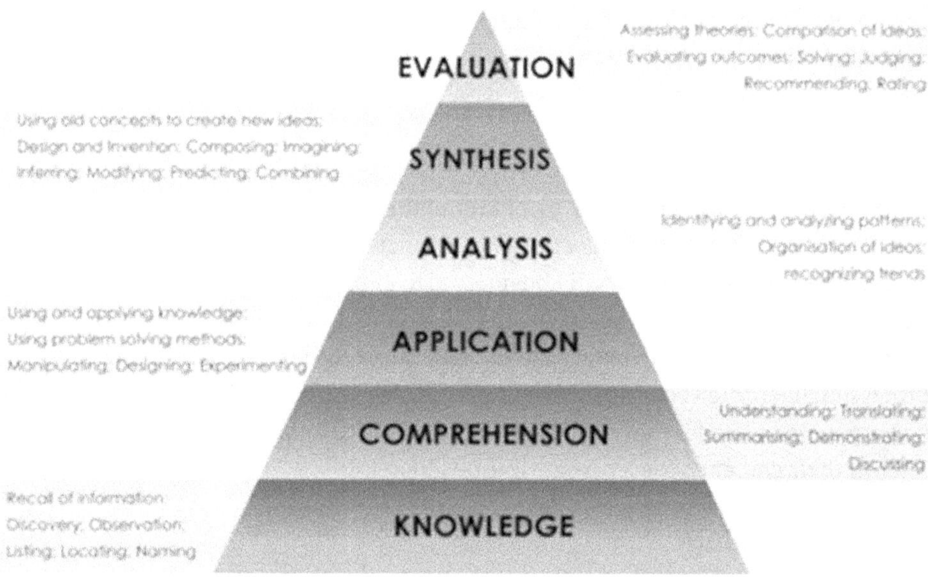

Professional Skepticism

Perhaps one of the most well-known soft skills attributed to accountants and auditors is professional skepticism. In auditing the concept is well ingrained into the auditor's day to day operations but also is a skill that internal financial and management accountants must possess. Accountants and auditors, by the nature of the work and the standards they follow, are more skeptical than others because they see more situations where business partners may want to slant the presentation of information to support their position. The professional standards define professional skepticism as "an attitude that includes a questioning mind, being alert to conditions that may indicate possible misstatement due to fraud or error, and a critical assessment of audit evidence." Clearly a nebulous concept that cannot be easily measured and can take some time to perfect. [2]

True it is a skill that can be improved upon through experience, but businesspeople do expect newly graduated accountants to be adept in this regard. The perception is important, and it has its roots in understanding that professional skepticism comes from a position of knowledge and analysis ability. In many ways one of the pillars of skills necessary to help ensure that financial reporting is accurate and properly depicts the results of a company. In the application of this skill, we tend to view professional skepticism as an attribute that people with good street smarts can learn to implement in a business framework. In this world of the proliferation of information, whether the information be accurate or not, in the many aspects of our expanding eWorld it is important that logic be applied to data and data driven conclusions.

Professional skepticism is considered a soft skill because the effect challenges the veracity of someone's assertion; so, diplomacy must be exercised as well as being open to discussing the issue in more depth. It is one of the challenging skills to expect from a recent college graduate because students are more likely than now fed the educational truth in their studies. For graduates to be effective using professional correlate disparate pieces of data to connect the dots and ensure the information is providing a consistent response. Professional skepticism is the practical application of critical thinking. and is a high order skill that encompasses different attributes such as analysis, synthesis, and logic, The appropriate use of professional skepticism leads to a proper evaluation for a critical decision.

Leadership

Increasing business complexity has been changing the scope of the responsibilities of the Chief Financial Officer (CFO) to take on functions that in the past were the purview of the Chief Operations Officer. These increased responsibilities are more cross functional, and they require strong management and leadership skills to be effective. Companies expect their future leaders to come through their financial and accounting departments as they develop broad experience in diverse areas of finance, accounting, and operations throughout their career. The recognition of the importance and skill set of financial organizations will resonate when developing staff requirements and recruiting for accounting graduates. Companies recognize that new graduates may not have the skills necessary for management yet, but there is an expectation that the graduates are more organized, analytical and have teamwork skills. Identifying budding leadership skills in inexperienced staff is both a desirable and challenging task.

Graduates may not have enough experience to demonstrate strong leadership skills yet but there are promising attributes that businesses seek and expect students to have developed during their college years. These attributes include: the ability and willingness to ask questions, effective time management skills, using prioritization to multi-task and meet goals and objectives and a thirst for learning exhibited through curiosity and willingness to take on new tasks.

Willingness to Ask Questions

The confidence to ask questions demonstrates a questioning mind that helps to identify someone that seeks to learn, grow, and have an open mind to developing solutions. Confidence is critical for future leaders and when considered with the associated learning of profound issues, the ability to question is a skill that business want to foster. The ability can help identify those that are open to innovative ideas and is necessary in business's changing risks and opportunities.

Time Management Skills

Many new staff have difficulty managing their time and may have little experience in doing so. However, students that are competent in time management may point to employment experience while attending college or participation in extracurricular activities such as student chapters in professional organizations and athletics Such students have already begun to master the skill of juggling conflicting priorities. Time management is critical for future leaders dealing with satisfying many internal and external constituents and stakeholders that are all subject to well-defined timelines and deadlines.

Prioritization

Prioritization is a skill that is intricately linked with strong time management skills but comprises the culmination of all of Bloom's Taxonomy to the top of the pyramid at the evaluation level. To prioritize which project or objective to focus on in real time manner is necessary to judge the immediacy, importance, and associated efforts necessary to deliver on objectives. Prioritization is a skill that full-time students must develop to ensure that they meet the overlapping demands of all their professors.

Thirst for Learning

Business is about learning and applying what you have learned to help a company meet its goals or objectives. This can be demonstrated using learning to apply innovative technology or through the application of external current events into the business environment. Intellectual curiosity is a key driver for those that have a true thirst for learning. High grades inherently demonstrate that students are good at learning, but curiosity demonstrates that they are willing to understand the concepts behind the facts. The importance of the drive to learn cannot be understated because for successful people the learning does not stop, and that is what businesses seek. When individuals rise to the top of their peer group, they drive companies to attain their greatest success. Finance organizations are seen as change agents and therefore must be at the forefront of new concepts whether they be technology related or not.

Technology Gaps

This is a gap that has been identified by industry for quite some time and is inherent in the speed of innovation in this age of technological change spurred on by business' constant objective to reduce costs and enhance overall efficiencies. The demands from business are no longer limited being adept at spreadsheet software and use of popular Enterprise Resource and Planning Systems. There is greater emphasis on understanding and utilizing sophisticated data bases, data visualization, and mechanized process improvement systems and applications. The greatest difficulty from an academic perspective is to balance education amongst data analysis and information technology structure and controls with application of technology products commonly used in business. Future discussions could analyze in depth the educational gap in technology in the following areas:

- Data analysis tools and techniques such as Excel, BI Computing and Alteryx
- Data visualization from simple excel charts to more sophisticated tools
- Process driven automation tools including Robotic Process Automation, BlockChain, Artificial Intelligence, Machine Learning, and the top Enterprise Resource Planning Systems

CONCLUSION

As the old expression goes, the only constant in life is change is inevitable. The changes in society, technology, and business forces us all to be better educated and be able to change and to maximize our potential for success. The world has grown smaller due to globalization and the competition for good career-based jobs has become fiercer as technology takes over some of the more mechanical tasks off the staff's hands. These changes force us all to strengthen soft skills to succeed, including critical thinking, professional skepticism, communication skills and to skillfully synthesize disparate pieces of data into decision making information. Academia works closer with industry to have more interaction to drive teaching topics, internships through increased presentations from businesspeople that further solidify the needs that business people demand from new graduates.

REFERENCES

Albrecht, W., & Sack, R. (2001). The Perilous Future of Accounting Education. *The CPA Journal*, (March), 18.

Beard, D., Schwieger, D., & Surendran, K. (2008). Integrating Soft Skills Assessment through University, College and Programmatic Efforts at an AACBSB Accredited Institution. *Journal of Information Systems Education, 19*(2).

Gabbin, A. (2019) Warning Signs about the Future Supply of Accounting Graduates. *The CPA Journal.*

Himstreet, W., Baty, W., & Lehman, C. (1993). Business Communications: Principles and Methods, PWS-Kent Publishing.

Koncz & Collins. (2007) *News for Media Professionals*. NACEWeb. http://www.naceweb.org/press/display.asp?year=2007&pri d=270.

Ovaska-Few, S. (2017) What large firms expect from new accounting grads? *Journal of Accountancy*. https://www.journalofaccountancy.com/issues/2017/mar

KEY TERMS AND DEFINITIONS

Bloom's Taxonomy: A hierarchy of skills that define and distinguish different levels of cognition.

Emoji: A pictogram, logogram, ideogram, or smiley representation used in written communications.

Functional Area: Typical organization structure of a business.

Hard Skills: Skills that focus on specific procedural skills and technical expertise.

Knowledge-Based Tasks: Tasks that require specific and specialized knowledge for completion.

Soft Skills: Non-technology skills. Skills that are typically focused on communication, analysis, and organizational.

Training: Additional learning that fills the gap between education obtained from an institution of higher learning to an understanding of specific procedures and processes necessary utilized by a specific employer.

ENDNOTES

1 Image Source: Armstrong, P. (2010). Bloom's Taxonomy. Vanderbilt University Center for Teaching. Retrieved from https://cft.vanderbilt.edu/guides-sub-pages/blooms-taxonomy/

2 See https://pcaobus.org/oversight/standards/archived-standards/pre-reorganized-auditing-standards-interpretations/details/AU316_13

Chapter 11
Can Accounting Programs at Smaller Universities Survive?

Cynthia Scarinci
CUNY College of Staten Island, USA

Mark Martinelli
Synchrony Bank, USA

ABSTRACT

The accounting profession has undergone a major transformation, and while the academic community does its best to educate students and provide them with the core competencies required to ultimately achieve success in the profession, the traditional "tool kit" is in need of updating. The speed of change and the ever-increasing demands of business have further widened the expectations gap on newly graduated students' skills and on the universities that are preparing them for their careers. Larger universities have successfully addressed this issue by partnering with public accounting firms. While these collaborations have proven to be very effective for the students at larger and more established universities, smaller programs without such access are at a disadvantage. The road ahead for smaller accounting programs is going to be a challenging one, but creativity and outreach are the keys.

INTRODUCTION

The accounting profession has undergone a major transformation, and while the academic community does its best to educate students and provide them with the core competencies required to ultimately achieve success in the profession, the traditional "tool kit" that has succeeded for decades is in need of updating. The

DOI: 10.4018/978-1-6684-5483-1.ch011

Copyright © 2023, IGI Global. Copying or distributing in print or electronic forms without written permission of IGI Global is prohibited.

speed of change and the ever-increasing demands of business have further widened the expectations gap on newly graduated students' skills and on the universities that are preparing them for their careers.

CPAs today require a varied technical skill set that includes analytical abilities, IT aptitude, digital savvy, and social intelligence. The academic community may be able to provide expertise in some areas, but the rapid pace of change, combined with limited financial and faculty resources, makes this process extremely challenging and in the long term untenable. While faculty can update their skills and the curriculum, the process is lengthy, costly, and time-consuming.

Larger universities have successfully addressed this issue by partnering with public accounting firms. These firms call upon the skills of specialists that provide collaborative learning experiences for the students in the program and ultimately provide career opportunities benefiting the students, the firms, and in the longer-term the profession. Others call upon the talents of alumni or the local business community as guest lecturers, mentors, advisors, and financial supporters.

While these collaborations have proven to be very effective for the students at larger and more established universities, those without such access are at a competitive disadvantage. The result is that students at smaller universities have greater difficulty in obtaining the required skills and ultimately placement in accounting and related financial positions. Another longer tailed consequence is that the number of students enrolling in accounting programs in such institutions is on the decline further impacting the smaller universities revenues and ability to compete.

The Downward Trend

Based on a search at collegefactual.com, on a nation-wide basis, there are a little over 1,000 colleges/universities of various enrollment sizes offering bachelor's degree programs in Accounting. (Collegefactual.com 2022)[1] Many of these programs have been facing growing struggles with student enrollment. Unfortunately, the AICPA 2021 Accounting Trends Report has revealed some daunting statistics. Accounting degree completions have been on a downward trend since 2016. The 2019–2020 academic year revealed additional decreases of 2.8%. Thirty-nine percent of the respondents to the Accounting Trends survey anticipate future enrollment to continue the downward trend, with 62% of universities offering accounting programs indicating that they do not offer accounting specializations.[2] With the advent of the CPA Evolution process and the introduction of three disciplines, this is of major concern, specifically for smaller accounting programs.

The report also indicated that the total hiring of accounting undergraduates has decreased by 10%. In many instances, CPA firms have been hiring both accounting and non-accounting undergraduates to fill positions that were traditionally held by accounting majors. In comparing 2022 to 2021, the survey respondents indicated that they anticipate the number of non-CPA professional staff hired into accounting/finance functions to increase by 37%, while 49% indicated that they would hire the same number of non-accountants as they did in 2021.[2]

Naturally, this downward trend in the number of accounting graduates and potential employment is having an impact on the accounting programs in universities throughout the country. Unfortunately, the smaller accounting programs are the ones who will bear the brunt of this downward spiral, as they are the ones with the fewest students, faculty and resources.

What do the Enrollment Numbers Say?

Table 1 presents enrollment trends for accounting degrees completed by U.S. institutional size over a five-year period. The data were compiled from The Integrated Postseconday Education Data System (IPEDS), which is the data collection program for the National Center for Education Statistics.[3] The data present degrees completed by institution size measured by enrollment size; Panel 1 represents all degrees completed by year, which include associate, bachelor, and master's degrees in the accounting discipline. Panel 1 presents the data for only bachelor's degrees.

Panel 1 shows that for all institutions, degrees completed declined from 78,446 in 2017 to 72,396 or 7.7% in 2021. Panel 1 confirms that the smaller institutions sustained the most significant declines completed from 2017 to 2021 of 13.7% and 14.8%, respectively for Group 1 and Group 2 institutions. It is important to note that these categories represent mostly private institutions (not tabulated); Group 3, which represents mostly public institutions, sustained a 3.9% decline for all degrees completed within its group from 2017 to 2021. As a percentage of total degrees completed in the years 2017 and 2021, respectively, Group 1 and Group 2 degrees declined by 3% (37% vs. 34%). That loss was absorbed by Group 1, which increased by 3% (63% vs. 66%). Group 1 and Group 2 represent approximately 77% or 820 of institutions awarding all degrees; Group 3 represents approximately 23% or 250 of all degrees completed. Overall, although there are significantly more institutions with less than 10,000 students enrolled (820), they represented only slightly more than one-third of the degrees awarded during the years 2017 through 2021. In spite of their volume, institutions with less than 10,000 students enrolled sustained significant declines in awarding associate, bachelor, and master's degrees.

A closer look at the degrees completed is presented in Panel 2, which presents comparable data for the bachelor degree, which is considered the pipeline to the profession. Overall, all institutions sustained a 6% decline in degrees competed from 2017 to 2021. Most of that decline is attributable to Group 1 and Group 2, representing 12.8% and 14.9%, respectively, declines within their group. Group

3 barely declined by 1.1% within its group from 2017 to 2021. The percentage of degrees awarded still reflects about a one-third, two-thirds split between Groups 1 and 2 verses Group 3 despite significantly more institutions in the Group 1 and Group 2 categories. Overall, the data presented in Table 1 signals that the smaller institutions, despite of their dominance in volume, are the most vulnerable to the challenge of declining enrollments in the accounting discipline. That vulnerability may be further exacerbated by the challenges CPA Evolution presents to curricula development.

Reasons for Decreased Enrollment

Naturally, the first step in developing the solution to this dilemma is to identify the reasons for the downward trend in the accounting enrollment. The Illinois CPA Society conducted a survey of accounting students, graduates, and accounting professionals under the age of 35. The results of their survey revealed that approximately one third of the respondents did not see the CPA credential as offering value to their careers. A little less than a third indicated that prospective employers do not

Table 1(a). Number of accounting degrees completed by institutions

	Number of Accounting Degrees Completed by Institutions										
Panel 1: All degrees	**2021**	**2020**	**2019**	**2018**	**2017**	**2021 vs. 2017**	**No. of Institutions**	**Percentage of Institutions**	**Percentage of Degrees 2017**	**Percentage of degrees 2021**	**Change in Percentage of degrees**
Group 1 less than 5000	13,953	14,624	15,548	16,229	16,169	-13.7%	641	59.9%	20.6%	19.3%	-1.3%
Group 2 5000-9999	10,987	11,606	11,864	12,521	12,892	-14.8%	179	16.7%	16.4%	15.2%	-1.3%
Subtotal less than 10000	**24,940**	**26,230**	**27,412**	**28,750**	**29,061**	-14.2%	**820**	**76.6%**	**37.0%**	**34.4%**	**-2.6%**
Group 3 greater than 9999	47,456	48,267	49,159	49,606	49,385	-3.9%	250	23.4%	63.0%	65.6%	2.6%
Total all institutions	**72,396**	**74,497**	**76,571**	**78,356**	**78,446**	**-7.7%**	**1,070**	**100.0%**	**100.0%**	**100.0%**	**0.0%**
Group 1 and 2 to total	34%	35%	36%	37%	37%						
Group 3 to total	66%	65%	64%	63%	63%						

Table 1(b). Number of accounting degrees completed by institutions

Panel 2: Bachelor's only	2021	2020	2019	2018	2017	2021 vs. 2017	No. of Institutions	Percentage of Institutions	Percentage of Degrees 2017	Percentage of Degrees 2021	Change in Percentage of degrees
Group 1 less than 5000	9,022	9,540	10,028	10,343	10,351	-12.8%	641	59.9%	21.1%	19.6%	-1.5%
Group 2 5000-9999	7,235	7,637	7,864	8,341	8,505	-14.9%	179	16.7%	17.3%	15.7%	-1.7%
Subtotal less than 10000	**16,257**	**17,177**	**17,892**	**18,684**	**18,856**	-13.8%	**820**	**76.6%**	**38.4%**	**35.2%**	**-3.2%**
Group 3 greater than 9999	29,874	30,306	30,067	30,247	30,210	-1.1%	250	23.4%	61.6%	65%	3.2%
Total all institutions	**46,131**	**47,483**	**47,959**	**48,931**	**49,066**	**-6.0%**	**1,070**	**100.0%**	**100.0%**	**100.0%**	**0.0%**
Group 1 and 2 to total	35%	36%	37%	38%	38%						
Group 3 to total	65%	64%	63%	62%	62%						

require the credentials or support it, and that other credentials would potentially be more valuable to their careers.[4] With the embedding of technology in everyday accounting and finance processes, increasingly employers are looking for newly branded technology certifications in cloud and web services such as Amazon Web Services Cloud Practitioner, cybersecurity and network certifications (e.g., Certified Information Security Manager) as well as graduate degrees specific to data sciences and specialized programming. Additionally, other more specialized certifications are being pursued by accountants and auditors in the non–public accounting sector that are further crowding the once impregnable CPA certification domain. These include the Certified Internal Auditor (CIA) accreditation, the Certified Fraud Examiner (CFE) and the Certified Anti-Money Laundering accreditation (CAMS). These non-financial certifications are gaining prominence as employers are looking for a higher degree of specialization and industry expertise that are also driven by regulatory expectation.[5]

The 150-credit hour requirement added another barrier in the road to CPA licensure. The introduction of this requirement increased coursework and reduced the experience requirement in most states to one year. It was anticipated that most students would obtain a master's degree in an area of specialization like tax or information technology, to complement their accounting degree. Some universities introduced a 5-year program where their students would graduate with a bachelor's and master's Degree. The difficulty is that some smaller institutions may not have the resources nor the funding to develop such a program. Additionally, students relying on financial aid were impacted, because, other than student loans, government financial aid that is typically available for undergraduate studies, cannot be obtained for advanced degrees. To meet the 150-credit requirement, some students take the 30 credits in additional undergraduate courses. It should be noted that because there are no specifics on the type of courses needed to fulfill this requirement, students are at liberty to take 30 credits in any courses they wish, business-related or not. In smaller institutions with fewer course offerings, students have even fewer options for these credits. The 150-credit hour requirement increased the amount of time accounting students are in school and not earning money. Students majoring in Finance, Data Analytics and Information Technology are also hired by CPA firms after completing only 120 credits (depending on the institution) thus the appeal of the accounting program is waning.

To make matters worse, Maurer (2020) highlight the fact that in 2019 only a little over a third of CFOs of the largest public companies in the United States, are CPAs. Additionally, in many accounting firms, highly prestigious roles are often held by individuals who are CISAs and not CPAs. Lastly, the push to institute non-CPA ownership in CPA firms is further diluting the reverence for the profession AICPA (2012)[6].

Large Universities Partnering With Big 4 Accounting Firms

To ensure that students are obtaining the skills required to contribute effectively, once they enter the workforce, the larger public accounting firms are collaborating with larger universities. These collaborations have proven to be extremely effective in providing students with the education required to successfully complete the CPA exam, as well as helping them to hone a skillset that will serve them as accounting professionals. The following is a synopsis of the programs offered by the Big 4 in collaboration with select universities. The form of the programs varies, but the objectives are the same.

KPMG

The Villanova School of Business joined forces with KPMG in establishing the KPMG Master of Accounting with Data and Analytics Program. According to Joyce E. A. Russell, PhD, Dean of the Helen and William O'Toole Villanova

School of Business (VSB), "It is important for the nation's top universities and companies to work together to properly prepare our students to become effective future business leaders. VSB is proud to join with KPMG to provide these students with the tax knowledge and experience necessary to make an immediate positive impact." The program allows for selected accounting students to earn a tuition free master's degree, while enjoying free room and board. Students participate in a fully integrated curriculum of accounting, tax, and audit, and they are provided the opportunity to utilize technologies used at the firm to solidify their skills in analytics. While obtaining their education, students are provided with an internship opportunity during summer and winter sessions to gain real-world experience from their future employer. This makes for a much smoother transition into the workplace because KPMG offers these students full time employment upon their successful completion of the program. The person who spearheaded this initiative is alumnus Roger O'Donnell of KPMG. According to O'Donnell, "This program is changing the paradigm of how we're looking at recruiting." KPMG has established similar programs at the Ohio State University's Max M. Fisher College of Business, as well as another 7 other universities nationwide. Recently, KPMG has expanded their partnerships with international schools of higher education (see https://kpmg.com/uk/en/home/services/kpmg-alliances/university-partnerships/kpmg-and-university-academy-92.html and https://www.accountingtoday.com/opinion/kpmg-announces-data-and-analytics-masters-programs-with-ohio-state-university-and-villanova).

Deloitte

Similarly, Deloitte has partnered with several universities. According to Deloitte's website, "Our University Program focuses on preparing the best and brightest young people to drive innovation in business analytics theory, perform cutting-edge analytics research, and create tomorrow's solutions today." These institutions include, The University of Maryland's (UMD) Robert H. Smith School of Business which has created a Business Analytics Consortium, The Wharton School of the University of Pennsylvania, The Pamplin College Center for Business Intelligence and Analytics, The University of Virginia's McIntire School of Commerce which launched the Center for Business Analytics, The Institute for Business Analytics (IBA) at Indiana University's Kelley School of Business and The University of Texas McCombs School of Business which developed a Master's degree concentrating on Business Analytics. Deloitte has agreed to provide resources, mentoring, internship, and employment opportunities for students through specific agreements made with each of the universities.

PwC

PwC has collaborated with Northeastern University to create the *While You Work* fellowship, whereby PwC fully subsidizes a one-year fully online master's degree program for selected college seniors and students who recently graduated. The Master of Science, earned by these students focuses on a concentration in accounting analytics. The program is targeted for minority students, to increase opportunities in public accounting. As a fellow, these students work part-time and earn a salary at PwC. Upon successful completion of this program, there is the possibility of full-time employment at PwC. Additionally, PWC has partnered with the University of Binghamton School of Management through a funded PWC Scholars Program (see https://www.binghamton.edu/som/scholars/index.html).

In a very significant initiative with Saint Peter's College in New Jersey, PWC established a 30 credit post-bachelorette program whereby work experience at PWC will enable accounting students to earn the necessary credits to be licensed through a work for credit program. The program, which has been approved by the State Board of New Jersey (see https://www.njconsumeraffairs.gov/acc/Minutes/accountancy-minutes-051922.pdf), is currently the only CPA licensing jurisdiction that allows the work for credit program as an alternative path to CPA licensure (see https://www.saintpeters.edu/news/2022/10/06/saint-peters-university-establishes-pilot-program-for-accounting-students/).

EY

The 150-credit hour requirement to earn CPA licensure is a hurdle many aspiring CPAs face. EY created the EY Career Path Accelerator, a hands-on program providing accredited business and elective post-baccalaureate courses, to help remove this barrier. The EY program is partnered with Hult International Business School. The program equips learners with future skills and subject matter knowledge necessary to attain CPA licensure eligibility (see https://techrseries.com/career-development/ey-launches-career-path-accelerator-to-eliminate-the-barriers-to-entry-and-enhance-talent-diversity-in-the-accounting-profession/).

AICPA Recent Initiatives

The AICPA has initiated an aggressive plan to enhance the pool of candidates to the CPA pipeline. Specifically, the plan involves a united effort from stakeholders that include the profession, academia, state societies, and state boards. The plan includes recommendations not previously considered such as, expand college education savings plans for CPA -related exam costs, collaborate with state and local government officials for hiring best practices in the public sector and similarly for offshore talent, and improve CPA branding especially to middle and high school students (AICPA 2023).

What Can Smaller Programs Do to Survive?

Naturally, it is difficult for smaller universities to compete with these collaborative programs. According to Dr. Katherine Newman, Provost of University of Massachusetts Amherst and Senior Vice-Chancellor for Academic Affairs, "The northeast of the US has the densest number of higher education institutions and the fastest population decline. It's the worst combination. We are already seeing the collapse of the smaller, less-endowed, private institutions."[7] Some universities will need to scale back the number of courses offered, do not replace retiring professors and substitute retirees with less costly adjunct faculty. At a minimum, these scenarios could potentially negatively impact the learning experience of accounting students and at worst, deter new college level students from choosing accountancy as a course of study.

Resource and Budget Constraints

Most higher learning institutions struggle with resource and budget constraints, but smaller universities are at a considerable disadvantage, often. They have fewer, if any, endowments, and less alumni, making it difficult to supplement funding for accounting program improvements. Naturally, as enrollment continues to decline, further budget strains persist. CPA Evolution will require broad range program changes, but limited faculty and other resources will make it difficult to make effective changes. Smaller programs are tasked with identifying their available options if their programs are to survive.

Impact of Online Education

Online education has transformed the educational landscape and has accelerated during the pandemic. With most universities offering online courses to the masses, the smaller universities are further challenged to compete. The ease of participating in an online course, particularly those conducted asynchronously may be more appealing to potential students; yet, still require additional resources to deliver. In 2017, Harvard Business School professor Clayton Christensen predicted that, of the total 4,000 colleges and universities in the United States, more than half will file for bankruptcy. In addition, his belief is that "online education will become a more cost-effective way for students to receive an education, effectively undermining the business models of traditional institutions and running them out of business."[8]

While this presents a very bleak view of the future, Christensen's research also revealed that successful students who donated to their alma maters did so because of a connection with a faculty member. This "ability to change their (students) lives"[6] leaves a lasting impact (Hess 2017). This is where smaller institutions may have a tangible advantage. In smaller programs, with smaller classes, it is conducive to interact with students as individuals and thus create life-long connections.

Visiting Experts/Alumni

Many universities are calling upon their alumni to take on the role of Guest Lecturers to share their expertise with students. Some of these guest lecturers will teach a course for an entire semester, whereas others will teach a specific topic in a course. This has proven to be extremely successful because these lecturers provide "state of the art" real-time experience that would otherwise be missing from the curriculum. It also provides students with professional contacts outside of the university. Guest lecturers are alumni, who are dedicated to assist the university and its current student base. Alumni guest lectures provide a source for internship and employment opportunities, as well.

While alumni are an excellent resource, in smaller or commuter schools, alumni may not be as connected to their alma mater; therefore, making these arrangements a bit more difficult to establish and thereafter maintain. The other challenge is that more recent graduates are preferable because they can better relate to students. Unfortunately, the recent grads are challenged by limited time availability. The demands of public accounting are intense, leaving many employees trying their best to manage what little time they must focus on passing the CPA exam. If alumni do return as guest lecturers, their participation may be limited to a single class. While this is helpful, it is more productive if alumni can recurringly serve as adjuncts allowing for alumni/student connections to solidify. Creative arrangements could be made between an alumnus firm and the university whereby the employee/alumnus is paid by the firm to teach or is given time away from the office to donate their time to their alma mater. Although such a program is not as expansive as the programs the Big 4 university partnerships, it could give the smaller accounting programs the assistance that they need to compete.

Local CPA Firms, Businesses, Government Agencies

Another source for guest lecturers is local CPA firms, businesses, and governmental agencies. Students are always reminded that careers in accounting are not limited to public accounting. Demand for internal audit have continued to grow post the 2008 financial crisis.[9]

Guest lecturers from different career paths provide insights into a variety of skillsets and introduce students to career options that they may not have considered. While time limitation is always a consideration, if the guest lecturer works locally, time constraints become less of an issue. In addition, many firms and businesses are happy to provide some sort of community outreach. Again, it enables students to connect with individuals in their chosen profession for mentoring and employment opportunities. The advent and acceptance of videoconferencing for working and teaching provides an avenue for having guest speakers and professors provide remote capabilities that will reduce the need for in-person lectures and professors. This will add versatility in finding and accommodating tight time schedules and assist the smaller universities in finding speakers who will no longer be exclusively bound with in- classroom presence.

Retired CPA Firm Members

CPA's who have retired from the profession could be welcomed additions to university faculty. Their years of experience and relationship with their former firm and its employees make them an invaluable resource. Retired CPAs are often looking to find ways to give back to their communities and their alma mater. Moreover, their change in lifestyle from working full time to being retired presents them with a need to find fulfilling ways to remain productive. They can provide a great deal of insight and many times offer recommendations on how to modify curriculum to address both current and emerging skills gap. If they have the financial resources, smaller institutions hiring retired firm members is one allows competitiveness with a larger university. In lieu of hiring, the retired CPA may be able to consult with the university to offer suggestions and alternatives to keep their programs sustainable. This is often done through accounting department advisory boards or committees that are formed through connections the universities' deans and accounting professors have with alumni or local businesspeople.

These boards serve as a departmental think tank, providing formal and informal feedback and advice to the department from the perspective of accounting professionals engaged in real-world business activities. They can help provide thought leadership in the field of accounting, auditing, and tax, enhance undergraduate and graduate programs, and enrich the educational experience of the department's students. They are also an excellent avenue to be able to establish connectivity to non-alumni further establishing the smaller universities networking footprint.

Skilling Up Professors

Unfortunately, the accounting curriculum at smaller universities may be challenged in maintaining a relevant curriculum in an environment with ever-changing skill sets for CPAs. Digital transformation, business and societal expectations and the speed of technological change have accelerated not only the demands of learning, but the expectations for educators. The CPA Evolution Initiative aims to transform the CPA licensure model to recognize the rapidly changing skills and competencies the practice of accounting requires today and will require in the future (see https://www.thiswaytocpa.com/) The challenge is to now update the accounting curriculum to better prepare students for the new CPA exam, as well as provide them with the skills they need to succeed as accounting professionals. It must be understood that the Evolution process is in its infancy. The profession is at the forefront of a future of continuous change. Emerging technologies have transformed the way accountants operate. The change is for the better, because it allows accountants to perform more analysis, while relying on technology to address the more rote and time-consuming tasks.

The challenge is two-fold. Universities are tasked with updating their curriculum to adhere to the new requirements for the exam and licensure within their licensing jurisdiction. They are also faced with the dilemma of utilizing their existing faculty to teach these courses. Professors require training in new skill sets. For some, several years have passed since they were employed in public accounting or have obtained training in new skill required for newly licensed CPAs. In smaller programs, the challenges are magnified. It is not uncommon for a handful of professors to teach a variety of courses in the program rather than teaching multiple sections of one course, which may be typically found at a larger university. Evolution is fast approaching that require changes in programs, and training for professors in an environment of limited resources.

The larger universities who have partnered with the Big 4 firms are at a distinct advantage. Their programs have already been modified and their students are already receiving the benefit of the new curriculum. Their students have also begun utilizing their new skillsets as they work as interns or new hires for the firm that has trained them.

The questions that must be addressed for the smaller accounting programs are:

- How are instructors skilled up so that they can teach their students?
- How is the curriculum going to be transformed?
- How much time will be required to do so?
- Where are the resources to undertake this transformation?
- Who will instruct the instructors?

For the universities that do not have the advantage of a faculty with diverse skill sets, it will be necessary to "skill-up" those that they have. Fortunately, there is little concern about capability. The concern is how this can be accomplished in the most efficient and cost-effective manner.

Returnships

Returnships are traditionally programs for individuals who have left the workforce and are looking to revamp their skills to return to the workplace. Many companies advertise these programs for individuals that have left the workforce to raise children or to care for sick or elderly family members. Some companies use this platform to hire retirees, as well. Although the programs offered vary, generally a returnship resembles a paid internship. The objective is to provide an experienced individual with a new set of skills. These have proven to be very successful. According to AARP, there are nearly 100 such programs in existence and these programs are very popular on both a national and global basis.

Accounting firms could provide returnships to faculty members who are trying to skill up. If established well, it would be beneficial for the firm, the faculty member, and the university. The firm would be working with a faculty member CPA who would have a foundation for this re-education. Older methodologies can be replaced with new ones and then introduced in the classroom. It is beneficial for the accounting firm because a former practitioner is being retrained. The newly trained faculty member returns to the university with the skillset they can now share with their students. A skillset that is required of interns and new hires. It is beneficial to the university because they do not have to stress over replacing faculty.

It is also beneficial because, much like the programs that the larger firms have established with the larger universities, it solidifies a relationship between the university and the firm or firms that their faculty are "training" with. This provides a channel for internships and full-time employment for students.

The timing and cost of the retraining must be considered. The timing can be coordinated between the firm and the faculty member and university. Many professors do not teach during the summer, the returnship could be offered following a Spring semester, and continue thought-out the summer. Firms may take advantage of downtime for an opportunity for retraining programs.

Faculty members may use sabbatical opportunities to engage in a returnship. This would enable the faculty member to be immersed in the returnship for a semester or even an entire year. This would be beneficial since an immersion of an entire year in the work environment could better solidify the returnship experience. The "returnee" would have the advantage of training during the slower season and utilizing their newly earned skillset during the busy season with the firm they partner with. This could prove helpful to the firm because they now have the temporary benefit of an additional employee.

There is a cost associated with the returnship that would be require negotiation between the university and the accounting firm. Agreements include the university pays the employee during the returnship, or the accounting firm can pay a salary or stipend. If the faculty member uses a sabbatical, the university can opt to pay their professor for the sabbatical. The firm and the university can agree to a mutually beneficial arrangement. If the faculty considering the returnship involves union membership, the arrangement would have to be crafted to ensure that there is no violation of the union contract.

Firms Providing University Training

Another way that universities can partner with accounting firms to skill up their faculty, is to coordinate training with a firm or firms. Basically, if "Mohammed can't get to the mountain, bring the mountain to Mohammed." Faculty members can participate in training sessions on campus with a "trainer" from the accounting firm. Much of the training provided to new firm employees is through computerized training modules. Perhaps a licensing agreement with a partnered firm can be established whereby these training modules can be accessed by faculty members. The advantage of this scenario is that the faculty members can complete the training when they have availability, much like employees within the firms do.

Universities Partnering With Tech Companies

Another option for universities is to reach out to the companies that provide the technology utilized by accounting firms. These firms can train faculty members to utilize their products, and in turn train the students at the university. It is understood that not all firms use the same technology, but the foundation for the technology and how it is applied in the workplace is the most essential piece of the learning experience. It can be argued that there are different types of technology used in every firm out there. Employees today change jobs with greater frequency than they did in the past. The technology utilized in one firm may be different that that found in the next firm, but the purpose and functionality will be undoubtedly similar, as the objective is the same. For example, the audit software used in one firm may differ from that used in the next, but the purpose it serves, and the analyses and reports required will be similar.

As many have pointed out, the objective of the Evolution is to train the next generation of accountants to master critical thinking. This can be accomplished using varying platforms.

Education and Training Offered by the AICPA and State CPA Societies

CPA Evolution resources are vast for both training and course instruction. As an example, scheduled Faculty Hours, hosted by the AICPA provide faculty with updates on CPA Evolution, as well as the opportunity to learn and ask questions. The AICPA also offers certificate programs for faculty interested in solidifying their skills on specific topics.[10]

State Societies are also offering members assistance with the evolution process. There a committees dedicated specifically to academics so that processes and methodologies to accomplish program modifications can be discussed and shared amongst members.[11] These education and volunteer opportunities represent minimal cost choices to further faculty education and training necessary to deliver a relevant education.

Smaller Universities Partnering Programs

Another option for smaller universities to accomplish the upskilling of their faculty is for them to partner with other smaller universities. The new curriculum calls for students to select a specific discipline track. Of course, smaller universities will not have the resources to provide courses in all three tracks. By partnering their program with another university, they can provide more options to students. This will enhance the course offering and perhaps make their program as appealing as those offered by larger schools, potentially at a lower tuition cost.

Another option is for universities to partner with universities on a national or global basis. That is, partnering and offering online courses to students in other locations. This would replicate a "study abroad" kind of scenario, only the students would take part of the program from their own location and part from another location here in the US or a global location. This could introduce another revenue stream for the university, which could offset the cost of revamping their accounting program to meet the new requirements. This partnering or 'coalition approach' may ultimately prove to the most viable solution to address the challenge facing smaller organizations. It could lower costs and leverage scale of resources while heling retains their identities.

CONCLUSION

The road ahead for smaller accounting programs is going to be a challenging one, but creativity and outreach are the keys to success. The data show that smaller colleges and universities still have a significant role in providing accounting education, but that role is eroding. There are many smaller programs that are struggling to compete for a declining number of students. A distinct advantage would be to conceptualize a unique program, that is affordable and appealing to the population they serve. The smaller institutions must act to maintain their relevance in accounting education.

REFERENCES

Trends Report. (2021). https://www.aicpa.org/professional-insights/download/2021-trends-report

Best Accounting Bachelor's Degree Schools. (n.d.). Retrieved July 15, 2022, from https://www.collegefactual.com/majors/business-management-marketing-sales/accounting/rankings/top-ranked/bachelors-degrees/

AICPA. (2012). *State Regulatory and Legislature Affairs. State Non-CPA Ownership Provisions*. https://us.aicpa.org/content/dam/aicpa/advocacy/state/statecontactinfo/uaa/downloadabledocuments/non-cpa_ownership.pdf

AICPA. (2023). https://www.aicpa-cima.com/news/article/aicpa-publishes-detailed-plan-to-boost-pool-of-prospective-cpa-candidates

Hess, A. (2017, November 15). *Harvard Business School professor: Half of American colleges will be bankrupt in 10 to 15 years*. CNBC. https://www.cnbc.com/2017/11/15/hbs-professor-half-of-us-colleges-will-be-bankrupt-in-10-to-15-years.html

Maurer, M. (2020). Why You Don't need to Be an Accountant to Be a CFO. *The Wall Street Journal*.

KEY TERMS AND DEFINITIONS

Asynchronous: An online learning platform that students approach a course at their own time while meeting course requirements.

CPA Evolution: The CPA exam format that starts in January 2024 and consists of 3 core exams and a choice of one discipline-based exam.

Integrated Postsecondary Education Data System (IPEDS): Which is the data collection program for the National Center for Education Statistics

Jurisdiction: Licensing authority for the Certified Public Accountant.

Online Education: A format of education that delivers a course using remote access. Unlike a correspondence course, online education requires significate interaction between faculty and students and between students and students.

Returnships: Faculty returning to employment with the intention to obtain relevant and current skills.

Small Schools: Student population of less than 10,000.

ENDNOTES

1 *2022* Best Accounting Bachelor's Degree *Schools*. (n.d.). Www.collegefactual.com. Retrieved July 15, 2022, from https://www.collegefactual.com/majors/business-management-marketing-sales/accounting/rankings/top-ranked/bachelors-degrees/

2 *2021 Trends report*. (2021). Aicpa.org. https://www.aicpa.org/professional-insights/download/2021-trends-report

3 See https://nces.ed.gov/ipeds/

4 See https://www.icpas.org/information/professional-issues/decoding-the-decline

5 See https://www.roberthalf.com/blog/salaries-and-skills/finance-and-accounting-certifications-employers-want-to-see

6 On May 30, 2023, the New York State Assembly and Senate overwhelmingly passed a non-CPA ownership bill, which now sets 50 jurisdictions allowing non-CPA ownership once the NYS governor signs the bill to become law. See https://www.nysscpa.org/news/publications/the-trusted-professional/article/new-york-state-legislature-passes-non-cpa-ownership-bill-053023 for recent press release.

7 See https://assets.ey.com/content/dam/ey-sites/ey-com/en_gl/noindex/ey-future-of-higher-education-report.pdf

8 Hess, A. (2017, November 15). *Harvard Business School professor: Half of American colleges will be bankrupt in 10 to 15 years*. CNBC; CNBC. https://www.cnbc.com/2017/11/15/hbs-professor-half-of-us-colleges-will-be-bankrupt-in-10-to-15-years.html

9 See https://www.cpapracticeadvisor.com/2016/04/20/demand-and-salaries-are-high-for-internal-auditors/21715/ The U.S. Bureau of Labor Statistics projects that employment growth for internal auditing professionals will grow faster than the average for all occupations from 2014 to 2024.

10 See https://www.aicpa-cima.com/cpe-learning/webcast/aicpa-and-cima-faculty-hour-series as an example.

11 See https://www.nysscpa.org/membership/committees#sthash.3Y3mclBZ.dpbs as an example.

Compilation of References

Trends Report. (2021). https://www.aicpa.org/professional-insights/download/2021-trends-report

Best Accounting Bachelor's Degree Schools. (n.d.). Retrieved July 15, 2022, from https://www.collegefactual.com/majors/business-management-marketing-sales/accounting/rankings/top-ranked/bachelors-degrees/#:~:text=1%2C063%20Colleges%20in%20the%20United%20States%2052%2C477%20Bachelor%27s

AACSB International – The Association to Advance Collegiate Schools of Business. (n.d.) *2013 Eligibility Procedures and Accreditation Standards for Business Accreditation.* AACSB. https://www.aacsb.edu/-/media/documents/accreditation/2018-business-standards.pdf?la=en&hash=B9AF18F3FA0DF19B352B605CBCE17959E32445D9

AACSB. (2018). 2018 Standards For Accounting Accreditation. AACSB. https://www.aacsb.edu/-/media/documents/accreditation/accounting/standards-and-tables/accounting2018standards-july-1-2022.pdf

AACSB. (2020). 2020 GUIDING PRINCIPLES AND STANDARDS FOR BUSINESS ACCREDITATION. AACSB. https://www.aacsb.edu/-/media/documents/accreditation/2020-aacsb-business-accreditation-standards-jul-1-2022.pdf

AACSB. (2021). *About Us.* AACSB. https://aacsb.edu/about-us

AACSB. (2022). 2022 State of Accreditation Report. AACSB. https://www.aacsb.edu/insights/reports/2022-state-of-accreditation-report

Abbe, A., & Brandon, S. E. (2014). Building and maintaining rapport in investigative interviews. *Police Practice and Research, 15*, 207–220. doi:10.1080/15614263.2013.827835

ACBSP. (2021). *About.* ACBSP. https://acbsp.org/page/about-who-we-are

Açıkgöz, B. & Mutlu, M. D. (2022). Muhasebe Mesleğinde Dijital Dönüşüm: Covid-19 Pandemi Döneminde Uzaktan Çalışma Uygulamaları. *İnsan ve Toplum Bilimleri Araştırmaları Dergisi, 11*(2), 52-69.

AICPA (2020) *Where Opportunity Meets Value: Business Model Trends for Accounting Advisory Services*. CPA.com

AICPA. (2012). *State Regulatory and Legislature Affairs. State Non-CPA Ownership Provisions*. https://us.aicpa.org/content/dam/aicpa/advocacy/state/statecontactinfo/uaa/downloadabledocuments/non-cpa_ownership.pdf

AICPA. (2013, October). *Accounting for the sustainability cycle: how the accounting profession can add value to sustainability-oriented activities*. AICPA. https://documents.pub/document/accounting-for-the-sustainability-cycle-dcclean-for-the-sustainability-cycle.html?page=1

AICPA. (2020). *How to Help Your Students Become Better Critical Thinkers*. AICPA. https://thiswaytocpa.com/program/CriticalThinking

AICPA. (2021a). *Accounting Competencies*. AICPA. https://www.aicpa.org/interestareas/accountingeducation/resources/accounting-core-competencies-functional.html

AICPA. (2021b). *Uniform CPA Examination Blueprints*. AICPA. https://us.aicpa.org/content/dam/aicpa/becomeacpa/cpaexam/examinationcontent/downloadabledocuments/cpa-exam-blueprints-effective-july-2021.pdf

AICPA. (2022). AICPA releases updated Foundational Competencies Framework for Aspiring CPAs. AICPA. https://www.aicpa.org/news/article/aicpa-releases-updated-foundational-competencies-framework-for-aspiring-cpas

AICPA. (2022). *Exposure Draft: Proposed 2024 CPA Exam changes*. AICPA. https://www.aicpa.org/resources/download/exposure-draft-proposed-2024-cpa-exam-changes AICPA/NASBA.

AICPA. (2023). https://www.aicpa-cima.com/news/article/aicpa-publishes-detailed-plan-to-boost-pool-of-prospective-cpa-candidates

AICPA. (December, 2022). *Maintaining the Relevance of the Uniform CPA Examination – Aligning the Exam with the CPA Evolution Licensure Model: Practice Analysis Final Report Practice Analysis*. AICPA. https://www.aicpa.org/resources/download/learn-what-is-tested-on-the-cpa-exam

AICPA/CIMA. (2022). The AICPA Foundational Competencies Framework for Aspiring CPAs. *This Way To CPA*. https://thiswaytocpa.com/collectedmedia/files/foundational-competencies-framework-pdf.pdf

Albert, E. (2016). China-Taiwan Relations. *Council on Foreign Relations, 7*.

Albrecht, W., & Sack, R. (2001). The Perilous Future of Accounting Education. *The CPA Journal*, (March), 18.

Allen, A., & Woodland, A. M. (2006). The 150- Hour Requirement and the Number of CPA Exam Candidates, Pass Rates, and the the Number Passing. *Issues in Accounting Education*, *21*(3), 173–193. doi:10.2308/iace.2006.21.3.173

American Institute of Certified Public Accountants & National Association of State Boards of Accountancy. (2021). *CPA Evolution Model Curriculum*. CPA.

American Institute of Certified Public Accountants. (n.d.). *150 hour requirement for obtaining a CPA license*. AICPA. https://us.aicpa.org/becomeacpa/licensure/requirements.html#why

Amernic, J., & Craig, R. (2004). Reform of accounting education in the post-Enron era: Moving accounting 'out of the shadows.'. *Abacus*, *40*(3), 342–378. doi:10.1111/j.1467-6281.2004.00162.x

Angelo, T. A., & Cross, K. P. (1993). Classroom assessment techniques: A handbook for college professors. Jossey-Bass.

Arens, A. A., Beasley, M. S., Elder, R. J., & Hogan, C. E. (2020). *Auditing and assurance services: an integrated approach* (17th ed.).

Association of Charted Certified Accountants and the International Federation of Accountants. (2021). *Groundbreakers: Gen Z and the future of accountancy*. ACCAI. file:///C:/Users/user/Downloads/GEN-Z-GROUNDBREAKERS.pdf

Auksztol, J., & Chomuszko, M. (2020). A data control framework for SAF-T reporting: A process-based approach. *Journal of Entrepreneurship Management and Innovation*, *16*(1), 13–40. doi:10.7341/20201611

Ayboğa, H. (2003). Globalleşme sürecinde ülkemizde muhasebe mesleği ve meslek mensuplarının eğitimi. *Marmara Üniversitesi İktisadi ve İdari Bilimler Dergisi*, *18*(1), 327–359.

Aydemir, O. (2015). Muhasebe meslek mensuplarının karşılaştıkları sorunlar ve beklentiler. *Muhasebe ve Finansman Dergisi*, (67), 71–84. doi:10.25095/mufad.396577

Azaltun, M., Aktaş, A., Yavuzaslan Söylemez, S., Tekbaş, İ., & Atasoy, A. (2022). COVID-19 Pandemisinin Muhasebe Mesleği Ve Muhasebe Meslek Mensuplarına Etkileri Üzerine Bir Araştırma. *Mali Çözüm Dergisi*, *32*(171), 65–101.

Bahador, K. M. K., & Haider, A. (2012). Information technology skills and competencies—A case for professional accountants. In Abramowicz, W., Domingue, J., Węcel, K., (eds.) Business Information Systems Workshops, pp. 81–87. Springer: Berlin/Heidelberg.

Baldwin, J. (1993). Police interview techniques: Establishing truth or proof? *British Journal of Criminology*, *33*, 325–351.

Bannon, S., Ford, K., & Meltzer, L. (2011). Understanding millennials in the workplace: Certified public accountant. *The CPA Journal*, *81*(11), 61–65.

Beard, D., Schwieger, D., & Surendran, K. (2008). Integrating Soft Skills Assessment through University, College and Programmatic Efforts at an AACBSB Accredited Institution. *Journal of Information Systems Education*, *19*(2).

Bebbington, J. (1997). Engagement, education, and sustainability. A review essay on environmental accounting. *Accounting, Auditing & Accountability Journal*, *10*(3), 365–381. doi:10.1108/09513579710178115

Bebier, A. (2015). Crimea and the Russina-Ukranian Conflict. *Romanian Journal of European Affairs*, *15*(1), 35–54.

Beder, N. (2021). Muhasebe Meslek Mensuplarının Yeni Dünya ile İmtihanı. *Anadolu Üniversitesi Sosyal Bilimler Dergisi*, *21*(1), 163–184. doi:10.18037/ausbd.902591

Bootsma, M., Jeffrey, C., & Perkins, J. D. (2021). Is there learning in service learning? Measuring the extent to which VITA participation improves student technical competence and soft skills. *Issues in Accounting Education*, *36*(2), 21–42. doi:10.2308/ISSUES-19-113

Braun, R. L., & Stallworth, H. L. (2009). If You Need Love, Get a Puppy: A Case Study on Professional Skepticism and Auditor Independence. *Issues in Accounting Education*, *24*(2), 237–252. doi:10.2308/iace.2009.24.2.237

Brook, C. A., & Willoughby, T. (2015). The Social Ties That Bind: Social Anxiety and Academic Achievement Across the University Years. *Journal of Youth and Adolescence*, *44*(5), 1139–1152. doi:10.100710964-015-0262-8 PMID:25691148

Brown, A. (2022). The CPA exam curriculum is changing. *Accounting Today*, *36*(1), 24.

Bryant, S. M. (2019). Bridging the gap between the classroom and career readiness for new accounting graduates. *The CPA Journal*. https://www.cpajournal.com/2019/02/01/bridging-the-gap-between-the-classroom-and-career-readiness-for-new-accounting-graduates/

Bublitz, M., Oetomo, F., Sahu, S., Kuang, A. X., Fadrique, L., Velmovitsky, P., & Morita, P. (2019). Disruptive technologies for environment and health research: An overview of artificial intelligence, blockchain, and internet of things. *International Journal of Environmental Research and Public Health*, *16*(20), 3847. doi:10.3390/ijerph16203847 PMID:31614632

Bui, B., & Porter, B. (2010). The expectation-performance gap in accounting education: An exploratory study. *Accounting Education*, *19*(1-2), 23–50. doi:10.1080/09639280902875556

Bull, R., & Soukara, S. (2010). A set of studies of what really happens in police interviews with suspects. In G. D. Lassiter & C. Meissner (Eds.), *Interrogations and confessions* (pp. 81–96). American Psychological Association.

Burns, H. (2022). *The enrollment cliff is coming for higher education, making affordability even more important*. The Business Journals.

Buyruk Akbaba, A. N., & Bulut, N. (2021). Pandemi Sürecinde Muhasebe Meslek Mensuplarının Mesleki Tükenmişlik Düzeylerinin İncelenmesi. *EUropean Journal of Managerial Research (EUJMR)*, *5*(Özel), 35-48.

Cambridge dictionary. (2022, May 2). Business Model. *Cambridge Dictionary*. Cambridge. https://dictionary.cambridge.org/it/dizionario/inglese/business-model

Carnegie, G. D. (2014). The present and future of accounting history. *Accounting, Auditing & Accountability Journal*, *27*(8), 1241–1249. doi:10.1108/AAAJ-05-2014-1715

Carnegie, G. D., & Napier, C. J. (2012). Accounting's past, present and future: The unifying power of history. *Accounting, Auditing & Accountability Journal*, *25*(2), 328–369. doi:10.1108/09513571211198782

Carungu, J., Di Pietra, R., & Molinari, M. (2021). The impact of a humanitarian disaster on the working approach of accountants: A study of contingent effects. *Accounting, Auditing & Accountability Journal*, *34*(6), 1388–1403. doi:10.1108/AAAJ-08-2020-4789

Ceylan, R., & Hacıhasanoğlu, T. (2022). A Qualitative Study on the Problems of Accounting Professionals in Covid-19 Period in Yozgat Province. *Cumhuriyet Üniversitesi İktisadi ve İdari Bilimler Dergisi*, *23*(3), 774–789. doi:10.37880/cumuiibf.1109191

Chabus, R. (2021). Top soft skills for accounting professionals. *Journal of Accountancy*. https://www.journalofaccountancy.com/newsletters/2021/jun/top-soft-skills-accounting-professionals.html

Chamorro-Premuzic, T., & Bersin, J. (2018). *4 ways to create a learning culture on your team*. Harvard Business Review. https://hbr.org/2018/07/4-ways-to-create-a-learning-culture-on-your-team

Cherryman, J., & Bull, R. (2001). Police officers' perceptions of specialist investigative interviewing skills. *International Journal of Police Science and Management*, *3*, 199– 212. https://doi.org/. 1177%2F146135570100300302 doi:10

Clancy, A. (2012). How to accommodate millennial accountants. *Long Island Business News*. https://www.proquest.com/trade-journals/how-accommodate-millennial-accountants/docview/1017591689/se-2

Clarke, C., & Milne, R. (2001). National Evaluation of the PEACE Investigative Interviewing Course. *Police Research Award Scheme Report No. PRAS/149*. London: Home Office.

Cleary, H. M. D., & Bull, R. (2019). Jail inmates' perspectives on police interrogation. *Psychology, Crime & Law*, *25*, 157–170. doi:10.1080/1068316X.2018.1503667

Collison, D., Ferguson, J., & Stevenson, L. (2007). Sustainability accounting education. In J. Unerman, J. Bebbington, & B. O'Dwyer (Eds.), *Sustainability accounting and accountability* (pp. 327–344). Routledge.

Combs, D. G., & Mattix, C. (2021). Sustainability Accounting in the United States Higher Education System. *Quarterly Review of Business Disciplines*, *8*(1), 19–40.

Coombs, T. W. (2014). *State of Crisis Communication: Evidence and the Bleeding Edge*. Research Journal of the Institute for Public Relations.

Copley, P., & E. Douthett (2020). The Enrollment Cliff, Mega-Universities, COVID-19, and the Changing Landscape of U.S. Colleges. *The CPA Journal*.

Coulson, A., & Thomson, I. (2006). Accounting and sustainability, encouraging a dialogical approach; integrating learning activities, delivery mechanisms and assessment strategies. *Accounting Education*, *15*(3), 261–273. doi:10.1080/09639280600850695

Coville, T. (2023). *The Neglected Need for and the Effects of Sustainability in Accounting Curriculum*. Journal of Global Awareness.

CPA Practice Advisor. (2021). *Report Examines Decline in Number of CPAs*. CPA. https://www.cpapracticeadvisor.com/2021/06/14/report-examines-decline-in-number-of-cpas/44293/

Creel, T., & Paz, V. (2018). Teaching Sustainability in an Accounting Classroom. In Discourse and Communication for Sustainable Education, 9(1) 79-85. doi:10.2478/dcse-2018-0006

Cunha, T., Martins, H., Carvalho, A., & Carmo, C. (2022). Not Practicing What You Preach: How Is Accounting Higher Education Preparing the Future of Accounting. *Education Sciences*, *12*(7), 432. doi:10.3390/educsci12070432

Deloitte University. (n.d.) *Leadership Center*. Deloitte University. https://www2.deloitte.com/us/en/pages/about-deloitte/articles/deloitteuniversity-leadership-center.html?icid=top_

Dodds, W. (2019). Disease Now and Potential Future Pandemics. The World's Worst Problems, (pp. 31-44). Springer. doi:10.1007/978-3-030-30410-2_4

Dorata, N. (2021). Changes ahead for the big test. *Accounting Today*, *35*(6), 32.

Duckworth. (2016). *Grit: the power of passion and perseverance*. Scribner.

Duncan, J., & Schmutte, J. (2006). Change in Accounting Programs: The Impact of Influences and Constraints, 16.

Duska, R. F. (2015). The responsibilities of accountants. *The Geneva Papers on Risk and Insurance. Issues and Practice*, *30*(3), 410–424. doi:10.1057/palgrave.gpp.2510042

Elam, D., & Mendez, F. (2010). Career Expectations Of Accounting Students. *American Journal of Business Education*, *3*(5), 71–80. doi:10.19030/ajbe.v3i5.430

Erol, M., & Ayboğa, H. (2021). Kovid-19'un Muhasebe Meslek Mensuplarının Mesleki Faaliyetlerine Etkisinin Belirlenmesine Yönelik Ampirik Çalışma. *Uluslararası Beşerî ve Sosyal Bilimler İnceleme Dergisi*, *5*(1), 1–12.

Fei Gong, Y., Kim, S., & Harding, N. (2014). Elevating professional scepticism. *Managerial Auditing Journal*, *29*(8), 674–694. doi:10.1108/MAJ-08-2013-0914

Fernandez, D., & Aman, A. (2018). Impacts of robotic process automation on global accounting services. *Asian J. Account. Gov.*, *9*, 123–132. doi:10.17576/AJAG-2018-09-11

Fico, J., & Walsh, D. (n.d.). *A review of the accounting and forensic auditing literature as it applies to interviewing people as part of the job role.*

Frumuşanu, N. M., Marin, A. M., & Martin, M. (2020). The impact of COVID-19 pandemic on the activity of the professional accountant. *ANNALS ECONOMIC SCIENCES SERIES*, *XX*(2), 922.

Gabbert, F., Hope, L., Luther, K., Wright, G., Ng, M., & Oxburgh, G. E. (2021). Exploring the use of rapport in professional information-gathering contexts by systematically mapping the evidence base. *Applied Cognitive Psychology*, *35*, 329–341. doi:10.1002/acp.3762

Gabbin, A. (2019) Warning Signs about the Future Supply of Accounting Graduates. *The CPA Journal.*

Gordon, I. M. (1998). Enhancing students' knowledge of social responsibility accounting. *Issues in Accounting Education*, *13*(1), 31–46.

Grabski, S. V., Leech, S. A., & Schmidt, P. J. (2011). A Review of ERP Research: A Future Agenda for Accounting Information Systems. *Journal of Information Systems*, *25*(1), 37–78. doi:10.2308/jis.2011.25.1.37

Gray, R. (2013). Sustainability + Accounting Education: The Elephant in the Classroom. *Accounting Education*, *22*(4), 308–332. doi:10.1080/09639284.2013.817795

Gray, R., Bebbington, J., & McPhail, K. (1994). Teaching ethics in accounting and the ethics of accounting teaching: Educating for immorality and a possible case for social and environmental accounting education. *Accounting Education*, *3*(1), 51–75. doi:10.1080/09639289400000005

Gray, R., & Collison, D. (2002). Can't see the wood for the trees, can't see the trees for the numbers? Accounting education, sustainability and the public interest. *Critical Perspectives on Accounting*, *13*(5-6), 797–836. doi:10.1006/cpac.2002.0554

Griffiths, A., Milne, B., & Cherryman, J. (2011). A question of control? the formulation of suspect and witness interview question strategies by advanced interviewers. *International Journal of Police Science & Management*, *13*(3), 255–267. doi:10.1350/ijps.2011.13.3.219

Griffiths, A., & Milne, R. (2006). Will it all end in tiers? Police interviews with suspects in Britain. In T. Williamson (Ed.), *Investigative interviewing: Rights, research and regulation* (pp. 167–189). Willan.

Griffiths, A., & Walsh, D. (2018). Qualitative analysis of qualitative evaluation: An exploratory examination of investigative interviewers' reflections on their performance. *Psychology, Crime & Law*, *24*(4), 433–450. doi:10.1080/1068316X.2017.1390115

Güngör Karyağdı, N. (2021). Muhasebe Meslek Mensuplarının Covid-19 Pandemi Krizini ve Etkilerini Mesleki Açıdan Değerlendirmelerine Üzerine Bir Çalışma: Muş İlinde Bir Araştırma. *Siirt Üniversitesi Sosyal Bilimler Enstitüsü Dergisi*, *9*(17), 20–40.

Guragai, B., Hunt, N. C., Neri, M. P., & Taylor, E. Z. (2017). Accounting information systems and ethics research: Review, synthesis, and the future. *Journal of Information Systems*, *31*(2), 65–81. doi:10.2308/isys-51265

Hadar, L. L., Ergas, O., Alpert, B., & Ariav, T. (2020). Rethinking teacher education in a VUCA world: Student teachers' social-emotional competencies during the Covid-19 crisis. *European Journal of Teacher Education*, *43*(4), 573–586. doi:10.1080/02619768.2020.1807513

Haller, A. (2002). Financial accounting developments in the European Union: past events and future prospects. *European Accounting Review*, *11*(1), 153-153-190.

Hart, L. (July 2018). Should students learn sustainability accounting? *Journal of Accountancy*. https://www.journalofaccountancy.com/newsletters/extra-credit/sustainability-accounting-education.html

Haskin, D. L., & Burke, M. M. (2016). Incorporating Sustainability Issues Into the Financial Accounting Curriculum [AJBE]. *American Journal of Business Education*, *9*(2), 49–56. doi:10.19030/ajbe.v9i2.9611

Hassall, T., Joyce, J., Montaño, J. L. A., & Donoso Anes, J. A. (2005). Priorities for the development of vocational skills in management accountants: A European perspective. *Accounting Forum*, *29*(4), 379–394. doi:10.1016/j.accfor.2005.03.002

Haven, L. T., & Van Grootel, D. L. (2019). Preregistering qualitative research. *Accountability in Research*, *26*(3), 229–244. doi:10.1080/08989621.2019.1580147 PMID:30741570

Hazelton, J., & Haigh, M. (2010). Incorporating sustainability into accounting curricula: Lessons learnt from an action research study. *Accounting Education*, *19*(1-2), 159–178. doi:10.1080/09639280802044451

Hess, A. (2017, November 15). *Harvard Business School professor: Half of American colleges will be bankrupt in 10 to 15 years*. CNBC. https://www.cnbc.com/2017/11/15/hbs-professor-half-of-us-colleges-will-be-bankrupt-in-10-to-15-years.html

Himstreet, W., Baty, W., & Lehman, C. (1993). Business Communications: Principles and Methods, PWS-Kent Publishing.

Holmberg, U., & Christianson, S.-A. (2002). Murderers and sexual offenders' experiences of police interviews and inclination to admit or deny crimes. *Behavioral Sciences & the Law*, *20*, 31–45. PMID:11979490

IAESB International Education Standards Board. (2014). *IES 4, Initial Professional Development—Professional Values, Ethics, and Attitudes*. IFAC.

IESBA. (Dec. 2022). *December 2022 Sustainability Update*. IESBA. https://www.ifac.org/system/files/publications/files/IESBA-December-2022- Sustainability-Update.pdf

IFAC. (2023). *The State of Play in Sustainability Assurance*. IFAC. https://www.ifac.org/knowledge-gateway/contributing-global-e conomy/discussion/state-play-sustainability-assurance

IIA. (2022). *Internal Auditing Education Partnership (IAEP) Program Program Guidelines and Operating Framework*. IIA. https://www.theiia.org/globalassets/documents/about-us/initiatives--awards/academic-relations/iaep-program-requirements-and-operating-framework.pdf

IIA. (2022). *Internal Auditing Education Partnership (IAEP)*. Program Program Guidelines and Operating Framework.

IIA. (2022). The IIA's Global Model Internal Audit Curriculum. IIA.

IIA. (2022). The IIA's Global Model Internal Audit Curriculum. IIA. https://www.theiia.org/globalassets/documents/about-us/initi atives--awards/academic-relations/global-model-internal-audi t-curriculum.pdf

Investor Responsibility Research Center Institute (IRRC). (2018). *State of Sustainability & Integrated Reporting 2018*. CPB. https://cpb-us-w2.wpmucdn.com/sites.udel.edu/dist/8/12944/fi les/2022/07/2018-SP-500-Integrated-Reporting-FINAL-November-20181.pdf#:~:text=State%20of%20Sustainability%20%26%20Integr ated%20Reporting%202018%204,their%20corporate%20identities%2 0and%20approach%20business%20in%20general

IOSCO. (Jan. 2019) https://www.iosco.org/library/pubdocs/pdf/IOSCOPD619.pdf

IPEDS. (2021). *National Center for Education Statistics*. NCES. https://nces.ed.gov/ipeds/use-the-data

ISACA. (2012). *ISACA Model Curriculum for Information Security Management*. ISACA.

ISACA. (2012). *ISACA Model Curriculum for IS Audit and Control*. ISACA.

ITEN. (2015). Critical Thinking Toolkit. *Learning, A: A Guide to Professional Skepticism*. ITEN. https://www.acilearning.com/blog/professional-skepticism-for -auditors

Izotovas, A., Kelly, C. E., & Walsh, D. (2021). The Domains of PEACE: Examining interviews with suspected sex offenders. *Journal of Police and Criminal Psychology*.

Jackling, B., & De Lange, P. (2009). Do accounting graduates' skills meet the expectations of employers? A matter of convergence or divergence. *Accounting Education, 18*(4-5), 369–385. doi:10.1080/09639280902719341

Jankelová, N., & Mišún, J. (2021). Key Competencies of Agricultural Managers in the Acute Stage of COVID-19 Crisis. *Agriculture, 11*(1), 59. doi:10.3390/agriculture11010059

Johnson, S., & Pike, B. (2018). Employee retention: The state of engagement in public accounting firms and why it matters. *The CPA Journal, 88*(12), 64–66.

Kaka, E. J. (2020). the Covid-19 Crisis, Risk Compliance and Its Aftermath on Professional Accountants. *Indonesian Journal of Accounting and Governance, 4*(1), 65–81. doi:10.36766/ijag.v4i1.61

Kassin, S. M., & Gudjonsson, G. H. (2004). The Psychology of Confessions: A Review of the Literature and Issues. *Psychological Science in the Public Interest, 5*(2), 33–67. doi:10.1111/j.1529-1006.2004.00016.x PMID:26158993

Katkat Özçelik, M. (2021). Covid-19 Salgınının Muhasebe Mesleğine Etkisi Üzerine Bir Olgubilim Çalışması. In T. Öndeş, C. Yerdelen Kaygin (eds.) Covid-19'un Muhasebe ve Finans Yansımaları. Gazi Kitabevi.

Kebbell, M. R., Hurren, E. J., & Mazerolle, P. (2006). Sex offenders' perceptions of police interviewing: Implications for improving the interviewing effectiveness. *The Canadian Journal of Police & Security Services, 4*, 67–75.

Kelly, C. E., Miller, J. C., Redlich, A. D., & Kleinman, S. M. (2013). A taxonomy of interrogation methods. *Psychology, Public Policy, and Law, 19*(2), 165–178. doi:10.1037/a0030310

Kim, J., Walsh, D., Bull, R., & Bergstrom, H. (2018). Planning ahead? Factors influencing investigators' attitudes towards planning for interviews with suspects. *Journal of Police and Criminal Psychology, 33*, 158–174. doi:10.100711896-017-9243-z.104

Kim, S. J. (2021). Crisis leadership: An evolutionary concept analysis. Applied nursing research. *ANR, 60*(1), 151454. PMID:34215477

King, A. Z., & King, H. (2021). Developing team skills in accounting students: A complete curriculum. *Journal of Higher Education Theory and Practice, 21*(7), 116–146.

Kingsinger, P., & Waich, K. (2012, July 9). *Living and leading in a VUCA world.* Thunderbird University. http://knowledgenetwork.thunderbird.edu/research/2012/07/09/kinsinger-walch-vuca/

Kokina, J., & Davenport, T. H. (2017). The Emergence of Artificial Intelligence: How Automation is Changing Auditing. *Journal of Emerging Technologies in Accounting, 14*(1), 115–122. doi:10.2308/jeta-51730

Koncz & Collins. (2007) *News for Media Professionals.* NACEWeb. http://www.naceweb.org/press/display.asp?year=2007&pri d=270.

Köse, E., Altunay, M. A., & Bekci, İ. (2022). Covid-19 Salgınının Muhasebe Meslek Mensuplarına Etkisi. *Vergi Raporu*, *272*, 138–155.

Krathwohl, D. R. (2002). A revision of Bloom's taxonomy: An overview. *Theory into Practice*, *41*(4), 212–218. doi:10.120715430421tip4104_2

Lahey, J. (2015). *The gift of failure: How parents learn to let go so their children can succeed.* HarperCollins Publishers.

Lai, A., & Stacchezzini, R. (2021). Organisational and professional challenges amid the evolution of sustainability reporting: A theoretical framework and an agenda for future research. *Meditari Accountancy Research*, *29*(3), 405–429. doi:10.1108/MEDAR-02-2021-1199

Leahy-Harland, S., & Bull, R. (2017). Police strategies and suspect responses in real-life serious crime interviews. *Journal of Police and Criminal Psychology*, *32*(2), 138–151.

Lee, J., Waldeck, D., Holliman, A. J., Banerjee, M., & Tyndall, I. (2022). Feeling socially anxious at university: An interpretative phenomenological analysis. *Qualitative Report*, *27*(4), 897–919. doi:10.46743/2160-3715/2022.5270

Leinicke, L. M., Ostrosky, J. A., Rexroad, W. M., Baker, J. R., & Beckman, S. (2005). Interviewing as an Auditing Tool. *The CPA Journal*, *75*(2), 34.

Lin, H., & Hwang, Y. (2021). The effects of personal information management capabilities and social-psychological factors on accounting professionals' knowledge-sharing intentions: Pre and post COVID-19. *International Journal of Accounting Information Systems*, *42*, 100522. doi:10.1016/j.accinf.2021.100522

Makridakis, S. (2017). The forthcoming Artificial Intelligence (AI) revolution: Its impact on society and firms. *Futures*, *90*(1), 46–60. doi:10.1016/j.futures.2017.03.006

Mangion, D. (2006). Undergraduate education in social and environmental accounting in Australian universities. *Accounting Education*, *15*(3), 335–348. doi:10.1080/09639280600850844

Marshall, T. E., & Lambert, S. L. (2018). Cloud-based intelligent accounting applications: Accounting task automation using IBM Watson Cognitive Computing. *Journal of Emerging Technologies in Accounting*, *15*(1), 199–215. doi:10.2308/jeta-52095

Martin, T. N. (2019). Review of Student Soft Skills Development Using the 5Ws/H Approach Resulting in a Realistic, Experiential, Applied, Active Learning and Teaching Pedagogical Classroom. *Journal of Behavioral and Applied Management*, *19*(1), 41–57.

Mathews, M. R. (1997). Twenty-five years of social and environmental accounting research. Is there a silver jubilee to celebrate? *Accounting, Auditing & Accountability Journal*, *10*(4), 481–531. doi:10.1108/EUM0000000004417

Maurer, M. (2020). Why You Don't need to Be an Accountant to Be a CFO. *The Wall Street Journal*.

Mazman İtik, Ü. (2021). Covid-19 Pandemi Sürecinde Serbest Muhasebeci Mali Müşavirlerin Yaşadığı Sorunlar Üzerine Sivas İlinde Bir Araştırma. *Akademik Sosyal Araştırmalar Dergisi, 9*(120), 78–91.

McCabe, S. (2022, May 6). PwC U.S. announces $2.4B employee investment. *Accounting Today.* https://www.accountingtoday.com/news/pwc-us-announces-2-4b-employee-investment

McCrea, B. M. (2019). Leveling up your accounting and finance credentials. *Insight.* https://www.icpas.org/information/copy-desk/insight/article/spring-2019/leveling-up-your-accounting-and-finance-credentials

Mcpeak, D. W., Pincus, K. V., & Sundem, G. L. (2012). The International Accounting Education Standards Board: Influencing Global Accounting Education. *Issues in Accounting Education, 27*(1), 743–750. doi:10.2308/iace-50121

McPhail, K. (2001). The other objective of ethics education: Re-humanising the accounting profession – a study of ethics education in law, engineering, medicine, and accountancy. *Journal of Business Ethics, 34*(3/4), 279–298. doi:10.1023/A:1012576631990

Middle States Commission on Higher Education. (2015). *Standards for Accreditation and Requirements of Affiliation.* MSCHE. https://msche.box.com/shared/static/6upfla8coxha663p0j10u3gatow38jel.pdf

Mihai, F., Stan, M., Radu, G., & Dumitru, V. F. (2020). Heavy work investment for the accounting profession in Romania at time of coronavirus pandemic. *Amfiteatru Economic, 22*(14), 1121–1139.

Milne, R., & Bull, R. (1999). *Investigative interviewing: Psychology and practice.* Wiley.

Mintz, S. (2017). Reimagining Ethics Education. *The CPA Journal, 87*(9), 8–9. https://jerome.stjohns.edu/login?url=https://search.ebscohost.com/login.aspx?direct=true&db=buh&AN=124942823&site=ehost-live

Mintz, S. (2018). Accounting in the Public Interest. (cover story). *The CPA Journal, 88*(3), 22–29. https://jerome.stjohns.edu/login?url=https://search.ebscohost.com/login.aspx?direct=true&db=buh&AN=128446872&site=ehost-live

Mohamed, E. K. A., & Lashine, S. H. (2003). Accounting knowledge and skills and the challenges of a global business environment. *Managerial Finance, 29*(7), 3–16. doi:10.1108/03074350310768319

Moston, S., Stephenson, G. M., & Williamson, T. (1992). The effects of case characteristics on suspect behaviour during police questioning. *British Journal of Criminology, 32*, 23–40.

NACE. (2021). *Competencies for a Career-Ready Workforce.* NACE Web. https://www.naceweb.org/uploadedfiles/files/2021/resources/nace-career-readiness-competencies-revised-apr-2021.pdf

NASBA. (2020). *Candidate Performance on the Uniform CPA Examination*. NASBA. https://nasbareport.com/

NASBA. (2020). *UAA Model Rule Requirements - Education*. NASBA. https://nasba.org/app/uploads/2020/10/Oct-20-UAA-Model-Rule-5-1-Education.pdf

NASBA. (2020). *Uniform Accountancy Act Model Rules*. NASBA. https://nasba.org/wp-content/uploads/2021/03/REV-Mar-2021-Nov-2020-Model-Rules-FINAL-edited.pdf

NASBA. (2020a). *Candidate Perfomance On The Uniform CPA Examination 2019 Edition*. NASBA.

NYSED. (2022). Registration of Curricula, Part 52.13 Accountancy. NYSED. https://www.op.nysed.gov/professions/certified-public-accountants/laws-rules-regulations/part-52

Ovaska-Few, S. (2017) What large firms expect from new accounting grads? *Journal of Accountancy*. https://www.journalofaccountancy.com/issues/2017/mar

Oxburgh, G. E., Myklebust, T., & Grant, T. (2010). The question of question of question types in police interviews: A review of the literature from a psychological and linguistic perspective. *International Journal of Speech Language and the Law*, *17*, 45–66.

Oxburgh, G. E., Williamson, T., & Ost, J. (2006). Police officers' use of emotional language during child sexual abuse investigations. *Journal of Investigative Psychology and Offender Profiling*, *3*, 35–45.

Özdemir, L & Balkan, M. (2010). *The Positive and Negative Effects of Crisis on Organizations: An Application*. Research Gate.

Papadopoulou, S., & Papadopoulou, M. (2020). The Accounting Profession Amidst the COVID-19 Pandemic. *International Journal of Accounting and Financial Reporting*, *10*(2), 39–59. doi:10.5296/ijafr.v10i2.17001

Parker, K., & Igielnik, R. (2020). *On the cusp of adulthood and facing an uncertain future: What we know about Gen Z so far*. Pew Research Center. https://www.pewresearch.org/social-trends/2020/05/14/on-the-cusp-of-adulthood-and-facing-an-uncertain-future-what-we-know-about-gen-z-so-far-2/

Pathways Commission. (2012). *Final report*. American Accounting Association.

Payne, E. (2022, April 15). *What it takes to keep top talent: 3 areas of focus*. Benefits Pro. https://www.benefitspro.com/2022/04/15/what-it-takes-to-keep-top-talent-3-areas-of-focus/?slreturn=20220429125753

PCAOB. (2012). *Maintaining and Applying Professional Skepticim in Audits*. PCAOB. https://pcaobus.org/Standards/QandA/12-04-2012_SAPA_10.pdf

Pincus, K. V. (1997). Is teaching debits and credits essential in elementary accounting? *Issues in Accounting Education*, *12*(2), 575–579.

Pintrich, P. R. (2002). The role of metacognitive knowledge in learning, teaching, and assessing. *Theory into Practice*, *41*(4), 219–225. doi:10.120715430421tip4104_3

Pippin, S. E., Stallings, M. A., Weber, J. L., & Wong, J. A. (November 2021). Integrating Sustainability into the Accounting Curriculum: Meeting an Emerging Student Demand. *CPA Journal*. https://www.cpajournal.com/2021/11/12/integrating-sustainability-into-the-accounting-curriculum/

Pippin, S. E., Weber, J. L., Wong, J. A., & Bergner, J. (June 2016). The Inclusion of Sustainability in the Accounting Curriculum. *CPA Journal*. https://www.cpajournal.com/2016/06/17/inclusion-sustainability-accounting-curriculum/

Porco, B. (2018). *Importance of Sustainability Reporting*. [Video]. Youtube. https://www.youtube.com/watch?v=tonVGMZ8guo

Porco, B. M., & Hedley, T. P. (2019). Seven Easy Ways to Introduce Sustainability Reporting into Existing Accounting Curricula. *CPA Journal*. https://www.cpajournal.com/2019/10/11/seven-easy-ways-to-introduce-sustainability-reporting-into-existing-accounting-curricula/

Porter, S. F., & Crumbley, D. L. (2012). Teaching interviewing techniques to forensic accountants is critical. *Journal of Forensic & Investigative Accounting*, *4*(1), 122–146.

Pratama, A. (2015). Bridging the gap between academicians and practitioners on accountant competencies: An analysis of International Education Standards (IES) implementation on Indonesia's accounting education. *Procedia: Social and Behavioral Sciences*, *211*(1), 19–26. doi:10.1016/j.sbspro.2015.11.004

Prawitasari, P. P. (2022). Will Accountants Still Exist? Challenges of The Accountant Profession In Facing Technological Disruption In The New. In *International Conference on Industrial Revolution 4.0* (pp. 326–350).

PwC. (2023). Higher Apprenticeship Program. PwC. https://jobs-au.pwc.com/au/en/higher-apprenticeship

Rachlew, A., Loken, G.-E., & Bergestuen, S. T. (2022). *A Guide to the Professional Interview*. Anthem Press.

Rafoth, M. A. (2020). *Independent Study*. State University. https://education.stateuniversity.com/pages/2080/Independent-Study.html

Rebele, J. E., & St. Pierre, E. K. (2019). A commentary on learning objectives for accounting education programs: The importance of soft skills and technical knowledge. *Journal of Accounting Education, 48*, 71-79. doi:10.1016/j.jaccedu.2019.07.002

Richins, G., Stapleton, A., Stratopoulos, T., & Wong, C. (2017). Big data analytics: Opportunity or threat for the accounting profession? *Journal of Information Systems, 31*(3), 63–79. doi:10.2308/isys-51805

Ritter, T., & Carsten, P. L. (2020). Analyzing the impact of the coronavirus crisis on business models. *Industrial Marketing Management, 88*(1), 214–224. doi:10.1016/j.indmarman.2020.05.014

Robley, W., Whittle, S., & Murdoch-Eaton, D. (2005). Mapping generic skills curricula: A recommended methodology. *Journal of Further and Higher Education, 29*(3), 221–231. doi:10.1080/03098770500166801

Rouiller, J. Z., & Goldstein, I. L. (1993). The relationship between organizational transfer climate and positive transfer of training. *Human Resource Development Quarterly, 4*, 377–399.

Russano, M., Narchet, F., Kleinman, S., & Meissner, C. (2014). Structured interviews of experienced HUMINT interrogators. *Applied Cognitive Psychology, 28*. 847– 859. doi:10.1002/acp.3069.

Şahin, O. N., & Kumaş, C. (2022). COVID-19 Sürecinde Muhasebe Meslek Mensuplarına Yönelik Alanya Örneğinde Bir Araştırma. *Anadolu İktisat ve İşletme Dergisi, 6*(2), 142–166.

Schislyaeva, E. R., & Saychenko, O. A. (2022). Labor market soft skills in the context of digitalization of the economy. *Social Sciences (Basel, Switzerland), 3*(11), 91. doi:10.3390ocsci11030091

Schroeder, R. (2001). A Second Demographic Cliff Adds to Urgency for Change. *Inside Higher Ed.*

Schroth, H. (2019). Are you ready for Gen Z in the workplace? *California Management Review, 61*(3), 5–18. doi:10.1177/0008125619841006

Seidman, I. (2006). *Interviewing as qualitative research: A guide for researchers in education and the social sciences*. Teachers college press.

Seipp, E., & Lindberg, D. L. (2012). A Guide to Effective Audit Interviews. *The CPA Journal, 82*, 26.

Selimoğlu, S. K., Cengiz, A. A., Özdemir, A., & Begüm, Y. A. L. I. (2021). COVID-19 İle Birlikte Muhasebe Mesleğindeki Stresin Yeni Halleri. *Muhasebe ve Denetime Bakış, 21*(63), 1–18.

Shepherd, E., & Griffiths, A. (2012). *Investigative interviewing*. Oxford University Press.

Shortridge, R. T., & Smith, P. A. (2009). Understanding the changes in accounting thought. *Research in Accounting Regulation, 21*(1), 11–18. doi:10.1016/j.racreg.2008.11.010

Singleton, T. (2014). *IS Audit Basics: The Core of IT Auditing*. ISACA Journal.

Soukara, S., Bull, R., Vrij, A., Turner, M., & Cherryman, J. (2009). What really happens in police interviews with suspects? Tactics and confessions. *Psychology, Crime & Law, 15*, 493–506.

Stacey, H., & Page, A. (2013). *Investigative interview: a guide for the workplace*. Publicious Publishing.

Stanciu, V., Pugna, I. B., & Gheorghe, M. (2019). New coordinates of accounting academic education. A Romanian insight. Paper presented at *the 14th International Conference on Accounting and Management Information Systems (AMIS IAAER)*. Bucharest Univ.

Strawser, J. A., Flagg, J. C., & Holmes, S. A. (2000). Job perceptions and turnover behavior of tenure-track accounting educators. *Journal of Accounting Education*, *18*(4), 315–340. doi:10.1016/S0748-5751(01)00004-5

Sull, D., Sull, C., & Zweig, B. (2022). Toxic Culture Is Driving the Great Resignation. *MIT Sloan Management Review*, *63*(2), 1–9.

Taleb, N. N. (2012). *Antifragile: Things that gain from disorder*. Random House.

Thibodeaux, J., Deutsch, A., Kitsantas, A., & Winsler, A. (2017). First-year college students' time use: Relations with self-regulation and GPA. *Journal of Advanced Academics*, *28*(1), 5–27. doi:10.1177/1932202X16676860

Tollefson, J. (2020). Why deforestation and extinctions make pandemics more likely. *Nature*, *584*(7820), 175–176. doi:10.1038/d41586-020-02341-1 PMID:32770149

Tomastik, M., Strohmadl, J., & Cech, P. (2015). Managerial competency of crisis managers. *Procedia: Social and Behavioral Sciences*, *174*, 3964–3969. doi:10.1016/j.sbspro.2015.01.1141

Topcu, N., & Demirkol, V. (2021). Covid-19 Pandemi Sürecinin Muhasebe Meslek Elemanları Üzerindeki Etkisi: Yalova Örneği. *Journal of Academic Value Studies*, *7*(3), 344–353. doi:10.29228/javs.52026

Trigo, A., Belfo, F. P., & Estébanez, R. P. (2014). Accounting Information Systems: The Challenge of the Real-time Reporting. *Procedia Technology*, *16*(1), 118–127. doi:10.1016/j.protcy.2014.10.075

Tuğay, O., & Dokur, Ş. (2020). Koronavirüs (Kovid-19) Salgınının Muhasebe Meslek Mensuplarının Çalışma Alışkanlıkları Üzerine Etkileri: Bir Araştırma. *Akademik Sosyal Araştırmalar Dergisi*, *8*(105), 75–86.

Tulgan, B. (2016). Bridging the soft-skills gap. *Employment Relations Today*, *42*(4), 25–33. doi:10.1002/ert.21536

Vafeas, N. (2009). Is accounting education valued by the stock market? Evidence from corporate controller appointments. *Contemporary Accounting Research*, *26*(4), 1143–1174. doi:10.1506/car.26.4.6

Vanderhallen, M., Vervaeke, G., & Holmberg, U. (2011). Witness and suspect perceptions of working alliance and interviewing style. *Journal of Investigative Psychology and Offender Profiling*, *8*(2), 110–130. doi:10.1002/jip.138

Venter, E. R., Gordon, E. A., & Street, D. L. (2018). The role of accounting and the accountancy profession in economic development: A research agenda. *Journal of International Financial Management & Accounting*, *29*(2), 195–218. doi:10.1111/jifm.12080

Vien, C. (2021). Wanted: More systems and analytics training for accounting students. *Journal of Accountancy*. https://www.journalofaccountancy.com/news/2021/mar/systems-analytics-training-accounting-students.html

Walsh, D., & Bull, R. (2010). The interviewing of suspects by non-police agencies: What's effective? What is effective! *Legal and Criminological Psychology*, *15*, 305–321.

Walsh, D., & Bull, R. (2011). Benefit fraud investigative interviewing: A self-report study of investigation professionals' beliefs concerning practice. *Journal of Investigative Psychology and Offender Profiling*, *8*, 131–148.

Walsh, D., & Bull, R. (2012a). How do interviewers attempt to overcome suspects' denials? *Psychiatry, Psychology and Law*, *19*, 151–168.

Walsh, D., & Bull, R. (2012b). Examining rapport in investigative interviews with suspects: Does its building and maintenance work? *Journal of Police and Criminal Psychology*, *27*, 73–84.

Walsh, D., & Bull, R. (2015). The association between evidence disclosure, questioning strategies, interview skills, and interview outcomes. *Psychology, Crime & Law*, *21*, 661–680. doi:10.1080/1068316X.2015.1028544

Walsh, D., King, M., & Griffiths, A. (2017). Evaluating interviews which search for the truth with suspects: But are investigators' self-assessments of their own skills truthful ones? *Psychology, Crime & Law*, *23*, 647–665. doi:10.1080/1068316X.2017.1296149

Walsh, D., & Milne, R. (2007). Giving PEACE a Chance. *Public Administration*, *8*, 525–540.

Walsh, D., & Milne, R. (2008). Keeping the PEACE? A study of investigative interviewing practices in the public sector. *Legal and Criminological Psychology*, *13*, 39–57.

Walsh, D., Milne, R., & Bull, H. (2016). One way or another? Criminal investigators' beliefs regarding the disclosure of evidence in interviews with suspects in England and Wales. *Journal of Police and Criminal Psychology*, *31*, 127–140.

Walsh, D., Oxburgh, G., Redlich, A., & Myklebust, T. (2016). *International developments and practices in investigative interviewing and interrogation*. Routledge.

Wang, Y., Chiu, T., Wang, T., & Debreceny, R. S. (2020). A Classroom Exercise on Building Auditors' Interview Skills. *Journal of Emerging Technologies in Accounting*, *17*(2), 93–101. doi:10.2308/JETA-19-07-07-31

Wells, J. T. (2013). *Principles of Fraud Examination*. John Wiley & Sons, Inc.

Wertheim, P., Clements, C., & Stovall, O. (2022). *School Characteristics, Teaching Areas, and Other Factors Affecting the Impact from Pending Retirements of Accounting Faculty*. (Working paper presented at the Academy of Business Research, San Antonio, Texas).

Wessels, P. L. (2005). Critical information and communication technology (ICT) skills for professional accountants. *Meditari Account. Res.*, *13*(1), 87–103. doi:10.1108/10222529200500006

Willis, D. S. (2018). *On the road to champion.* https://www.insidehighered.com/advice/2018/03/26/advice-how-become-diversity-equity-and-inclusion-leader-opinion#.Ys7Yns HPsv8.link

Wolters, & Brady, A. C. (2020). College students' time management: A self-regulated learning perspective. *Educational Psychology Review, 33*(4), 1319–1351. https://doi.org/ doi:10.1007/s10648-020-09519-z

World Economic Forum – International Business Council's. (2020). Measuring Stakeholder Capitalism: Towards Common Metrics and Consistent Reporting of Sustainable Value Creation. WEF. https://www.weforum.org/reports/measuring-stakeholder-capitalism-towards-common-metrics- and-consistent-reporting-of-sustainable-value-creation .

Yorke, M. (1992). Quality in higher education: A conceptualization and some observations on the implementation of a sectorial quality system. *Journal of Further and Higher Education, 16*(1), 90–103. doi:10.1080/0309877920160210

About the Contributors

Nina T. Dorata earned a Ph.D. in accounting from Rutgers, The State University of New Jersey in 2003. She holds a B.S. in Accounting and a M.B.A. in Taxation from St. John's University. Dr. Dorata is a registered certified public accountant in New York. Before joining the faculty at St. John's University, Dr. Dorata taught at the State University of New York at the College of Old Westbury, where she served as chair of the Accounting and Business Law Department. Additionally, Dr. Dorata taught at St. Joseph's College where she co-founded the Accounting Club. Dr. Dorata has taught numerous courses in financial and managerial accounting in both graduate and undergraduate curriculums. Dr. Dorata's professional experience includes working as an auditor for Price Waterhouse & Co. where she serviced clients in the financial services and manufacturing industries. She was an Assistant Vice President of Corporate Accounting for E.F. Hutton & Co. Inc. and a Director of Financial Reporting at Staff Builders Inc., which are both registrants of the Securities and Exchange Commission. Her professional experience also includes consulting for various clients and has served on audit committees. Dr. Dorata's research interest is primarily financial reporting, capital markets and corporate governance. Recent research initiatives include governance structures in public finance, particularly public school districts. She has presented numerous papers to academic forums at national and international venues. She has published in peer reviewed journals such as Journal of Accounting, Auditing and Finance, Journal of Applied Business Research, Managerial Finance, Accounting Forum, Review of Business, and The CPA Journal. Dr. Dorata serves as a Technical Expert in Business Combination accounting for CCH and has authored a book titled "Accounting for Business Combinations, Goodwill, and Other Intangible Assets. Interpretations of U.S. and International Accounting Standards." She is the recipient of the 2007 Best Paper Award at the Financial Services Institute Symposium. Dr. Bikki Jaggi advised her dissertation, "The Impact of Post-Acquisition Activities on Bid Premium in the Market for Corporate Acquisitions." Dr. Dorata received several academic honors and teaching awards. In 2008, Dr. Dorata received the Dr. John Dobbins Professor of the Year Award from Student Government. She is also a recipient of the 2008 Beta Alpha Psi Outstanding Faculty Member of the Year Award for dedication to students. She is the recipient of the 2008-2009 Dr. John W. Dobbins Outstanding Service Award from the Peter J. Tobin College of Business in connection with the Volunteer Income Tax Assistance (VITA) program in the Department of Accountancy, which is now a campus-based virtual VITA program. She is also a co-recipient of the 2019 PwC INQuires Grant, the recipient of the 2010-2011 PWC Faculty Fellowship for Recognition of Teaching Excellence, and the recipient of Ernst and Young Inclusive Excellence Award for Accounting and Business School Faculty 2010 Honors. In August 2011, St. John's University recognized Dr. Dorata with the Outstanding Faculty Service Medal and in 2015, the Outstanding Faculty Achievement Medal. In 2020, Dr. Dorata was selected as the VIP nominee for Values and Inclusion University award. Dr. Dorata is the 2022 winner of the NYSSCPAs Dr. Emanuel Saxe Outstanding CPA in Education Award. Dr. Dorata is a member of the American Institute of Certified Public Accountants, the New York State Society of Certified Public Accountants, and the American Accounting Association and currently serves as Chair of the New York State Society of CPAs Future of Accounting Education Committee.

Richard C. Jones is an Associate Professor in the Department of Accounting at the Frank G. Zarb School of Business at Hofstra University. Dr. Jones is a CPA (PA, non-practicing) and has a B.S. in accounting from Drexel University and a Ph.D. in accounting from Rutgers University. Dr. Jones's business experience includes six years as a vice president at a large global banking corporation, where he was a Divisional Controller in Private Banking and, before taking on that assignment, a Vice President in the bank's Accounting Policy Group. Before entering banking, Dr. Jones was a member of the staff of the Financial Accounting Standards Board where he specialized in public utility issues. Dr. Jones began his professional career as an auditor in the Melville, NY office of Arthur Andersen and Company. Dr. Jones has served as a presenter and/or discussant for numerous academic and professional accounting conferences and has authored or co-authored numerous articles and manuscripts that have been published in professional and academic accounting and reporting journals. He has also co-authored a book on revenue recognition and, over the years, has reviewed and edited accounting and reporting publications and manuscripts for the CPA Journal and the American Institute of CPAs. Dr. Jones is an active member of the NYSSCPAs, where he is a member of several professional committees, including the Future of Accounting Education Committee, the Sustainability Committee, Auditing Standards, and the International Accounting and Auditing Committee, where he is the outgoing committee chair. As an educator, Dr. Jones has received several awards for teaching excellence, including the Hofstra University Distinguished Teacher of the Year Award in 2001.Dr. Jones is member of the NYSSCPAs and the American Accounting Association.

Jennifer Mensche has been an accounting professional since 1998, providing auditing, financial accounting and tax preparation services to various commercial, personal and not-for-profit organizations. In 2005, she transitioned to providing consulting services to various not-for-profit organizations specializing in programs for individuals with developmental disabilities. She began teaching as an adjunct instructor at St. Joseph's University in 2017 and then secured a full time faculty position in September of that same year. She is currently the Accounting Department Chair, teaching courses that range from the fundamentals of financial accounting to Graduate level research and accounting theory. Jennifer is a member of the New York State Society of CPAs, the American Institute of Certified Public Accountants and the American Accounting Association.

Mark M. Ulrich is an Assistant Professor in the Business Department at Queensborough Community College of the City University of New York. Prior to his academic appointment at Queensborough, he served as a senior auditor at KPMG LLP and a budget director at a large private university in New York City. He received bachelors and MBA degrees in accounting from St. John's University, and is a Certified Public Accountant in the State of New York. Professor Ulrich teaches financial accounting and cost accounting. He has been teaching accounting at the college level for over 12 years. His research interests include accounting education pedagogy and the CPA licensure process. At Queensborough, Professor Ulrich serves as a senator on the Academic Senate and serves as co-chair on the Senate's Assessment and Institutional Effectiveness committee. He also serves as a faculty fellow in the CUNY Career Success Fellows program where he researches career and salary outcomes of CUNY graduates with the goal of ensuring that all CUNY graduates earn a living wage out of college. He currently serves in numerous leadership capacities at the New York State Society of CPAs (NYSSCPA), including Past President of the Queens/Brooklyn Chapter and Director on the statewide Board of Directors. He is also a member of its Future of Accounting Education committee. He was named one of NYSSCPA's "40 Under 40" winners in 2020, and one of the NYSSCPA's "Emerging Leaders" in 2022. He also serves as the American Institute of Certified Public Accountants Academic Champion for Queensborough.

* * *

Gianluigi Baldacci holds a Bachelor's degree in Economics and Management and a Master's degree in Global Management and Politics from LUISS Guido Carli in Rome. He also participated in the Double Degree programme realised in collaboration with the Nova School of Business and Economics in Carcavelos where he obtained a Master's Degree in Management.

Ellen Bartley earned her PhD in Higher and Post-Secondary Education, with a concentration in Business Education, from New York University. She currently teaches principles, managerial and intermediate accounting at Farmingdale State College. Ellen served two terms as Secretary/Treasurer for the Gender Issues and Worklife Balance section of the American Accounting Association and on the Board of Directors of the Long Island, New York Chapter of the Institute for Management Accountants. She currently serves as chair of the Finance Committee of the Board of Trustees for The Learning Connection, a 501(c)3 organization that provides tools for the empowerment of women who are undereducated, lack a high school diploma, or speak languages other than English.

Cecília Margarita Rendeiro do Carmo has a PhD in Accounting from the University of Aveiro (2014), a master's degree in Accounting and Finance from Aberta University (2004) and a degree in Business Management from University of Beira Interior (1997). She is an Adjunct Professor in the University of Aveiro, at the Higher Institute of Accounting and Administration. She lectures subjects of Financial Accounting and Financial and Nonfinancial Reporting in undergraduated and graduated courses of Accounting.

Amélia Carvalho is a PhD in Management from School of Economics and Management of the University of Porto (FEP), with specialization in Accounting and Management Control. Master in Accounting and Management from the University of Minho (EEG) and Bachelor in Economics (UPT). Research areas: Accounting, and Financial and Non-Financial Reporting, Management and Accountability in the Third Sector, Transparency and Governance. Lecturer for more than two decades at the Escola Superior de Tecnologia e Gestão do Politécnico do Porto (ESTG-P.PORTO), in the areas of Business Sciences present in the Undergraduate and Master Degrees. She was Vice-President ESTG-P.PORTO and also Director of the Degree in Business Sciences. She collaborated as a teacher in other institutions of Higher Education, particularly in the area of Accounting and Taxation of the Third Sector. Currently, she is President of the Scientific-Technical Council of ESTG-P.PORTO. Integrated member of CIICESI-Center for Innovation and Research in Business Sciences and Information Systems. Member of the Scientific Committee in several international and national conferences and congresses, as well as in international journals. Extensive experience in guiding master's theses/projects and participation in juries of public examinations. Author and co-author of several scientific articles and reviewer in several journals. She was active in the e-Learning and Pedagogical Innovation Unit of the Polytechnic of Porto (EIPP) and held for several years the position of public manager and director in regional organizations.

David Chan earned a Ph.D. in Management with a concentration in Accounting Information Systems from Rutgers, The State University of New Jersey. He also holds a Master of Science in Accounting and Bachelor of Science in Finance from St. John's University. Dr. Chan is a licensed Certified Public Accountant (CPA) in the State of New York, Certified Internal Auditor (CIA), Certified Information Systems Auditor (CISA), and Certified Fraud Examiner (CFE). Dr. Chan's teaching interest includes financial auditing, internal auditing, fraud examination, and information technology auditing. His research interest includes auditing, auditing technology, and the application of technology in accounting and auditing.

Timothy Coville holds a Ph.D. in Business Management from Rutgers University. He earned an M.B.A. in Finance from New York University and is a Phi Beta Kappa key-holder having graduated Summa Cum Laude from S.U.N.Y. Albany with a B.S. double-majoring in both Accounting & Economics. He is a licensed Certified Public Accountant in the State of New York. Most recently, he became one of the first cohort of less than a hundred individuals internationally to earn the Fundamentals of Sustainability Accounting (FSA) credential sponsored by the Sustainability Accounting Standards Board (SASB). Dr. Coville was able to obtain his undergraduate education thanks to the support of the G.I. Bill from his service as a paratrooper with the U.S. Army's 82nd Airborne Division. Dr. Coville has published in Advances in Public Interest Accounting, the International Journal of Disclosure and Governance, the Review of Business, and the Academy of Business Research journals. He has also presented research papers in Europe and the USA and published in such international, national and regional conference proceedings as the INFORMS section on Group Decision and Negotiation and the American Accounting Association's Annual National Meeting, its Mid-Atlantic and North East Regions Annual Meetings, and its Auditing Section Midyear Conference. Dr. Coville came to academia after a successful 20 year career as a controller and risk manager for international derivatives trading firms. His banking career entailed a number of extended assignments and travel in Europe, Asia, and South America as well as the USA. His research interests are in corporate governance, international financial reporting standards, derivative products, financial literacy and sustainability. He has taught at both the undergraduate and graduate level in the following accounting disciplines: Financial Accounting, Managerial Accounting, Auditing and Sustainability.

Tiago Cunha is a Researcher and Collaborating Member at CIICESI-Centro de Inovação e Investigação em Ciências Empresariais e Sistemas de Informação. Assistant Professor at the School of Technology and Management of the Polytechnic Institute of Porto (ESTG-P.PORTO). Ph.D student in Economic Analysis and Business Strategy at the Faculty of Economic and Business Sciences of the University of Vigo.

Joan Fico is an assistant professor of accounting at the University of Delaware. Dr. Fico is a certified public accountant in New Jersey. Dr. Fico graduated from Rutgers University with her BA, MBA, and PhD in accounting. Her research interests are presently focused on forensic interviewing. She has presented her research at professional accounting conferences.

Adrian P. Fitzsimons holds a Ph.D. from the New School for Social Research and a Bachelor of Science and Master of Business Administration from St. John's University. He is licensed as a Certified Public Accountant in the State of New York, is a Chartered Financial Analyst, a Certified Fraud Examiner, a Certified Information Systems Auditor, a Chartered Global Management Accountant, and a Certified Management Accountant. Dr. Fitzsimons has taught at St. John's for over 35 years and has served as Chair of the Department of Accounting and Taxation for 14 years and Associate Dean for Academic Programs for 5 years. Dr Fitzsimons has written extensively on accounting and auditing topics. He served as a Vice President and as a Director for the New York State Society of CPAs (NYSSCPA) and as President, President-Elect and Treasurer of the Queens-Brooklyn Chapter of the NYSSCPAs and as Corresponding Secretary and a Director of the ISACA - the Information Systems Audit and Control Association.

Ahmet Kaya is an assistant professor at the Akdeniz University (Turkey), Faculty of Applied Sciences. He received bachelor's degree in business administration and master's degree in business administration from Gaziantep University (Turkey). He received a PhD. in business and administration from Kahramanmaras Sutcu Imam University, 2019. In his doctoral dissertation study, he investigated the establishment of an Analytic Hierarchy Process (AHP) based lean cost management (Value Stream Costing) system in enterprises applying lean production techniques, the correct distribution of common expenses to value streams and more accurate calculation of product cost. He is interested in investor behoviour, decision-making and behaviorul finance. In particular, he has conducted important studies on value stream costing and activity-based costing, and recently he has also conducted research on accounting professionals. In addition, although he has publications on business performance and sustainability, he has generally used multi-criteria decision-making techniques in these publications.

Feden Koç, who works as a lecturer in the Department of Office Management and Executive Assistant at Uşak University Karahallı Vocational School, has national and international research and books at national and international level on financial accounting, international accounting and auditing.

Frank Manzi, CPA, currently serves as the Chair of the Department of Accounting, Business and Economics at The College of Mount Saint Vincent and is an Accounting professor. Frank earned a bachelor's degree in economics from Columbia University and a Master's in Business Administration with a concentration in accounting from Pace University and is a practicing CPA in New York. Prior to joining academia Frank operated in the business world for 35 years in the fields of Accounting, Finance and Operations with increasing levels of responsibilities in the public accounting, telecommunications, advertising, and supply chain operations industries. 0Frank is a member of New York State Society of CPA's and serves as the Assistant Chair on the Future of Accounting Education Committee. Frank has several articles published in the CPA Journal focusing on the many diverse skills a CFO must have and how to improve those skills for future business requirements.

Mark Martinelli, CPA, CGMA, CAMS Mark spent nine years as Synchrony Financial's Chief Audit Executive before announcing his retirement in 2022. Since that time, Mark has been an Executive Advisor to Synchrony assisting the CEO and the Board's Audit Committee. He led the audit function following Synchrony's 2014 IPO and spin-off from GE. Prior to Synchrony, Mark had a twenty-year career at HSBC where he was SEVP and Chief Auditor for North America. Prior to that he was President and Chief Executive Officer of HSBC.com and its Chief Financial Officer. Mark held executive positions in Finance, Strategy, Planning and Audit. Prior to joining HSBC, he was a Senior Manager with KPMG LLP. Mark kas been an Adjunct Professor at Baruch College. He served on the Audit Committee of New York Clearing House and was its Chairman from 2011 to 2013. Mark is an active board member and advisor for several academic institutions and professional associations, including Baruch College/Zicklin School of Business (Member, Stan Ross Accountancy Board), Baruch College Fund (Trustee, Audit Committee Vice Chair, Cyber Security Risk Sub-Committee Chair), St. John's University, (Executive Advisory Board Member, Department of Accounting & Taxation/Advisor, Peter Tobin School of Business), and New York State Society of Certified Public Accountants (Internal Audit, Nominating & Future of Accounting Education committees). He is a member of the Editorial Review Board of the CPA Journal. Mark earned his B.S. in Accounting from St. John's University. He lives in the Greater New York City area with his wife. Greater New York City Area.

Helena Martins is a lecturer in Human Resources Management at the Instituto Politécnico de Setúbal and the Nova School of Business and Economics in Portugal. She is an integrated member of the CEOS.PP research centre and her research interests focus the development of soft skills for crisis situations especially for leaders and managers. She holds a PhD in Management (University of Porto, Portugal), a Masters in Work, Organizational and Personnel Psychology (University of Coimbra, Portugal and University of Valencia, Spain) and a Bachelors in Psychology (University of Minho, Portugal). Member of the Scientific Committee in several international and national conferences and congresses, and international journals. Extensive experience in guiding master's theses/projects and participation in juries of public examinations. Author and co-author of several scientific articles and book chapters and reviewer in several journals.

Cynthia Scarinci is an Associate Professor of Accounting for the Lucille and Jay Chazanoff School of Business, College of Staten Island, City University of New York. She has been an accounting professor for more than twenty years, teaching auditing, financial accounting and cost accounting. Cynthia was the 2013 recipient of the Dr. Emanuel Saxe Outstanding CPA in Education Award from the New York State Society of Certified Public Accountants (NYSSCPA). She has been an active member of the NYSSCPA for over 20 years and has served in several roles, including Society Vice President of Chapters, member of the Board of Directors and Chair of the Education committee, as well as Chapter President. Prior to her academic career, Cynthia was employed in both public and private accounting, specializing in auditing and accounting information systems, including contingency and continuity planning. Cynthia earned her BBA and MBA from Pace University, New York City. Cynthia and her husband are New York residents.

Vincent Shea received his PhD in Business - Accounting from Kent State University. He has published articles in several journals including: the Journal of Information Systems, International Journal of Accounting Information Systems, Information Systems Frontier, Issues in Accounting Education, Journal of Forensic Accounting, Journal of Accounting Education and the CPA Journal.

Dave Walsh's research focuses on the investigative interviewing of victims (including children), witnesses and suspects, as well as decision making of investigators. He has published extensively these areas. He was a founding member of the International Investigative Interviewing Research group (see). Among his many current projects include how the pandemic has affected policing practice as it applies to the interviewing of witnesses. He is also working with researchers, practitioners and policy makers across the world concerning the implementation of the UN's Mendez Principles on Effective Interviewing in Investigations.

Index

D

E

F

G

H

I

J

K

L

O

P

Q

R

S

T

U

V

W

Recommended Reference Books

IGI Global's reference books are available in three unique pricing formats:
Print Only, E-Book Only, or Print + E-Book.

Order direct through IGI Global's Online Bookstore at **www.igi-global.com** or through your preferred provider.

ISBN: 9781799887096
EISBN: 9781799887119
© 2022; 413 pp.
List Price: US$ **250**

ISBN: 9781799874157
EISBN: 9781799874164
© 2022; 334 pp.
List Price: US$ **240**

ISBN: 9781668440230
EISBN: 9781668440254
© 2022; 320 pp.
List Price: US$ **215**

ISBN: 9781799889502
EISBN: 9781799889526
© 2022; 263 pp.
List Price: US$ **240**

ISBN: 9781799885283
EISBN: 9781799885306
© 2022; 587 pp.
List Price: US$ **360**

ISBN: 9781668455906
EISBN: 9781668455913
© 2022; 2,235 pp.
List Price: US$ **1,865**

Do you want to stay current on the latest research trends, product announcements, news, and special offers?
Join IGI Global's mailing list to receive customized recommendations, exclusive discounts, and more.
Sign up at: **www.igi-global.com/newsletters.**

Publisher of Timely, Peer-Reviewed Inclusive Research Since 1988

IGI Global
PUBLISHER of TIMELY KNOWLEDGE

www.igi-global.com Sign up at www.igi-global.com/newsletters facebook.com/igiglobal twitter.com/igiglobal

Ensure Quality Research is Introduced to the Academic Community

Become an Evaluator for IGI Global Authored Book Projects

The overall success of an authored book project is dependent on quality and timely manuscript evaluations.

Applications and Inquiries may be sent to:
development@igi-global.com

Applicants must have a doctorate (or equivalent degree) as well as publishing, research, and reviewing experience. Authored Book Evaluators are appointed for one-year terms and are expected to complete at least three evaluations per term. Upon successful completion of this term, evaluators can be considered for an additional term.

If you have a colleague that may be interested in this opportunity, we encourage you to share this information with them.

Easily Identify, Acquire, and Utilize Published Peer-Reviewed Findings in Support of Your Current Research

IGI Global OnDemand

Purchase Individual IGI Global OnDemand Book Chapters and Journal Articles

For More Information:

www.igi-global.com/e-resources/ondemand/

Browse through 150,000+ Articles and Chapters!

Find specific research related to your current studies and projects that have been contributed by international researchers from prestigious institutions, including:

Massachusetts Institute of Technology

HARVARD UNIVERSITY

COLUMBIA UNIVERSITY IN THE CITY OF NEW YORK

Australian National University

- Accurate and Advanced Search
- Affordably Acquire Research
- Instantly Access Your Content
- Benefit from the InfoSci Platform Features

"It really provides an excellent entry into the research literature of the field. It presents a manageable number of highly relevant sources on topics of interest to a wide range of researchers. The sources are scholarly, but also accessible to 'practitioners'."

- Ms. Lisa Stimatz, MLS, University of North Carolina at Chapel Hill, USA

Interested in Additional Savings?

Subscribe to

IGI Global OnDemand *Plus*

Learn More

Acquire content from over 128,000+ research-focused book chapters and 33,000+ scholarly journal articles for as low as US$ 5 per article/chapter (original retail price for an article/chapter: US$ 37.50).

7,300+ E-BOOKS. ADVANCED RESEARCH. INCLUSIVE & AFFORDABLE.

IGI Global PUBLISHER of TIMELY KNOWLEDGE

IGI Global e-Book Collection

- **Flexible Purchasing Options** (Perpetual, Subscription, EBA, etc.)
- Multi-Year Agreements with **No Price Increases** Guaranteed
- **No Additional Charge** for Multi-User Licensing
- No Maintenance, Hosting, or Archiving Fees
- Continually Enhanced & Innovated **Accessibility Compliance Features** (WCAG)

Handbook of Research on Digital Transformation, Industry Use Cases, and the Impact of Disruptive Technologies
ISBN: 9781799877127
EISBN: 9781799877141

Handbook of Research on New Investigations in Artificial Life, AI, and Machine Learning
ISBN: 9781799886860
EISBN: 9781799886877

Handbook of Research on Future of Work and Education
ISBN: 9781799882756
EISBN: 9781799882770

Research Anthology on Physical and Intellectual Disabilities in an Inclusive Society (4 Vols.)
ISBN: 9781668435427
EISBN: 9781668435434

Innovative Economic, Social, and Environmental Practices for Progressing Future Sustainability
ISBN: 9781799895909
EISBN: 9781799895923

Applied Guide for Event Study Research in Supply Chain Management
ISBN: 9781799889694
EISBN: 9781799889717

Mental Health and Wellness in Healthcare Workers
ISBN: 9781799888130
EISBN: 9781799888147

Clean Technologies and Sustainable Development in Civil Engineering
ISBN: 9781799898108
EISBN: 9781799898122

Request More Information, or Recommend the IGI Global e-Book Collection to Your Institution's Librarian

For More Information or to Request a Free Trial, Contact IGI Global's e-Collections Team: eresources@igi-global.com | 1-866-342-6657 ext. 100 | 717-533-8845 ext. 100

Are You Ready to Publish Your Research?

IGI Global
PUBLISHER of TIMELY KNOWLEDGE

IGI Global offers book authorship and editorship opportunities across 11 subject areas, including business, computer science, education, science and engineering, social sciences, and more!

Benefits of Publishing with IGI Global:

- Free one-on-one editorial and promotional support.
- Expedited publishing timelines that can take your book from start to finish in less than one (1) year.
- Choose from a variety of formats, including Edited and Authored References, Handbooks of Research, Encyclopedias, and Research Insights.
- Utilize IGI Global's eEditorial Discovery® submission system in support of conducting the submission and double-blind peer review process.
- IGI Global maintains a strict adherence to ethical practices due in part to our full membership with the Committee on Publication Ethics (COPE).
- Indexing potential in prestigious indices such as Scopus®, Web of Science™, PsycINFO®, and ERIC – Education Resources Information Center.
- Ability to connect your ORCID iD to your IGI Global publications.
- Earn honorariums and royalties on your full book publications as well as complimentary content and exclusive discounts.

Join Your Colleagues from Prestigious Institutions, Including:

Australian National University

Massachusetts Institute of Technology

Johns Hopkins University

Harvard University

Tsinghua University

Columbia University in the City of New York

Learn More at: www.igi-global.com/publish

or by Contacting the Acquisitions Department at: acquisition@igi-global.com

www.ingramcontent.com/pod-product-compliance
Lightning Source LLC
LaVergne TN
LVHW061536290926
849162LV00004B/810